Rethinking Religion and Politics in a Plural World

Rethinking Religion and Politics in a Plural World

The Bahá'í International Community and the United Nations

Julia Berger

BLOOMSBURY ACADEMIC
LONDON • NEW YORK • OXFORD • NEW DELHI • SYDNEY

BLOOMSBURY ACADEMIC
Bloomsbury Publishing Plc
50 Bedford Square, London, WC1B 3DP, UK
1385 Broadway, New York, NY 10018, USA

BLOOMSBURY, BLOOMSBURY ACADEMIC and the Diana logo
are trademarks of Bloomsbury Publishing Plc

First published in Great Britain 2021

Cover design: Nicole Corea
Cover image © Shakiba Kazemi

A catalogue record for this book is available from the British Library.

A catalog record for this book is available from the Library of Congress.

ISBN: HB: 978-1-3501-3032-6
       ePDF: 978-1-3501-3033-3
       eBook: 978-1-3501-3034-0

Typeset by Integra Software Services Pvt. Ltd.

…regard ye not one another as strangers.
Ye are the fruits of one tree, and the leaves of one branch.

– Bahá'u'lláh

Contents

List of Figures

Preface

The ideas that gave rise to this book began to percolate in my mind in 2001. That summer, as part of my master's degree in education and international development, I completed an internship at the Bahá'í International Community's (BIC's) United Nations Office. The opportunity came about partly by accident. My husband had secured an internship at the United Nations Security Council, and I needed to find an internship in New York City related to my studies. Over the course of the summer, my interests began to shift away from education policy and toward the role of non-governmental organizations (NGOs)—specifically, religious ones—in international affairs. It was the summer before 9/11, the question of religion in international affairs was still under the radar, and the idea that religion was increasingly irrelevant to the forward march of modernity was largely accepted. But in my internship I observed a different reality, which sparked many questions: Why were so many religious and faith-based NGOs active and formally affiliated with the United Nations? Were there hidden proselytization agendas? Were their contributions valued or even taken seriously? Were they effective? In the years following 9/11, the question of religion and politics accelerated to the top of the research agenda.

In 2004, I began work as principal researcher for the BIC's United Nations Office in New York. For the next eleven years, I had a front-row seat to the multifaceted engagement of religious NGOs (RNGOs) with all matters on the UN agenda: human rights, social and sustainable development, poverty eradication, gender equality, peace and security, and UN reform, among others. During this time, I couldn't help but reflect on the distinct elements of the Bahá'í community's approach to interaction in the political arena. In the burgeoning studies of religion and politics, no one was describing the approach I witnessed at the BIC: a developmental view of history and religion; an understanding of modernity as a stage in humanity's advancement toward greater degrees of social unity; an avoidance of partisanship; an emphasis on the coherence between the means and ends of social transformation; and a keen attentiveness to principled processes of deliberation and decision-making and their place in the global and democratic institutional architecture of the worldwide Bahá'í community. This was religion in politics, but not in the familiar sense of "religion," nor the familiar sense of "politics." This was something different, something calibrated to a new understanding of human progress and human flourishing and intensely relevant to the pressing social, political, and economic questions of our time.

Twenty years after that first internship, we are seeing the world in a different light, chastened by the experience of a pandemic that has laid bare the frailties and the deep injustices embedded in our social order. We continue to struggle with gross inequality, social marginalization, protracted armed conflict, and the impotence of leaders at all levels to mend the fractures in the structures of society. Yet the heightened consciousness of these frailties has also ushered in a greater desire, an openness, a readiness to rethink established ways of being, doing, and organizing ourselves as a global community, as nations, as communities, and as neighbors. A spirit of refashioning and rethinking is palpable as the unquestionable reality of our interconnectedness comes to light. It is in this spirit—the search for new conditions of possibility, new conceptions of religion, and new modes of pursuing social change—that the inquiry in this book unfolds.

Acknowledgments

I imagine that when one sets out to write a book, especially the very first one, one really has no idea of the path that lies ahead. That was certainly my experience: I imagined that my PhD thesis on this subject would, with some effort but without painful struggle, eventually evolve into the manuscript that might be worthy of a "book." Instead, the seemingly endless shortcomings and deficiencies in one's thinking, analysis, assumptions, and process—one by one—come to light. A more seasoned writer would be more familiar with this pattern, which in the end, if we can bear it, is a gift. To stay with the difficult questions, to allow them to emerge in the full light of their complexity, to admit what we do not know, to ask more and better questions, to realize that the answers will not be found quickly or through our own striving but slowly and in community with others, to know that our contribution can only ever be quite small, limited as it is by our particular training and individual experience of the world, a world in which so many other voices and perspectives will refine and lend their wisdom to what we have tried to say, but that it is still a contribution worth making—these are the lessons I have learned along the way.

A wonderful community of mentors, scholars, family, and friends have made this journey possible and even thrilling at times. I am indebted to my colleagues at the BIC who responded generously to many queries and whose talents and dedicated work shaped the history in this book: Peter Adriance, Diane Ala'i, Lawrence Arturo, Bill Donworth, Bani Dugal, Jefferey Huffines, Ming Hwee Chong, Stephen Karnik, Nava Kavelin, Daniel Perell, Mary Power, Saphira Rameshfar, Mark Scheffer, Will van den Hoonaard, and Carolina Vasquez. Our conversations have been one of the highlights of this journey. I hope that you might find in this book, in some measure, a reflection of your tireless and inspired efforts to work, in concert with so many others, toward a more just, more kind, and equitable world.

I am grateful to scholars in the Bahá'í community who have helped me sharpen my thinking and persevere with challenging questions and who have accompanied me on various parts of this journey, especially Benjamin Schewel, Geoffrey Cameron, Caity Bolton, Nazila Ghanea, and Martha Schweitz. Your ideas, revisions, suggestions, and reflections strengthened and advanced this work in countless ways.

I greatly appreciate the research assistance extended to me by archivists Roger Dahl and Lewis Walker at the National Baháʼí Archives of the United States in Wilmette, Illinois, as well as the support of the Baháʼí World Centre in Haifa, Israel. Thank you also to Emma Tomalin and Richard King, whose example of incisive scholarship in the field of religious studies I drew on extensively, and whose feedback was instrumental in strengthening and clarifying the ideas presented in this book. I reserve a special measure of gratitude to Jeremy Carette, scholar of religion and philosophy, and an outstanding mentor who encouraged me to write this book and believed from the beginning that I had something important to say.

In the final stages of writing, I was blessed with the masterful editing assistance of Jennifer Janechek and Martha Schweitz, whose comments and deep experience have helped to tell this story more clearly, accurately, and in fewer words. Thank you also to Lucy Carroll, Lalle Pursglove, and Lily McMahon at Bloomsbury for supporting the publication of this work.

This book would not have been written without a village of support that helped keep our household running and my daughters cared for during the years of research and writing. Kathy Gerard, Farnoosh Famouri-Lee, Audris Wong, and Hata Velovic, I couldn't have finished this without you.

Thank you to my mother, Agnieszka Branecka, for her unflinching support at every step of this journey and for the example of fearless endeavor that she set in her personal and professional life. Thank you to my father, Marek Branecki, for introducing me to the Baháʼí Faith at the age of fifteen and never allowing me to settle for easy answers. I am grateful to my grandmother, Magdalena Esden Tempska, who first taught me English, fostered my love of reading and writing, and told me that one day I would write my own book. And to my grandfather, Jerzy Esden Tempski, for the example of your deep curiosity about the material and spiritual world.

Finally, I wish to thank my husband, Eric Berger—there would be no book without your love and selfless support. Your sharp intellect, generous heart, and deep rootedness in your spiritual tradition have been an abiding inspiration on this journey. To my sweet daughters, Ella and Sophia, thank you for your patience during my many absences and long periods of research and writing. This is the fruit of that work. I hope you will read it one day. And then write your own.

Abbreviations

BIC	Bahá'í International Community
CONGO	Conference of NGOs in Consultative Relationship with the UN
ECOSOC	United Nations Economic and Social Council
DPI	United Nations Department of Public Information
FBO	Faith-based organization
ICCPR	International Covenant on Civil and Political Rights
ICESCR	International Covenant on Economic, Social and Cultural Rights
NGO	Non-governmental organization
NSA	National Spiritual Assembly
OAW	Office for the Advancement of Women
OIC	Organization for Islamic Cooperation
RNGO	Religious non-governmental organization
UN	United Nations
UNAIDS	Joint United Nations Programme on HIV and AIDS
UNCED	United Nations Conference on Environment and Development
UNDP	United Nations Development Programme
UNEP	United Nations Environment Programme
UNFPA	United Nations Population Fund
UNHCR	United Nations Refugee Agency
UNICEF	United Nations Children's Fund

1

Ideas, Religion, and Social Change

In 1884, delegates from twenty-five countries met in Washington, DC, to approve a single "world time" organized around twenty-four time zones encompassing the globe. It was a remarkable achievement; only eighty years prior, every region, every city was setting its own time based on the position of the sun. Over the course of the next several decades, all countries would calibrate their clocks according to Greenwich Mean Time. A quiet revolution had unified the world around a common measure of time.

We, too, live in a time of revolutions, some quiet, some pronounced; dramatic and widespread shifts in thought and behavior arising from ideas that enter the public consciousness and alter the way in which we view and experience our human and social existence. Many such ideas arise not from the centers of power but from the periphery and gradually proliferate among the generality of people, altering thought and practice in fundamental ways. We might think of the printing press, women's suffrage, abolitionism, the internet, to name a few. The COVID-19 pandemic set the stage for further revolutions in thought and practice. In a world struggling with gross inequality and social marginalization, and the inability of leaders to mend the schisms and the wounds afflicting humanity, the pandemic has laid bare the frailties of our social order. Yet this heightened consciousness has also prompted a greater desire, an openness, a readiness to rethink established ways of relating to one another as human beings, as communities, and as nations.

It is in this spirit that the inquiry in this book unfolds: it traces the experience of a community whose ideas about social order and the mechanisms of social change refashion familiar notions of politics as well as religion. The book focuses its attention on the Bahá'í International Community (BIC), an international non-governmental organization (NGO), which represents the worldwide community of some 5 million Bahá'ís across 180 nations, in global fora—most notably, the United Nations. As a smaller religious community, Bahá'ís do not exert the kind of influence that is associated with "key players" in the international arena, such as powerful lobby groups that wield significant material resources and mobilize communities in protests and advocacy to achieve political aims. However, the Bahá'í example offers a particularly fruitful, unique test case for an approach to social change that goes beyond the divisive, antagonistic modes that typically characterize political processes to lay the foundations for new patterns of relationships among individuals, communities, and governing institutions—patterns that are keenly attuned to the needs of an evolving global community. Such an approach has given rise to a new polity, a new vision of political life, and a new logic of engagement animated by the reality of the profound interdependence of all peoples and nations.

On another level, this book is about the power of ideas to effect social change. I do not try to argue simply that ideas are powerful catalysts for driving change; this we know. We live in a world shaped by ideas that were once radical and dangerous and now widely accepted, such as universal suffrage, universal education, racial and gender equality, the system of nation-states, etc. As Victor Hugo once remarked: "An invasion of armies can be resisted; an invasion of ideas cannot."[1]

Specifically, I examine ideas that emerge from within a religious tradition and shape the interactions of a religious community with society as a whole. Perhaps we are not used to thinking of religions in terms of "ideas"; more commonly, we think of them in terms of "beliefs," laws, and social and cultural practices. But ideas matter. If we consider the history of religious thought dating back to Abraham, Moses, Zoroaster, Krishna, Buddha, Jesus, and Mohammad, one cannot but be struck by the deep influence of the teachings and ideas introduced by these figures on the development of human civilization. German sociologist Max Weber was among the first to posit a connection between Christian ideals and new patterns of behavior. In his famous treatise *The Protestant Ethic and the Spirit of Capitalism* (1930), Weber draws a connection between the ethics of ascetic Protestantism and the emergence of the capitalist spirit in the West. Specifically, he notes that Calvinist attitudes toward profit, wealth, and the dedicated pursuit of a craft or profession (seen as a "calling") are endowed with moral and spiritual significance.

Furthermore, the discipline of political theology has shed light on the relationship between ideas in religious teachings and engagement in public life, as exemplified in liberation theology, Catholic social teaching,[2] and more recently, feminist theology.[3] Political scientists Judith Goldstein and Robert Keohane have argued that ideas have the broadest impact when they take the form of worldviews, which, the authors note, can be rooted in religion as much as in scientific rationality. Of course, we can also point to organizations claiming to speak from a religious standpoint that have resorted to violent means to challenge dominant regimes (e.g., ISIS, Al-Qaeda, the Lord's Resistance Army, Buddhist groups in Myanmar and Sri Lanka, Hindu nationalist groups in India, among others).[4] Sadly, there is no lack of organizations, past or present, religious or secular, that have legitimized violence on philosophical grounds.

There are many different kinds of religious organizations. I focus specifically on a category of organizations known as "religious NGOs" or RNGOs. Broadly speaking, RNGOs are nonprofit voluntary organizations whose identity and mission are consciously shaped by the teachings of a religious or spiritual tradition, such as World Vision International, the Lutheran World Federation, Tzu Chi Foundation, Soka Gakkai International, Muslim Aid, American Jewish World Service, and many others. RNGOs have exercised their influence in the international arenas of policy-making and humanitarian aid and have demonstrated their impressive capacity to mobilize human and financial resources, as well as the ability to reach remote areas and populations. In this way, they have, over the years, become indispensable partners in development, relief, and peacemaking efforts.

But the way in which the teachings and ideas of these respective traditions are translated into action by RNGOs remains largely unknown. For example: How do the tenets of a religious/spiritual tradition shape an RNGO's view of the world and its understanding of the role it is to play in it? How do they influence the manner in which the RNGO diagnoses the world's social ills? How do the teachings shape the methods employed by the organization? What is the organization's understanding of foundational concepts such as peace, justice, progress, and human flourishing? To ask these questions is not to essentialize the aforementioned ideas and discount other influences on organizational behavior (e.g., finances, human resources, external sociocultural factors, etc.). Rather, it is a step toward examining more deeply the intellectual, conceptual, and epistemological dimensions of religious agency in the modern world.

Why Are These Questions Important, and Why Now?

Challenging Oppositional Conceptions of Religion and Modernity

Since the Enlightenment, religion has largely been defined in opposition to modernity: Friedrich Nietzsche's declaration that "God is dead" helped usher in the victory of scientific rationality over religious revelation.[5] The idea that the influence of religion would wane as the march of modernity advanced held sway over the social sciences until the 1960s.[6] Yet by the close of the twentieth century, one of the leading proponents of secularization theory recanted, observing that "[t]he world today, with some exceptions, … is as furiously religious as it ever was" and that the entire body of literature loosely labeled "secularization theory" was "essentially mistaken."[7] The pendulum had swung in the opposite direction, it seemed: religiously motivated activists, revolutionaries, social movements, and factions were mobilizing and asserting their place domestically and on the world stage.[8] This is "God's century," declared scholars[9]; in less than fifty years, religion had moved from a position of irrelevance to one of the "most influential factors in world affairs."[10] How, then, should we account for the role of religion in the present day?

This book adds to the efforts to examine the role of religion in the modern world by looking at religious agency from an internal, *emic* perspective. Complementary to the work that focuses on describing historical processes (e.g., the axial age,[11] multiple modernities,[12] narrative frameworks[13]), I seek to understand how a religious organization translates the ideas and teachings of its tradition to its actions in the international arena. In doing so, I challenge the construction of religion *in opposition to* modernity in order to explore its role as an active participant in the definition thereof.

Beyond the Focus on Religion and Violence

As one scholar points out, until recently, "the treatment of religion generally retained the old secular fixation with religiously based conflict or religiously inspired violence."[14] After the attacks of September 11, 2001, growing concerns about fundamentalism and radicalization directed research funding and attention to religious organizations to better understand the relationship between religious ideology and violence. However, this preoccupation with religiously motivated violence (which itself may be a misnomer, as political and personal interests play a defining role) has resulted in a partial and distorted view of religion in the international arena. Studies have associated organizations' deep rootedness in and adherence to a faith tradition with militant and violent actions.[15] This approach has reinforced a belief in the "irrationality" of religious actors, the notion that greater identification with a religious tradition leads to socially deviant and undesirable behavior, and the idea that religion has no place in broader discourse about the organization of human affairs and the social order.

At the same time, religious organizations pursuing social change in constructive, creative, effective, and law-abiding ways have received little attention. Isn't it possible that religious organizations can abide by the law and, at the same time, challenge the vision, rationality, and structures of power embedded in present-day society? Can organizations be revolutionary and law-abiding at the same time? And if so, how? In this book, I posit that by interrogating an RNGO's internal structures of thought, we can begin to examine how religious ideas combine to constitute a distinct logic—one that offers a new vantage point and lens for examining the present social order and the dynamics and relationships within it.

Beyond the Focus on Service Provision and Advocacy

Previous research about religious and faith-based organizations has conceptualized their roles along two lines: first, in terms of the provision of material and social services and, second, in terms of social justice advocacy. It is true that a large proportion of religious civil society organizations attend to the needs of underserved and vulnerable populations[16] and advocate for social justice in various domains. It is also true that many religious organizations have been able to provide financial and organizational resources, reach remote populations, and mobilize their congregations to support growing social movements.[17] Yet an exclusive focus on the service- and advocacy-oriented work obscures an important dimension of RNGO contributions—namely, their efforts "to confront and alter values that drive [contemporary society], and to shift power dynamics in contemporary politics."[18] Others concur that religion represents "a deep source for contesting development orthodoxy and providing alternatives" but note that this facet is poorly conceptualized and often ignored.[19] Do we see RNGOs simply as attending to those marginalized by the current world order, or do we also recognize their role in building the world anew?

Enlarging the Moral Imagination

It is too easy to forget that the philosophical foundations shaping our global order—our understanding of power, relationships between nations, individual responsibility, security, etc.—were not handed down to us but were created and constructed by people. It is these conceptual foundations that continue, often imperceptibly, to germinate and give rise to patterns of thinking and practice that appear very "normal" to us. It is difficult to picture another form of democracy, public education, or a market economy. Yet in the collective efforts to forge a more just social order, we must consider the intellectual contributions that arise outside of the prevailing order and not assume that all civil society actors wish to adopt the intellectual program of the Western liberal-democratic order. Scholars of international affairs have begun to explore "alternative understandings that can expand the meanings of power, institutions and ideas" in the context of world politics[20]; others describe a steady "transformation of the normative structure of international society" beyond its European origins[21] and examine new forms of rationality that "draw on both secular and religious imaginaries."[22] By studying the structures of thought of RNGOs, new forms of rationality are able to come to light, correcting the often-held assumptions about their proselytizing motives or the absence of critique or ideas regarding the structure and intellectual foundations of the present-day social order.

The Case for Studying the Bahá'í International Community

This book analyzes the influence of ideas on RNGO engagement in the international arena through a focused analysis of the BIC's United Nations Office seventy-year engagement with the United Nations. The Bahá'í Faith was founded in Persia (now Iran) in the mid-nineteenth century by Mírzá Husayn-'Ali, known as Bahá'u'lláh.[23] The teachings of this young Faith focus on the promotion of unity and justice in the context of an emerging and interdependent global community. The fundamental oneness of all human beings is the cornerstone of all Bahá'í teachings, which chart a course for the expression of this interdependence in all processes, relationships, and institutions that sustain society. The Bahá'í Faith is an independent religion, with communities established in over 100,000 localities around the world, numbering over 5 million adherents;[24] and today it is recognized as the second most widespread religion in the world.[25]

What makes the BIC such a compelling example to study? First, the sacred texts of the Bahá'í Faith address extensively, among other things, the institutional, legal, social, intellectual, and spiritual requisites of the emerging, increasingly interdependent, global community. Bahá'u'lláh spoke of a new "World Order" fully sixty years before Woodrow Wilson would use this expression in his "Fourteen Points."[26] In that sense, the Bahá'í Faith is qualitatively different than "ancient" faiths, as it addresses directly and explicitly the exigencies of the modern order. "Be anxiously concerned with the needs of the age ye live in," state the writings of the Bahá'í Faith, "and center your deliberations on its exigencies and requirements."[27] Furthermore, the development of the Bahá'í community in the nineteenth and twentieth centuries parallels the rise of nation-states and the modern political order.

Today, the BIC is an active and well-respected NGO at the United Nations and among its NGO peers, as attested to by independent reports as well as its history of being elected to leadership positions on numerous prominent NGO committees[28]; it has emerged as one of the leading voices in the areas of human rights, gender equality, and social development. A rich record for study emerges from its now seventy-five-year relationship with the United Nations.[29] The BIC is among very few RNGOs to represent the entire membership of a single religious community to the United Nations.[30]

Scholarship about the Bahá'í Faith has, over the years, shifted from a focus on the tenets and history of the Bahá'í Faith (often situated in the field of Middle Eastern studies)[31] to one that correlates the teachings of the Bahá'í Faith to a range of social issues and engages a wide variety of discourses. A number of scholars, both Bahá'ís and those in the larger community, have continued to shed new light on Bahá'í scriptures,[32] the history and practices of various Bahá'í communities,[33] and the persecution of the community in Iran.[34] Scholars have increasingly explored the application of Bahá'í principles to questions such as gender equality,[35] education,[36] governance, and peace.[37] As well, other publications have brought Bahá'í thought and practice into conversation with contemporary scholarship on religion and modernity.[38]

Another reason for the timeliness and urgency of this study is the need to advance scholarship beyond its comfort zone of Christian NGOs and organizations. While these comprise the majority of humanitarian, development, and advocacy NGOs worldwide, a continued focus on Christian organizations to the exclusion of other faiths continues the practice of transposing a normatively Christian understanding of religion onto the study of other faiths, whose theological and conceptual frameworks may be distorted, or rendered invisible, by such an analysis. As Richard King reminds us, one of the central tasks of scholars of religions outside of Christianity is to "[untangle] some of the Christian presuppositions that have framed the discussion so far."[39] Unlike the older world religions, the Bahá'í Faith engages directly with the category of "religion." In the Bahá'í writings, religion is described as a continually unfolding process that operates throughout the history of human civilization (and its present). "Bahá'u'lláh has not brought into existence a new religion to stand beside the present multiplicity of sectarian organizations," states a Bahá'í text; rather, "He has recast the whole conception of religion as the principal force impelling the development of consciousness."[40] Throughout this book, the Bahá'í conception of religion and its role in reshaping familiar understandings of social order and social change are explored in the context of the BIC's engagement in the international arena.

We must consider that new ideas and challenges to established modes of thinking and behaving tend to emerge not from the mainstream of a debate, but rather from the periphery—from groups of individuals who challenge prevailing patterns of thought and behavior and, perhaps most powerfully, establish alternative patterns for society to consider. One such alternative pattern, and one crucial to this discussion, is the orientation of the Bahá'í community toward the practice of politics. The centrality attached to the principle of the oneness of humankind in the Bahá'í writings extends to and shapes its view of politics. I use the term "politics" in a broad sense to denote processes and activities that encompass decision-making about the social order and the deliberation on issues facing society.[41] Efforts to contribute to the betterment of society must eventually navigate this terrain in some measure. Bahá'ís, however, draw a distinction between partisan political activity— activity characterized by association with, promotion of, or opposition to the interests of a particular group or political party—and unifying actions aimed at bringing about a social good. Partisan activity is traditionally concerned with the "retention or acquisition of power, in which all participants in the political arena are classified as either allies or opponents."[42] Grounded in the teaching of the oneness of humankind, the Bahá'í writings set forth a system of governance and decision-making that eschews partisan methods of any kind, methods that embody contests for power, however subtle (as will be discussed in detail in Chapter 3). The Bahá'í writings state: "If religion becomes a cause of dislike, hatred and division, it were better to be without it, and to withdraw from such a religion would be a truly religious act .... Any religion which is not a cause of love and unity is no religion."[43]

These specific parameters of engagement in political affairs are highly practical in nature as they preserve the unity of a growing, far-flung Baháʼí community, spread across different countries and under the authority of clashing governments. In a world slowly advancing toward unity, Baháʼís abstain from involvement in processes or systems that divide them into groups based on ideology (such as political parties) or social class (caste systems, for instance), as these maintain structures and ways of thinking that place individuals into oppositional and divisive relationships. On a practical level, this means that Baháʼís cannot identify as members of a political party or run for political office, though they can vote. Adherence to this principle is not meant as a criticism of those employing such methods but rather an acknowledgment of the limitations of such methods in trying to bring about greater unity. On the face of it, this may suggest an incompatibility between Baháʼí teachings and engagement with the United Nations, which is, after all, a political entity. Yet this is not the case. In the context of the United Nations, this directive means that Baháʼís cannot align with initiatives that support any one political platform or viewpoint. By analyzing the expression of several foundational elements of Baháʼí thought throughout seventy-five years of history at the United Nations, this book examines the emergence of a distinctive pattern of interactions in the political arena. Furthermore, the prohibition against engaging in partisan political processes does not prevent collaborating in other ways with those who use traditional political approaches to achieve noble ends. In fact, it implies working with broad and diverse arrays of partners (across on all "sides of the aisle"), where efforts can be combined to achieve constructive social change.

From the Vantage Point of the United Nations

The United Nations provides an important vantage point for the study of religious organizations in international affairs. Indeed, the presence of religious actors at the United Nations is more prominent today than at any other time and encompasses normative, institutional, operational, and discursive dimensions. Institutionally, intergovernmental and governmental delegations such as the Permanent Mission of the Organization for Islamic Cooperation (OIC) and the Permanent Observer Mission of the Holy See play a major representative role. The OIC is the largest intergovernmental organization with a mission to the United Nations, consisting of fifty-seven member states, while the Holy See represents the voice and experience of the worldwide Catholic community.[44] In addition, a number of UN member states have official religions that shape their foreign policy and perspectives on issues under consideration by the United Nations. Normatively, religion is addressed in the UN human rights framework as a non-derogable right[45] to freedom of religion or belief. In a less direct but widely acknowledged manner, both the Charter of the United Nations and the Universal Declaration of Human Rights are normatively rooted in values emanating from the world's religious traditions.[46] Of the over 5,000 NGOs that formally cooperate with the United Nations (through their "consultative status"[47]), approximately 10 to 15 percent have a religious affiliation and self-identify as "religious" or "spiritual."[48] Over the last fifteen years, various UN agencies have formalized their collaboration with a growing number of RNGOs and faith-based organizations, recognizing the value of their skills and resources (human, social, and financial) in achieving development and humanitarian goals.[49] As the UN Entity for Gender Equality and the Empowerment of Women notes:

> Faith-based[50] organizations are … among the most powerful agents of social change. The language of faith reaches to the deepest roots of human motivation. In addition, faith-based organizations and institutions are among the largest, most stable, and well-resourced social networks. Many of these networks transcend political, ethnic, and socio-economic boundaries…[51]

While only a decade ago, the question of religion and religious actors may have seemed out of place in the presumed secular domain of the United Nations, it is today—as outlined above—a well-established facet of its intellectual and operational environment.

A number of scholars have begun to examine the manner in which ideas rooted in religious traditions guide and motivate religious actors at the UN. Joseph Rossi, for example, identifies particular theological constructs that shaped Catholic engagement at the United Nations between 1946 and 1972; among them sovereignty of God, right conscience, human dignity, and the essential unity of the human race.[52] Similarly, in his 1965 address to the General Assembly, Pope Paul VI notes that "peace is not built merely by means of politics and a balance of power and interests. It is built with the mind, with ideas … the edifice of modern civilization has to be built on spiritual principles, for they are the only ones capable not only of supporting it, but of shedding light on it and inspiring it."[53] A more recent study of Christian NGOs at the United Nations, by Karsten Lehmann, asserts that "religiously affiliated actors cannot be properly analyzed without focusing upon the subjectively meaningful behavior of individuals."[54] The study attends to the manner in which the respective traditions of two RNGOs shaped their reading of international relations, their conceptions of human rights, the determination of organizational roles, and responsibilities vis-à-vis the social issues at hand, and the manner in which engagement with the United Nations was framed. Both Rossi's and Lehmann's studies highlight the dynamic relationship between theological reflection and the kind of strategies, approaches, and positions adopted by the RNGOs in question.

The Organizational Substrate: A New Analytical Tool

The central concern of this book is the identification and study of a distinct character of political activity as carried out by the BIC in its interactions with the United Nations. The inquiry draws inspiration from Robert Byrd's landmark study of Quaker engagement in foreign policy from 1647 to 1945 that seeks to identify a "body of cohesive principles which form the central structure" of the Quaker movement and which "give direction and moving power to it."[55] Examining Quaker efforts in the areas of abolishing slavery, promoting freedom of religion, as well as peacemaking and peacebuilding, Byrd delineates what he refers to as "the invisible skeleton" that consistently shaped the character of Quaker work for social justice over a period of three centuries.[56]

In the spirit of unearthing the hidden conceptual and epistemological frames shaping action, I introduce the concept of the *organizational substrate*. In order to grasp the nature and qualities of the political activity of the BIC, it is necessary to go beyond the external sociocultural determinants of behavior to explore the structures of organizational thought *from the inside*. This enables a better understanding of the manner in which the particular organization views the world and its role in it; as such, we begin to understand the entity not only as a political and social actor but *also* as a religious actor; not only as a consumer of political philosophies and structures of the liberal Western order but also as a creative agent of alternative formulations of progress and social order, a partner in the co-creation of the modern world.

If we understand religious traditions as organic, living phenomena, we must select (or develop) analytical tools that are attuned to these characteristics. As such, the *substrate* is a construct intentionally drawn from the fields of biology and chemistry, which themselves focus on organic phenomena. According to the *Oxford English Dictionary*, the term "substrate" refers to a foundational form—something that "underlies or forms the basis of another."[57] In biology, a substrate is a "surface or material on which any particular organism occurs or grows";[58] in chemistry, it is the "substance which a particular agent or reagent acts on ... bringing about a specific transformation."[59] Political theorist William Connolly highlights the utility of concepts drawn from biology for the study of phenomena in the political sphere. He argues that "bio-cultural connections should become more central to political inquiry," as this approach "appreciates the creative element in evolution" and may contribute to forms of "cultural interpretation that are even less reductionist in character."[60]

The creative and evolutionary element highlighted by Connolly is central to the analysis in this book, which attends to the generative (as opposed to deterministic) nature of the substrate as well as to the evolution of both the Bahá'í community and the United Nations between 1945 and 2020. The study identifies three elements of the organizational substrate of the BIC and examines their role in shaping the BIC's engagement with the United Nations. What emerges from the analysis is a distinctive kind of "politics" that challenges familiar notions of oppositional processes aimed at bringing about social change. The three elements are: (a) a developmental view of history, (b) the oneness of humankind, and (c) the Bahá'í system of governance (the "Administrative Order"). The elements of an organizational substrate not only bring to light the often hidden and unacknowledged factors shaping an organization's behavior, but it also enables us to consider the "conditions of possibility" (to borrow from Michel Foucault[61]) for new patterns and means of pursuing social change. Chapter 3 elaborates on this new analytical tool and its application in the study of the BIC.

Through the Lens of Seventy-Five Years of History

The case study of the BIC is presented through a historical lens: it is not a snapshot but rather an unfolding. As such, it is not an exhaustive account of the history of the organization's relationship with the United Nations (this would require several volumes to recount) but a study of the manner in which certain foundational elements of the Bahá'í Faith combine to give rise to a qualitatively different form of political activity.

There are of course many ways to tell this story and, with each approach, to reveal different facets of religious agency and engagement. One could, for example, organize the analysis according to various themes (for instance, engagement with civil society, capacity building) or issue areas (such as human rights or gender equality), and these too would yield useful insights. The rationale behind the historical approach is the desire to situate the BIC's engagement in the historical processes to which it is inextricably linked—the growth and development of civil society, the wider Baháʼí community, and the United Nations itself. Over the course of the seventy-five years covered by this volume, beginning in 1945 and concluding in 2020, we see the emergence of a new voice in international affairs—that of international civil society, through the work and organizing of thousands of NGOs spanning every issue, ideology, and constituency. We see the first seven decades of the first truly universal institution for deliberation among nation-states as it grows from 51 to 193 members. And we see the emergence of the BIC from obscurity—from an almost entirely unknown community in 1945—to an NGO elected to leadership positions of many of the largest NGO committees at the United Nations. As Byrd points out in his study of Quaker engagement in foreign policy, "The efficacy of this long-view approach is that the insights from each period are informed by the longer historical trajectory of engagement."[62]

To carry out the research, I drew on archival materials from the National Baháʼí Archives of the United States (Wilmette, Illinois), the archives of the BIC's United Nations Office (New York), the Dag Hammarskjöld Library (United Nations Headquarters, New York), the archives of the Baháʼí Office of Public Affairs (Washington, DC), as well as personal archives of past and present representatives of the BIC. Other sources include published primary sources such as Baháʼí sacred texts (print and online); online sources such as the official website of the BIC (www.bic.org), the official website of the worldwide Baháʼí community (www.Baháʼí.org), the BIC's YouTube channel, and the UN website. I also conducted open-ended interviews with past and present representatives of BIC, BIC delegates to various UN Commissions, as well as BIC staff.

How the Story Unfolds

In Chapter 2, I examine the history of the Baháʼí community, dating back to its origins in mid-nineteenth-century Persia in order to set the stage for its engagement with the structures of the emerging international order—the League of Nations and, subsequently, the United Nations. The chapter outlines the emergence of the Baháʼí community and its introduction of a novel concept of religion—a concept that stresses the progressive, evolutionary, unfolding nature of religious truth throughout human civilization; that religious revelation is not absolute but relative—that it is conveyed according to the exigences and capacity of humanity at varying times throughout history and will continue in this manner. Next the chapter traces the Bahá'í community's first encounter with the rulers and monarchs of the nineteenth-century world through letters written by Bahá'u'lláh exhorting them to adhere to the "highest principles in human and international relations,"[63] to eradicate corruption from their midst, to disarm, and to come together in a commonwealth of nations. Furthermore, it charts the community's efforts to support the world's nascent steps toward international peace and to begin to erect the structures of the social and governing order outlined in the Bahá'í writings, offering a model for a federated system of social organization capable of embodying the rich cultural and intellectual diversity of the world's people as well as building consensus and fostering unity at all levels of social organization.

Next, in Chapter 3, I introduce the concept of the organizational substrate and highlight the need to examine the BIC from the inside in order to identify and analyze the structures of thought that shape its behaviors in the international arena, thus shedding light on the organization as not only a political but also a religious actor. I stress the importance of attentiveness to the particularities of a given religious tradition, noting that too often Christian frameworks and templates have been used to study other religious traditions. This tendency has muted and rendered invisible some of the distinctive elements of these traditions, which are necessary to obtain a richer understanding of both the human experience of religion and also the broader question of the agency of religious actors in the modern world. The use of the term "substrate" underlines the organic, generative nature of its elements and highlights the evolution of the manner in which religious ideas are applied in response to various historical periods and exigencies. The three elements of the substrate are explored in detail: the developmental view of history, the oneness of humanity, and the Bahá'í Administrative Order.

The next four chapters examine the expression of the substrate throughout four distinct historical periods of the BIC–UN relationship, beginning in 1945 and ending in 2020. Chapter 4 opens with the creation of the United Nations and the BIC's early engagement as an "observer NGO;" it closes in 1970 when the BIC is granted the coveted "consultative status" with the United Nations. The chapter focuses on conceptions of history and time, and their implications for RNGO engagement in international affairs. The Bahá'í conception of history as a developmental and teleological process, unfolding over millennia and advancing toward the formation of a global community of nations, casts the United Nations in a new light. The chapter explores how such a view of history leads to an evolutionary understanding of the United Nations, its challenges, its promise, and its greater role in the advancement of human society as a whole. We begin to see the emergence of a new kind of agency—the RNGO not as a passive recipient of knowledge about the international order, but one that generates a distinct view of international relations, the processes shaping relationships between member states, the forces leading to integration and disintegration, and the protagonists in the unfolding order.

Turning to a dramatic period in the BIC–UN relationship (1970–86), Chapter 5 unfolds as the existence of the Bahá'í community in Iran is threatened by a government-backed campaign of violent persecution aimed at exterminating the community from its midst. In this period, the elements of the substrate give rise to a principled response to one of the most severe cases of religious persecution in the world at this time. In addressing the growing threats, the BIC is challenged to respond in a manner that "doesn't take [on] the characteristics of the oppressor" but that maintains a principled, nonpartisan, as well as swift and globally coordinated course of action to protect the beleaguered community in Iran. This highlights the Bahá'í approach to relating to secular government authorities, the building of capacity for global action, as well as the evolution of institutions and processes that consolidate the growing Bahá'í community into a coherent global order. Furthermore, the chapter explores the Bahá'í community's involvement in the UN Decade for Women (1976–85) and reveals the particular role of the Universal House of Justice and the Administrative Order in increasing the community's ability to contribute to the advancement of gender equality locally and on the world stage.

Spanning the period between 1986 and 2008, Chapter 6 introduces the distinct construct of peace pursued by the BIC. What emerges from this period is an understanding of peace in terms of processes that advance humanity's capacity for collective action and that are guided by a consciousness of the interdependence and oneness of humankind. The intimate relationship between unity and peace provides a new lens for reading society, primarily in terms of its capacity for social cohesion and collaboration on a global scale. The chapter discusses particular constructs that shape the BIC's understanding of and approach toward the pursuit of peace: unity in diversity, relationship between justice and unity, peace as process, different kinds of peace ("Lesser Peace" and the "Most Great Peace"), conceptions of time, and ends—means coherence. Furthermore, the chapter reviews the BIC's deep engagement in setting the stage for major UN conferences during this period (environment, social development, gender equality) as well as the BIC's epistemic and intellectual contributions to UN debates on issues of global and social concern.

Chapter 7 explores the operation of the substrate during the fourth and final period examined in this book, from 2008 to 2020. It uncovers a new orientation toward the BIC's engagement in the international arena, as introduced by the global governing body of the Bahá'í Faith—namely, "participation in the discourses of society." This shift embodies an approach toward social change that focuses on transformation at the level of thought, attitudes, and mental habits that constrain and shape the moral and social imagination. As the BIC asserts, "Attitudes, thoughts, and conceptions of fundamental issues need to be reshaped as a truly global community emerges and develops in its understanding of the nature of human flourishing as well as the social and material conditions required for such flourishing."[64] Such an orientation situates the BIC as a contributor to deliberative processes that shape the evolution of thought, practice, and policy-making. Furthermore, it highlights the collective dimension of the generation of insights and knowledge and the advancement of thought. The analysis reveals broader implications for the role of civil society in international affairs, conceptions of religion, the reconciliation of unity and difference, and the role of knowledge in advancing human flourishing.

Bringing together insights from the exploration of the BIC's seventy-five-year engagement with the United Nations, the final chapter probes the central questions of the book: How can we study the structures of thought that shape the engagement of RNGOs in the international arena in order to better understand religious agency in the world today? How do the BIC's structures of thought shape its encounter with the United Nations as it navigates different historical circumstances and opportunities? What insights can we glean about the changing role of religion in the modern world? While the volume focuses on the experience of the BIC, the questions raised and insights generated are not limited to the Bahá'í community. The book addresses itself to broader debates about the category of religion, pushing beyond Christian normativity in the study of civil society in international affairs, the unfoldment of civil society's relationship with the United Nations, the counter-rationality of religious organizations, and, ultimately, the complex, changing role of religion in the modern world.

Forging a Global Polity:
The Baháʾí Community on the World Stage

In order to understand the nature of the Baháʾí community's engagement with the United Nations, we must go back a full century before the intergovernmental organization's founding to the birth of the Baháʾí Faith in mid-1800s Persia (present-day Iran). Among the factors that make the Baháʾí community a particularly fascinating case study are the very timing and location of its origin. Its emergence in the full light of history, with the preserved and authenticated texts of its four successive leaders, gives us unprecedented access to the modern-day birth of a new religious tradition. The proceeding sections will provide a concise overview of the unfoldment of this new religion in three periods, organized according to the leadership of the Baháʾí community at the time: (1) the Báb[1] and Baháʾuʾlláh (1844–92); (2) ʿAbduʾl-Bahá (1892–21); and (3) Shoghi Effendi (1921–57).

Nineteenth Century: A New Revelation and a New Global Order

Let us pause for a moment to consider the world in the nineteenth century. At the turn of the century, the empire was the dominant form of social and political organization. It was an age of revolutions, which witnessed the growing contestation of traditional authority and the struggle for voice and power, such as the constitutionalist movements in Iran, Turkey, and Russia.[2] The Napoleonic Wars (1803–15) entangled nearly all European powers in a protracted battle for the domination of the continent;[3] the resulting Congress of Vienna (1814–15) redrew European borders and established a balance of powers among European monarchies.[4] The United States was embroiled in the War of 1812 and, later, in the American Civil War. It was the century of nation-state formation—one that saw the birth of international relations as we know it today.[5] It was also during this period that early forms of a global consciousness and organization began to take shape. The first international non-governmental organizations, such as the International Red Cross, started to form in the 1860s; the Second International Women's Conference took place in 1888 in Washington, DC; and the First Universal Peace Congress convened in Paris in 1889, among others. The "supra-national" consciousness of religious communities such as Christians and Muslims already existed at this time but without a corresponding political entity.[6] During this century, the contours of a new global order began to take shape.

Against the backdrop of revolutionary fervor, political upheavals, and intellectual flourishing, a new religion emerged in Persia. A young Persian nobleman, Mírzá Husayn-'Alí (1817–92), later known by the title of Bahá'u'lláh (Arabic for "Glory of God"), arose in the 1850s as the leader of a new religious community oriented toward the peaceful construction of a new social order.[7] As Ninian Smart has pointed out, "When religions start ... they [are not] concerned so much with maintaining equilibrium as with providing—in a revolutionary way—a new way of looking at the world and society."[8] Bahá'u'lláh taught that all of the world's religions come from the same divine source, that they comprise one continuous stream of guidance from God to humanity communicated through successive teachers, or "Manifestations of God" (as they are known in the Bahá'í Faith), including Zoroaster, Buddha, Moses, Abraham, Jesus, Krishna, Mohammad, and the Báb.[9] As this guidance comes in different periods of humanity's history, it necessarily differs according to the cultural and historical context within which it emerges. Bahá'u'lláh writes:

> O Son of Beauty! By My spirit and by My favor! By My mercy and by My beauty! All that I have revealed unto thee with the tongue of power, and have written for thee with the pen of might, hath been in accordance with thy capacity and understanding, not with My state and the melody of My voice.[10]

And thus comes the revolutionary message that religious truth is not absolute but relative—that it is conveyed according to the evolving exigencies and capacities of humanity, rather than an absolute expression of Divine Will.[11] "Every age hath its own problem," asserts Bahá'u'lláh, "and every soul its particular aspiration. The remedy the world needeth in its present-day afflictions can never be the same as that which a subsequent age may require."[12] From the age of thirty-five until his passing, Bahá'u'lláh was aggressively persecuted and exiled by Persian and Ottoman authorities for his leadership of a "heretical" religious movement that was gaining a steady following.

Throughout his ministry, Bahá'u'lláh penned thousands of letters and expositions on themes concerning the moral, spiritual, social, legal, and structural requisites of a just society; predominant among these (the alpha and the omega of his teachings) was the promotion of unity and justice among all the peoples of the world. "The earth is but one country," writes Bahá'u'lláh, "and mankind its citizens." He continues: "It is not for him to pride himself who loveth his own country, but rather for him who loveth the whole world."[13] Bahá'u'lláh urges his own countrymen and wider society alike, "Be anxiously concerned with the needs of the age ye live in, and center your deliberations on its exigencies and requirements."[14] Throughout the vast output of teachings issued during the course of his life (equivalent to about 100 volumes), he laid out the conceptual and moral scaffolding for the construction of a more just and unified world.

In the 1860s, having announced to his family, immediate followers, and community members, the nature of his station as the "Manifestation of God" for this stage in the life of humanity, Bahá'u'lláh turned his attention to kings and rulers around the globe, the centers of political and economic power of the nineteenth century.[15] Between 1866 and 1873, he addressed Queen Victoria (British Empire),[16] Emperor Napoleon III (French Empire), Tsar Alexander II (Russian Empire), Emperor Franz Joseph (Austro-Hungarian Empire), Kaiser Wilhelm I (German Empire), and Pope Pius IX (Head of Catholic Church).[17] He also addressed Sultan Abdu'l-Aziz (Ottoman Empire), Nasir al-Din Shah of the Qajar Dynasty (Persian Empire), and Álí Páshá, the Ottoman prime minister. In his letters, Bahá'u'lláh reveals his station as the Messenger of God for this day;[18] he exhorts the sovereigns to pursue just systems of government and to deal in a fair manner with their subjects, to adhere to the "highest principles in human and international relations,"[19] to eradicate corruption from their midst, to disarm, and to come together in a commonwealth of nations, warning rulers of catastrophic upheavals if they fail to establish peace. He addresses religious leaders and specifically monks, saying:

> Seclude not yourselves in your churches and cloisters. Come ye out of them by My leave, and busy, then, yourselves with what will profit you and others ....He that secludeth himself in his house is indeed as one dead. It behoveth man to show forth that which will benefit mankind.[20]

The letters convey the character of Bahá'u'lláh's mission and establish the "standard of justice that must govern the exercise of [sovereign] rule in this Day of God."[21] While the tone is pressing and authoritative, it is also an invitation to examine "in a spirit of open-mindedness"[22] the substance of his claims and exhortations.

While a detailed treatment of Bahá'u'lláh's correspondence is beyond the scope of this chapter, it is instructive to identify a number of relevant themes that emerge in the letters and the body of Bahá'u'lláh's work, among them: an embrace of constitutionalism,[23] an emphasis on the use of social discourse and peaceful deliberation to resolve disputes, an elaboration of the principle of obedience and loyalty to one's government, and a commitment to noninterference in partisan politics.[24] Many of these themes are also echoed in an 1875 treatise titled *The Secret of Divine Civilization*—commissioned by Bahá'u'lláh and penned by his eldest son, 'Abdu'l-Bahá—which addresses the degraded condition of Persia and outlines proposals for reforms in the area of governance, technology, education, and the intellectual and moral development of society as a whole.

By 1892, the year of his passing, Bahá'u'lláh's message had reached thousands and spread to fifteen countries. It attracted the attention of prominent figures; garnered the respect of political leaders, kings, and scholars; aroused the fears and jealousies of religious leaders; and laid the foundations for a new global religion.

Twentieth Century: Revolutions and the Groundwork for International Peace

In the early decades of the twentieth century, the Bahá'í community was led by Bahá'u'lláh's eldest son, 'Abdu'l-Bahá (meaning "Servant of Bahá"),[25] as the successor appointed by Bahá'u'lláh in his will and testament. The explicit appointment of a successor is not incidental to this narrative but rather central to the unfoldment of the story of the Bahá'í community on the world stage. The continuation of religious leadership after the passing of the founder of a new religious movement has always been a point of reckoning for a religious community—disagreements over who should lead a community have created schisms across most religious traditions. The Sunni–Shia divide in the Muslim world is one prominent example of this. By providing explicit instructions for the appointment of a successor, Bahá'u'lláh imparted the nascent Bahá'í community with a clear direction in which to turn after his passing.[26] 'Abdu'l-Bahá led the community until his passing in 1921.

The first two decades of the twentieth century witnessed the emergence of the nation-state project and the earliest efforts at devising the political architecture of international cooperation. At the same time, constitutionalist movements, such as those sweeping Turkey, Iran, and Russia, were pushing for major domestic legal reforms. It is instructive to consider 'Abdu'l-Bahá's guidance to the Baháʼí community during Iran's Constitutional Revolution (1905–11)—a movement spurred by the despotic rule of Nasir al-Din Shah (king of Persia from 1848–96) that advocated for the creation of a constitution and an elected parliament.[27] ʻAbduʼl-Baháʼs orientation toward the revolution was characterized by an affirmation of the principles of constitutionalism and, at the same time, a rejection of the confrontational nature of the interactions.[28] Some three decades earlier, in a treatise commissioned by Baháʼuʼlláh, he proposed the creation of a representative parliament composed of "consultative assemblies" of "elected representatives."[29] Rejecting the confrontational nature of the interactions between the Royalist and Constitutionalist camps, ʻAbduʼl-Bahá refused to sanction Baháʼís' participation in the uprisings and instead urged them to work to reconcile the two camps—as he was doing—or, if that was not possible, to withdraw. His response to the Constitutional Revolution in Iran embodied the principles of sociopolitical engagement established by Baháʼuʼlláh, "at the center of which was a belief in the power of discourse to change sociopolitical conditions and to reject violence as a means to sociopolitical ends."[30]

It was also during the first half of the twentieth century that representatives of the world's nations made pioneering attempts to lay the political groundwork for international peace. At the turn of the century, US President Theodore Roosevelt, in response to calls from leaders of peace movements, proposed a major peace conference, held in 1907, which was attended by representatives of forty-four governments and made important advances in the codification of laws in matters related to war.[31] No less than twenty-three international peace congresses were held between 1899 and 1913. During these years, ʻAbduʼl-Bahá, after forty years of imprisonment and exile to various parts of the Ottoman Empire, carried Baháʼuʼlláh's message of global solidarity and peace to the West, speaking to communities and leaders of thought in countries including France, England, Germany, Canada, and the United States. In 1912, throughout his eight-month stay in the United States, he gave over 400 public talks from coast to coast, addressing themes of international peace, racial, and ethnic equality, the full equality of women and men (including the importance of women's suffrage), and spent much of his time away from crowds and admirers, focusing on the plight of those living in sickness and in poverty.[32] He urged his listeners to consider that "religious, racial, political, economic and patriotic prejudices destroy the edifice of humanity" and that "until the minds of men become united, no important matter can be accomplished."[33] As he asserts, "The scope of Universal Peace must be such that all the communities and religions may find their highest wish realized in it."[34]

Among the central themes of 'Abdu'l-Bahá's messages in North America is a call to reflect critically on the role that religion had come to play in society. "Consider the record of religious warfare," he tells one audience, "the battle between nations, the bloodshed and destruction in the name of religion."[35] Furthermore, he names religion as "the greatest cause of human alienation."[36] 'Abdu'l-Bahá's forceful critique of divisive and harmful forms of religion was accompanied by an invitation—indeed, an exhortation—to consider religion in a new light. In his 1919 response to a letter from the Central Organization for a Durable Peace[37] at The Hague, he asserts that if religion "becomes the cause of estrangement then it is not needed, for religion is like a remedy; if it aggravates the disease then it becomes unnecessary."[38] Further, he states that religion "must be in conformity with science and reason, so that it may influence the hearts of men."[39]

This key element of Bahá'í guidance—developed by Bahá'u'lláh, 'Abdu'l-Bahá, and later Shoghi Effendi—brings about not merely a new religious tradition, but *a new conception of religion itself*, one suited to both the intellectual advances and the needs and exigencies of the age. As the Bahá'í writings state:

> Bahá'u'lláh has not brought into existence a new religion to stand beside the present multiplicity of sectarian organizations. Rather has He recast the whole conception of religion as the principal force impelling the development of consciousness. As the human race in all its diversity is a single species, so the intervention by which God cultivates the qualities of mind and heart latent in that species is a single process.[40]

It is a bold and revolutionary assertion that brings the great religions of the world together as elements or stages of one continuous, unfolding process— one stream of guidance from a divine source—thereby offering a vision for a harmonious social order. As Bahá'u'lláh says:

> The well-being of mankind, its peace and security, are unattainable unless and until its unity is firmly established.[41]

Thousands of tablets and letters are dedicated to the exposition of the deceptively simple concept of unity, a revolutionary idea necessitating that calls for "organic change" in the structure and life of society—such that relationships between all individuals, communities, and nations; between the people and their governing institutions; and between humanity and the natural environment can be transformed and organized in a manner that enables all people to play their part in helping to carry forward our human civilization. A religion that calls for the coming together of peoples and nations cannot itself be a source of division and work against its own self-identified civilizational imperative. Thus, the role of religion is not to divide, but rather—illumined by the lights of both faith and reason—to unite. As ʿAbduʾl-Bahá states:

> If religion becomes a cause of dislike, hatred and division, it were better to be without it, and to withdraw from such a religion would be a truly religious act.[42]

The implications of these convictions extend necessarily into the domain of politics—that arena of human endeavor concerned with the organization and governance of society. The principles of the Baháʾí Faith forbid engagement in antagonistic and contentious practices; unity must be pursued through means that are in themselves unifying and not partisan or oppositional in any way. Thus the stage is set for the emergence of a new religious community, a developing emerging global polity, spurred to action by the injunction to "be anxiously concerned" with the needs of the world and with the unequivocal examples of principled, forbearing, and unflinching engagement of Baháʾí leadership in the prevailing discourses and challenges of the age.

World War and a Second Wave of Peacekeeping Efforts

The early efforts of the world's nations to forge an international architecture that would secure the peace came to naught with the outbreak of the First World War in 1914 and the upheavals and destruction it brought upon the globe. A second wave of efforts following that war led to the signing of the Treaty of Versailles and the creation of the Covenant of the League of Nations—the first worldwide intergovernmental organization with a mission to maintain world peace. From the perspective of history, the League of Nations was an ambitious and earnest attempt to forge an international alliance in the name of securing universal peace. At the same time, its (fatal) deficiencies were also readily apparent and ultimately prevented it from staying the forces of nationalism, racism, and fascism paving the way for the Second World War.[43] The twentieth century saw the greatest number of deaths from war of any century in human history—over 100 million people perished.[44]

Yet the century also was marked by unprecedented intellectual and social breakthroughs and political developments that improved the quality of life for millions, a fact not unnoticed by historians who have examined this century in a broader perspective.[45] ʿAbduʾl-Bahá called attention to the crowning achievement of the twentieth century—laying the foundations for the unification of the peoples of the world:

In this day ... means of communication have multiplied, and the five continents of the earth have virtually merged into one .... In like manner all the members of the human family, whether peoples or governments, cities or villages, have become increasingly interdependent ... Hence the unity of all mankind can in this day be achieved. Verily this is none other but one of the wonders of this wondrous age, this glorious century.[46]

We can say, to borrow from Foucault, that 'Abdu'l-Bahá was highlighting newly emergent "conditions of possibility"[47] that had arisen in the twentieth century. Foucault used this term to refer to institutional supports and social practices that give rise to particular kinds of discourse and understandings of reality. In a similar way, 'Abdu'l-Bahá called attention to unprecedented and emerging material and social realities that contributed to the capacity to achieve the unity of humankind.

New Leadership and an Emerging Global International Order

The year 1921 saw the passing of 'Abdu'l-Bahá and the appointment of his eldest grandson, Shoghi Effendi—as stipulated in 'Abdu'l-Bahá's will and testament— as Head of the Bahá'í community.[48] Shoghi Effendi, until his passing in 1957, would lead the nascent community through one of the most turbulent periods of human history, marked by the rise of Nazism, fascism, and nationalism, anti-Semitism, the outbreak and carnage of the Second World War, and the persecution of the Bahá'í community in Iran under Mohammad Reza Pahlavi.

During Shoghi Effendi's thirty-six-year ministry, which unfolded throughout his 35,000 letters and epistles, the Bahá'í community emerged as a global religious body, expanding its presence in thirty-five countries in 1921 to 254 countries in 1957.[49] The Bahá'í Administrative Order—a unique system of democratic governance, whose fundamental structure and principles were outlined in the writings of Bahá'u'lláh and 'Abdu'l-Bahá—took on definitive shape with the formation of local and national administrative bodies (known as Local and National Spiritual Assemblies), buttressed by extensive elucidation on the principles of Bahá'í administration. Development of the Bahá'í administrative order at the local and national levels was essential to lay the foundation for members of the national bodies to eventually elect the Universal House of Justice. Among the key elements of Shoghi Effendi's prolific leadership was the translation of Bahá'í texts from the original Persian into English (having studied English at Oxford University), thus making authoritative translations available for the first time to the wider global community.

With the newly emerging institutions of the nascent international order, Shoghi Effendi recognized the opportunity for the Bahá'í community to contribute to the processes of global integration underway and encouraged the establishment of the International Bahá'í Bureau at the League of Nations headquarters in Geneva. The bureau, established in 1925 by American Bahá'í Jean Stannard, served as an informational distribution center and gathering place for Bahá'ís traveling to Geneva to participate in activities of the league and other international organizations.[50] In 1929, the bureau was formally recognized by the league. Grounded in the guidance of Bahá'u'lláh and 'Abdu'l-Bahá, both of whom outlined the features of an emerging global civilization, as well as the exhortation to engage earnestly and fully in the betterment of society, Bahá'ís in the twentieth century participated in "a great variety of congresses, associations, conventions, and conferences ... for the promotion of religious unity, peace, education, international cooperation, inter-racial amity and other humanitarian purposes."[51]

As the Bahá'í community found its voice in the international arena, Shoghi Effendi offered guidance in letters addressing a wide variety of issues; a particular focus concerned the establishment of institutions and processes necessary for the administration of a growing community.[52] A seminal passage from these letters encapsulates many themes that have particular relevance for the Bahá'í community's engagement with institutions on the world stage:

> The principle of the Oneness of Mankind—the pivot round which all the teachings of Bahá'u'lláh revolve—is no mere outburst of ignorant emotionalism or an expression of vague and pious hope. Its appeal is not to be merely identified with a reawakening of the spirit of brotherhood and good-will among men, nor does it aim solely at the fostering of harmonious cooperation among individual peoples and nations .... Its message is applicable not only to the individual, but concerns itself primarily with the nature of those essential relationships that must bind all the states and nations as members of one human family ... It constitutes a challenge, at once bold and universal, to outworn shibboleths of national creeds ... It calls for no less than the reconstruction and the demilitarization of the whole civilized world—a world organically unified in all the essential aspects of its life, its political machinery, its spiritual aspiration, its trade and finance, its script and language, and yet infinite in the diversity of the national characteristics of its federated units.[53]

This passage reveals that the pivotal tenet of the Bahá'í Faith is concerned with fostering harmonious relationships among peoples and nations and, more specifically, with binding them together into a coherent whole. It further shows that this vision is inextricably linked with institutional arrangements capable of embodying the oneness of humanity and that it requires that the whole civilized world be "reconstructed" in a manner that will render it capable of unifying all essential facets of collective life.

Contrasted with this vision, as the specter of a Second World War became a grim reality, was the ideological and moral bankruptcy that Shoghi Effendi identified as having brought about this state of affairs:

> The theories and policies, so unsound, so pernicious, which deify the state and exalt the nation above mankind, which seek to subordinate the sister races of the world to one single race, which discriminate between the black and the white, and which tolerate the dominance of one privileged class over all others—these are the dark, the false, and crooked doctrines for which any man or people who believes in them, or acts upon them, must, sooner or later, incur the wrath and chastisement of God.[54]

The extensive guidance from the pen of Shoghi Effendi outlining the evolutionary process through which a new global civilization would emerge—including the requisite transformation in the political, ecclesiastical, and social orders—provided Bahá'ís with a clearer understanding of the social forces at play in the world, as well as the direction of history and their role within it.

The Birth of the United Nations

The birth of the United Nations in 1945 offered new possibilities for engagement with the international community. Along with many other civil society organizations, buoyed with the hope and optimism that characterized the United Nations Founding Conference in San Francisco, the Bahá'í community participated through its official representatives, distributing thousands of copies of materials related to the Bahá'í peace program and the spiritual and social prerequisites of peace among the nations, as well as holding public meetings and talks on the subject of peace.[55] During his visit to Washington, DC, in 1912, over three decades earlier, 'Abdu'l-Bahá had auspiciously declared: "May this American democracy be the first nation to establish the foundation of international peace. May it be the first nation to proclaim the universality of mankind."[56] And further, during his visit to New York City that same year, he had stated, "There is no doubt that ... the banner of international agreement will be unfurled here to spread onward and outward among all the nations of the world."[57] Over the next decade, Shoghi Effendi would continue to shape the manner of Bahá'í engagement with the international community, developing a revolutionary framework for principled, nonpartisan participation in the sphere of global politics that would serve as a model for exercising religious agency in the modern world.

*

This chapter set out to accomplish an ambitious task—namely, to trace the historical and conceptual foundations of the Bahá'í community's engagement in the international arena. This historical account spans the birth of a new religious tradition and the establishment of a global religious community against the backdrop of two world wars, the fall of dynasties and empires, numerous revolutions and colonial revolts—indeed, one of the most turbulent and transformative periods of human history. While it is impossible to do justice to the multifaceted nature of the unfoldment of the Bahá'í philosophy and practice of engagement in the political arena, I have endeavored to outline, however incompletely, the major currents of thought and the important examples set by the successive leaders of the Bahá'í community as they sought to model a manner of engagement aligned with the needs of an emerging global community. We can discern in Bahá'u'lláh's writings and statements to the leaders of the day, 'Abdu'l-Bahá's public talks in Europe and North America, and Shoghi Effendi's assiduous guidance to the growing community and its emerging governing institutions a pattern of progressive, principled, and non-adversarial engagement, buttressed by the parallel evolution of a new community of discourse and practice occupied with the realization of the Bahá'í principles of justice and unity within their respective countries and modes of governance.

Shaping Organizational Behavior:
An Evolving and Generative Framework

Having surveyed the historical terrain that brought us from the inception of the Bahá'í Faith to the emergence of the United Nations, we return now to the central questions of this book: How do the conceptual foundations of the Bahá'í International Community (BIC) reshape familiar understandings of politics? What kinds of dispositions and approaches characterize a polity rooted in these foundations? My aim is to demonstrate that in order to more fully understand religious agency in the modern world, we must look beyond the material and sociocultural determinants of behavior to examine the internal logics of religious organizations. Such an approach takes seriously the religious dimensions of organizational life—that is to say the meaning-making, motivational, and epistemological dimensions—which are often bracketed out in studies working through the lens of secular social science.[1] This chapter will unfold in two parts: first, I will introduce and discuss the *organizational substrate*, a new analytical tool to examine the conceptual framework shaping organizational behavior. Second, I will identify three elements of the BIC's organizational substrate—view of history, oneness of humanity, and administrative order—whose expression throughout seventy-five years of the BIC's engagement with the United Nations, as I seek to demonstrate in this book, gives rise to a new global polity and a distinct manner of pursuing social change in the international arena.

When considering methodological approaches to the study of religion, it is necessary first to clarify the conception of religion itself, as this has important consequences for how it is studied. For example, if religion is understood as a set of static beliefs, then we might seek to analyze the consequences of those beliefs in various spheres of human life.[2] If, on the other hand, religion is seen as an unfolding tradition, we might look at the social practices of that community and see how they embody the beliefs in different social and historical contexts. These are not the only two ways of looking at religion of course, but they highlight an important distinction between "static" and "living" views of religion. The Bahá'í conception of religion—as introduced in Chapter 1—encompasses a dynamic, developmental notion of a process that unfolds throughout history as successive Revelations address themselves to the moral imperatives of the age in which they appear. From this perspective, religion is not regarded as a set of beliefs and practices, but as a continually unfolding source of knowledge that propels the advancement of human civilization.[3]

The Substrate and the Bio-Cultural Connection

In light of the above considerations, this book introduces the concept of the *organizational substrate* as a tool to study the structures of thought shaping organizational behavior and engagement in the political arena. The term "substrate" is intentionally drawn from the fields of biology and chemistry in order to highlight the dynamic and generative nature of the phenomenon being studied. In both disciplines, the substrate refers to a foundational form— something that "underlies or forms the basis of another."[4] In biology, a substrate is a "surface or material on which any particular organism occurs or grows";[5] in chemistry, it is the "substance which a particular agent or reagent acts on ... bringing about a specific transformation."[6] One can think of the substrate as performing a similar function to that of DNA in the human body. The DNA molecule carries most of the genetic instructions that shape the growth, development, and functioning of all living organisms. It constitutes the core identity of that being, and distinguishes it from other, even very similar, entities. However, DNA is not the sole determinant of such distinctions; just by knowing the DNA, one cannot fully know the organism's phenotype, which is shaped by both the expression of the organism's genes and the influence of environmental factors and the interactions between the two.

In the context of an organization, the substrate refers to the foundational concepts and commitments that make up the "DNA" of the organization; these play a vital, generative role in determining action, alongside social and material factors. One of the key features of the substrate is that it is generative: it is not a formula nor a prescription for a particular set of behaviors leading to a predetermined outcome. Rather, outcomes emerge as an organization, rooted in a substrate, responds to continually changing exigencies and opportunities, giving rise to a range of actions and behaviors. As Lehmann points out in his study of Christian NGOs, religious organizations are characterized by "very complex internal structures that are formed in constant exchange with their respective sociocultural contexts."[7] The substrate, then, is not absolute; whereas 1 + 1 will always equal 2, the substrate yields new behaviors and organizational forms as the organization negotiates continually shifting social and material contexts. The substrate constitutes the organization's conceptual framework, within which are coded the distinctive logics and patterns of behavior that characterize the organization.

The generative quality of the substrate is closely related to a second defining feature: its orientation toward evolution and change. This is of central importance as it differentiates the substrate from the related concepts of "paradigm" and "episteme." Recall, as was stated earlier, that the conception of religion has consequences for the manner in which it is studied. As the construct of religion introduced in the Bahá'í writings is one that unfolds and evolves through civilizational time, the manner in which such a phenomenon is studied, I am proposing, must grasp its essential evolutionary and dynamic quality. Thomas Kuhn's concept of the "paradigm" provides a useful mechanism for describing the nature and structure of thought in a particular discipline.[8] Yet a paradigm does not prefigure change; it is static: paradigms "shift" following a period of "crisis" during which increasing "anomalies" undermine confidence in a particular paradigm.[9] As rival paradigms emerge, they give rise to new criteria for evaluating the legitimacy of knowledge and observations, such as in the case of a transition from Newtonian to Einsteinian physics, which redefined, among other things, the nature of space and time and the relationship between them. As Kuhn describes, "when paradigms change, the world itself changes with them."[10] Foucault's "episteme" is another concept used to examine underlying structures of thought that shape intellectual life at particular points in time.[11] Foucault used this construct to describe the manner in which cultural, intellectual, and economic structures shaped and generated constructs, such as wealth[12] or mental illness[13] ("madness"), within a given society. Like the paradigm, the episteme, too, is a static construct: it does not evolve; it "ruptures" over longer time frames and is superseded by new epistemes.

While these constructs are helpful in shedding light on the structures of thought, they are associated with a predominantly static view of reality. Similarly, in the view of some authors, the discipline of theology configures religion as a phenomenon that must continually struggle to "sustain significant continuity with the past," fighting against "the constant changes and uprooting of modernity."[14] The implications of a static view of religion and social reality are particularly salient when studying a religion such as the Bahá'í Faith, whose vision of religion and epistemology are rooted in concepts of evolution (of ideas) and organic development. The substrate, with its explicit connection to the biological sciences, draws out this organic and evolutionary dimension; thus, it reframes the orientation toward the study of religion as a process not in conflict with modernity but rather one that unfolds and evolves in civilizational time.

Attentiveness to Particularism

As an analytical tool, the substrate allows for the expression of a tradition's lexicon and epistemology without imposing conceptual frameworks that are rooted in other traditions (predominantly Christianity) and importing assumptions about the category of religion that may not be relevant. Consider that the discipline of theology itself is not a neutral construct; it embodies a distinctively Christian intellectual and philosophical orientation and is not a term indigenous to other faith traditions. Islamic scholars, for example, are more likely to use the term "'Ilm al-Kalām" ("the science of discourse") or "Islamic jurisprudence" ("fiqh"). In Buddhism, the term "dharma" refers to the teachings of the Buddha. Hinduism has no equivalent for the concept of "theology." Jewish scholars refer to the study of the Torah and the Talmud.

In the writings of the Bahá'í Faith, the term "theology" is associated principally with patterns of thinking and disputation that obstruct intellectual and social progress. Bahá'u'lláh cautions against engaging in sciences that "begin with words and end with words" and that lead to "idle disputation."[15] Such sciences refer to "those theological treatises and commentaries that encumber the human mind rather than help it to attain the truth."[16] Similarly, 'Abdu'l-Bahá critiques "ancestral forms and theological interpretations ... which [do] not bear the analysis of reason."[17] Moving beyond critique, the Bahá'í writings explicitly outline the manner in which the study of the Bahá'í Faith is to be approached:

> Weigh not the Book of God with such standards and sciences as are current amongst you, for the Book itself is the unerring balance established amongst men ... the measure of its weight should be tested according to its own standard.[18]

This issues a challenge to scholars using interpretivist methods and endeavoring to portray the work of the organization through the eyes of its adherents. While it could be argued that a scholar could define theological inquiry in a manner sensitive to the particularities of the tradition being studied, I posit that the substrate provides an entry point into the lexicon and structures of thought of a particular organization in a manner that more readily disentangles the inquiry from intellectual assumptions and commitments associated with other religious traditions. It takes up the challenge issued by the Bahá'í writings by inviting scholars to examine closely the conceptual framework and mode of inquiry that arises from within a given tradition.

Further Considerations

There are two final points to highlight about the substrate. First, the elements of a substrate are *known* and can be consciously acted upon by individuals in a given organization[19] in response to opportunities and exigencies that arise. (While members of an organization may have varying levels of engagement in generating foundational frameworks, it is not the case that they operate in a subconscious manner.) In this sense, the substrate differs from similar concepts such as Foucault's episteme, which operates as a hidden cultural code that operates outside of conscious knowledge. It also differs from sociologist Pierre Bourdieu's related concept of "habitus." While habitus is similar to the substrate as it references "a system of ... dispositions,"[20] and functions as "the generative basis of structured, objectively unified practices,"[21] it is not consciously known; the dispositions and behaviors are reproduced unconsciously.[22] Conversely, the substrate is not "uncovered" by the researcher and "revealed" to the organization.

Second, while the substrate is being used to study the BIC in this book, as an analytical tool it eschews the religious–secular binary as a salient organizational characteristic. It focuses instead on the ideational dimensions of organizational life, which need not be categorized as "secular" or "religious." Even organizations that identify with the same religious tradition may not have identical substrates; to understand the structures of thought shaping their behavior, we need to go beyond the superficial categories of religious–secular or Muslim, Christian, Hindu, Jewish, etc., to examine the distinct intellectual foundations of their work as they are understood within the organizational context. The above mentioned characteristics of a substrate are summarized in Figure 3.1.

In summary, the substrate is particularly well-suited to the analysis of processes that are evolutionary and organic in nature. It advances understanding beyond that of previous studies in a number of ways: it discerns the meaning and

Figure 3.1 Insights from a substrate-based approach

Characteristics of prevalent approaches to the study of RNGOs	Characteristics of a substrate-based approach
Moral orientation viewed as a fixed set of beliefs	Moral orientation viewed as dynamic and generative; in dialogue with changing historical and cultural circumstances
Focus on the visible dimensions of behaviors and sociocultural determinants of behavior	Focus on the internal structures of thought and belief underlying behavior
RNGO viewed exclusively or primarily as a political actor	RNGO viewed as religious/moral *and* political actor
Religious beliefs seen in terms of clash with modernity; "non-religious" behaviors seen in terms of capitulation to secular norms	Evolution and change are prefigured
Use of Judeo-Christian frameworks to study religious organizations; Christianity assumed to be prototypical religion	Attentiveness to particularism of the religious/faith tradition
Religious/ideological commitments largely unexamined	Underlying religious/ideological commitments made explicit

logic shaping organizational dispositions and behaviors; moves beyond Christo-centric and Western-centric frames of reference; sets aside the religious–secular binary; renders "visible" behaviors that may not have been discerned using behaviorist or materialist frames of reference; and attends to the evolutionary, organic dimensions of organizational development and behavior.

Elements of the Substrate of the BIC

In the remaining part of this chapter, I identify three elements of the BIC's organizational substrate, which will serve as a useful framework for our study of its expression throughout seventy-five years of history to examine the nature of the polity and the approach to social change that emerges on the world stage. It is important to note that these three elements do not capture the substrate *in toto* (nor is that the aim); there are many other elements that could conceivably be included, such as conceptions of power, the nature of the human being, the relationship between material and spiritual dimensions of reality, etc. My aim is to take a first step in identifying the core philosophical and moral convictions that give rise to a qualitatively different type of interaction in the political arena as modeled by the BIC. A further aim of this endeavor is to set the stage for a consideration of the conditions of possibility that emerge—for the structures of an international order and the relationships that sustain it—from a particular set of conceptual foundations. This is not merely an intellectual exercise; it is an invitation to the very practical and necessary undertaking of examining the conceptual underpinnings of the present social order in order to identify its deficiencies and to continue the difficult work of reimagining and refashioning it in a more just and equitable way.

In order to identify the substrate of the BIC, or any religious organization, it is necessary to locate the source of authority whose guidance establishes the moral framework for the work of the organization. In the case of the BIC, the teachings of the central figures of the Baháʼí Faith are its unquestioned sources of moral authority; yet an even more precise authoritative document offers a concise accounting of convictions that bear directly on the Baháʼí community's interactions in the international arena. A letter penned by Shoghi Effendi in response to the UN Committee on Palestine in 1947 outlines the core convictions of Baháʼís vis-à-vis their role in the world. These include: (a) the concept of "progressive revelation," which states that religious Revelation is not absolute but relative and represents "successive stages in the spiritual evolution of humanity"; (b) the concept of the oneness of the human race; and (c) the uniqueness and centrality of the Administrative (governing) Order of the Baháʼí Faith.[23] For the purposes of this study, I have chosen to focus my attention on these elements and their expression in the seventy-five-year relationship between the BIC and the United Nations. Future scholars will wish to consider a larger number of elements to render their analysis with increasingly greater refinement and precision.

Developmental Perspective on History and Religion

The Baháʼí Faith views history in terms of a progression through successive stages of development. In these stages, the advancement of humanity can be likened to the stages in the development of a human being—childhood, adolescence, and maturity. While the term "developmental" is used to describe the Baháʼí perspective on history and religion, it is not intended in the vein of a narrow developmentalism or static prescriptivism, which implies a foreordained trajectory, such as, for example, in the case of global "development," which continues to be steeped in an ideology of a set of stages that culminate in the

European model of "development."[24] Rather, it unfolds in a manner that mirrors the natural world, including that of a human being, which occurs along a set of stages yet is also responsive to circumstance, experience, and choice.

Bahá'u'lláh's Revelation appears in the world at a time when humanity has arrived at the "threshold of maturity."[25] "Behind so much of the turbulence and commotion of contemporary life," writes the Universal House of Justice, "are the fits and starts of a humanity struggling to come of age."[26] Indeed, as outlined in the previous chapter, the world in the mid-nineteenth century, at the time of the announcement of Bahá'u'lláh's mission, had reached an unprecedented turning point—in terms of its intellectual, social, and political development. The very conceptions of a collective history, of time, of progress and modernity, as we know them today, had their origins in the nineteenth century.[27] "Inseparable from the Bahá'í perspective on politics," writes the Universal House of Justice, "is a particular conception of history, its course and direction."[28] In order to understand the BIC's interactions in the political arena, we must understand how it reads historical processes, how it understands the forces shaping contemporary life, and how it sees its place in this unfolding narrative.

The Bahá'í Faith differentiates between two parallel processes interacting throughout history: one characterized by disintegration and the other by integration. Elucidating the former, Shoghi Effendi, writing in 1934, draws attention to the "process of steady deterioration ... insidiously invading so many departments of human activity":

> the catastrophic fall of mighty monarchies and empires in the European continent; the decline ... in the fortunes of the S͟hí'ih hierarchy in His own native land; the fall of the Qájár dynasty ... the overthrow of the Sultanate and the Caliphate ... the wave of secularization which is invading the Muḥammadan ecclesiastical institutions in Egypt ... the humiliating blows that have afflicted some of the most powerful Churches of Christendom in Russia, in Western Europe and Central America; the dissemination of those subversive doctrines that are undermining the foundations ... of seemingly impregnable strongholds in the political and social spheres of human activity.[29]

Furthermore, the Universal House of Justice elucidates that processes of disintegration are evident in the "the impotence of leaders at all levels to mend the fractures appearing in the structure of society, in the dismantling of social norms that have long held in check unseemly passions, and in the despondency and indifference exhibited not only by individuals but also by entire societies that have lost any vital sense of purpose."[30]

Unfolding simultaneously are processes of integration—ones drawing together diverse peoples, social groups, nation-states, and opening new arenas for cooperation. This is not happening through a mere awakening of a spirit of solidarity and goodwill but rather through the maturation of intellectual, technological, social, and spiritual capacities for collaboration. For evidence of this, we need only consider how the prejudices and ideas that once seemed insurmountable—virulent nationalism, racial and ethnic prejudice, the oppression of women and girls, political, legal, and economic theories and practices privileging the advancement of the few—are now vigorously debated and denounced by growing masses of civil society, informed citizens, and courageous leaders who see themselves as protagonists and co-creators of a more just social order. The Bahá'í community strives to align itself with dynamics associated with these processes leading to greater solidarity and wider spheres of cooperation, "which, [it is] confident, will continue to gain in strength, no matter how bleak the immediate horizons."[31]

Embedded within this view of human history is a parallel developmental perspective on religion. As Shoghi Effendi explains:

> The fundamental principle enunciated by Baháʾuʾlláh is that religious truth is not absolute but relative, that Divine Revelation is a continuous and progressive process, that all the great religions of the world are divine in origin ... and that their missions represent successive stages in the spiritual evolution of human society.[32]

The historic figures we associate with the world's great religions—Abraham, Krishna, Zoroaster, Moses, Buddha, Jesus Christ, Muhammad, and (more recently) the Báb and Baháʾuʾlláh—form part of a continuous process of "progressive revelation" through which God (or whichever designation we accord to a transcendent source) conveys teachings to humanity in accordance with humanity's spiritual and social development and accompanying needs.[33] "All that I have revealed unto thee," writes Baháʾuʾlláh, "hath been in accordance with thy capacity and understanding, not with My state and the melody of My voice."[34] Thus the Baháʾí conception of religion is one that is intimately and inextricably associated with the spiritual and social maturation of humanity as a whole. While the source of Revelation stands outside of history, the Revelation itself appears *in history*—contingent and calibrated toward the needs and capacities of a particular time. "The All-Knowing Physician," writes Baháʾuʾlláh,

> hath His finger on the pulse of mankind. He perceiveth the disease, and prescribeth, in His unerring wisdom, the remedy. Every age hath its own

problem, and every soul its particular aspiration. The remedy the world needeth in its present-day afflictions can never be the same as that which a subsequent age may require.[35]

Finally, Bahá'u'lláh asserts that the Bahá'í Faith does *not* represent the final statement from God but rather the most recent, to be followed by further Revelation in the future.

Throughout the writings of the Bahá'í Faith, the dynamic qualities of religion come to the fore:

> Nothing is stationary in the material world of outer phenomena or in the inner world of intellect and consciousness. Religion is the outer expression of the divine reality. Therefore, it must be living, vitalized, moving and progressive.[36]

The historically contingent view of religion forms an essential component of the substrate.

The Oneness of Humankind

The Bahá'í writings state that the principle of the oneness of humankind is "the foundation of the Faith of God" and the "distinguishing feature of His Law."[37] It is the "operating principle and ultimate goal of the [Bahá'í] Revelation."[38] It refers not only to cooperation and goodwill among individuals but "concerns itself primarily with the nature of those essential relationships that must bind all the states and nations as members of one human family."[39]

The oneness of humankind emerges in the Bahá'í writings as a teleological principle. 'Abdu'l-Bahá highlights the historical imperative associated with this principle: "For none is self-sufficiency any longer possible, inasmuch as political ties unite all peoples and nations, and the bonds of trade and industry, of agriculture and education, are being strengthened every day."[40] Similarly, Bahá'u'lláh states: "The well-being of mankind, its peace and security, are unattainable unless and until its unity is firmly established."[41] While the achievement of unity is the overarching aim of every Bahá'í endeavor, it takes on a particular significance in the context of the Bahá'í community's engagement with the United Nations and in political affairs more broadly. In a 2006 letter, the Universal House of Justice writes:

> Human society has arrived at a stage in its evolution when unity of the whole human race is imperative. To not appreciate this reality is to not grasp the meaning of the current crisis in world affairs. The principle of the oneness of humankind identifies the code for resolving the far-reaching issues involved.[42]

It is important to note that the protagonists of this vision will not be the Bahá'ís themselves but rather the peoples of the world. Unity will not be achieved by a subset of the global community—by one group of people on behalf of the masses. The Bahá'í writings assert that "[a]ll men have been created to carry forward an ever-advancing civilization."[43] Thus, every nation and every group will make its unique contribution to the advancement of human civilization.

The core doctrinal tenets of the Bahá'í Faith, then, must be understood in the context of the broader goal of the achievement of the organic unity of the body of nations. As Shoghi Effendi elucidates, the principle of the oneness of humankind implies "an organic change in the structure of present-day society, a change such as the world has not yet experienced."[44] Together, Bahá'í principles and tenets seek to foster the spiritual, social, intellectual, structural, and material conditions conducive to the achievement of this unity. Among these, we may identify the following: the elimination of prejudice and discrimination, the achievement of universal education, gender equality, the elimination of the extremes of wealth and poverty, the harmony between science and religion, the freedom of religion, a universal auxiliary language, the centrality of justice to all human endeavors, and the independent investigation of truth. The principle of the oneness of humankind can be said to provide an overarching frame through which to view the collective progress of humanity.

This principle is also intimately related to the conception of religion introduced in the preceding section: "true religion" must be the cause of unity; actions carried out in the name of religion and leading to conflict and separation are contrary to its nature and purpose. As 'Abdu'l-Bahá unequivocally states: "If religion becomes a cause of dislike, hatred and division, it were better to be without it, and to withdraw from such a religion would be a truly religious act."[45]

The Bahá'í Administrative Order

The question of how the Bahá'í community is organized—its structures of governance, referred to as the Administrative Order—takes on paramount importance in the study of Bahá'í engagement in the political arena. The Bahá'í Administrative Order differs fundamentally from other religious institutions insofar as Bahá'u'lláh Himself elaborated its principles, established its institutions, and conferred the necessary authority on the body to "supplement and apply His legislative ordinances."[46] It is not a structure that stands apart from the teachings of the Bahá'í Faith; rather, as has been described by Shoghi Effendi, it is integral to the life of the community and the community cannot exist without it. Recall

Shoghi Effendi's assertion that the principle of the oneness of humankind "does not constitute merely the enunciation of an ideal, but stands inseparably associated with an institution adequate to embody its truth, demonstrate its validity, and perpetuate its influence."[47]

On a practical level, the Administrative Order provides the institutional context within which the BIC exists. At the local level, Bahá'ís over the age of twenty-one elect a nine-member governing body (the Local Spiritual Assembly)[48]; similarly, each year Bahá'ís elect a nine-member national-governing body (the National Spiritual Assembly [NSA]). Every five years, members of all NSAs gather to elect a nine-member international governing body (the Universal House of Justice). Among its features are the absence of clergy or any kind of professional priesthood and the election of governing bodies by universal suffrage.[49] Under the direction of the Universal House of Justice, the BIC relates to the United Nations as the representative of Bahá'í communities in over 180 nations. The BIC, then, must be understood in the context of this global administrative order, of which it is an inseparable part.

Another one of its distinguishing features, and indeed one with direct bearing on the manner of its engagement in politics, is the way in which the Administrative Order balances the imperatives of integrity and flexibility. On the one hand, the system of governance "guards the integrity of [Bahá'í] law" and provides for the continuity of guidance rooted in the faithful interpretation of the immutable teachings of Bahá'u'lláh; on the other, the Administrative Order, "as a living organism," is able to "expand and adapt to the needs and requirements of an ever-changing society."[50] As mentioned above, the members of the Universal House of Justice are invested with the authority to legislate on matters not explicitly addressed in the writings of Bahá'u'lláh.[51] Shoghi Effendi describes Bahá'í administrative bodies as "organic institutions" characterized by "elasticity" and able to incorporate "whatever is deemed necessary … in order to keep [the Administrative Order] in the forefront of all progressive movements."[52]

The system is further calibrated to maintain a dynamic interplay between the local and the global, guarding against the "evils of excessive centralization"[53] on the one hand and the lack of coordination and coherence on the other. Furthermore, it does not seek to compete with "legitimate allegiances," a "sane and intelligent patriotism," or national autonomy; nor does it seek in any way "to suppress the diversity of ethnical origins, of climate, of history, of language and tradition, of thought and habit, that differentiate the peoples and nations of the world."[54] Instead, Shoghi Effendi asserts,

[i]t calls for a wider loyalty, for a larger aspiration than any that has animated the human race. It insists upon the subordination of national impulses and interests to the imperative claims of a unified world. It repudiates excessive centralization on one hand, and disclaims all attempts at uniformity on the other. Its watchword is unity in diversity.[55]

This element of the substrate is highly relevant to our examination of religious NGOs in the political domain as it demonstrates alternative ways of "knowing the international"[56] and conceiving of the international order.

*

Having elaborated the above three elements of the substrate, the following four chapters examine their expression over seven decades of the BIC's engagement in the international arena. Each of the four historical periods covered in these chapters reveals a different facet of the operation of the substrate. Focusing on the period between 1945 and 1970, Chapter 4 first discusses the implications of the BIC's view of history for its relationship to the United Nations, including the BIC's understanding of the nascent international organization's significance within the broader arc of the advancement of human civilization. Chapter 5, which begins in 1970 and concludes in 1986, examines the operation of the substrate as the BIC seeks to defend the Bahá'í community in Iran from the violent attacks and oppression at the hands of the Iranian authorities; further, it explores the BIC's engagement in early efforts aimed at the advancement of women. Turning next to the period from 1986 to 2008, Chapter 6 examines the role of the substrate in the BIC's understanding and manner of pursuing peace. Chapter 7 rounds out the historical section by exploring the operation of the substrate in the BIC's reconceptualization of its engagement in the international arena between 2008 and 2020.

My aim in these four chapters is to demonstrate the very practical consequences of the ideas and convictions embodied in the substrate—the way in which they shaped aims, priorities, approaches, resource allocation, and interactions. All organizational action proceeds from certain beliefs about society, our role in it, the nature of progress, and how it is to be pursued. The examination of the substrate brings several of these convictions into sharp relief for the purposes of demonstrating that they have real implications in the social and material world. It is also a call to reflect on and question the assumptions that drive action in the political arena today and to remind ourselves that we are not only the recipients of a particular social order but also its co-creators.

A Distinct View of History, Time, and the Emerging Global Order:
The United Nations through a New Lens (1945–1970)

The examination of the seventy-five-year relationship between the BIC and the United Nations begins by looking at the question of history, especially the BIC's understanding of the processes of history and the significance of the formation of the United Nations within that history. There are many ways to conceive of the formation of the United Nations, to "read" its place in history; we might think of it as a necessity, a victory, a compromise, a machinery,[1] a promise, an idea, or perhaps an inflection point. An awareness of the particular reading of history is foundational: it forces actors in the arena of international politics and policy-making to grapple with the elemental questions of how the present came to be, the nature of the time in which we live, and the direction in which we are moving. In the words of one scholar, any analysis of political arrangements "must know what time it is—in short, it must grasp the age."[2]

There are of course many ways of narrating history and discerning meanings and intentions across historical time. Hegel, for example, conceived of history as the unfolding of human freedom. Enlightenment philosophers read history in terms of humanity's movement toward a more perfect civilization, others conceived of stages of human development, while others discerned the pattern of the rise and fall of civilizations. Although diverse cultures and traditions have carried forward their distinctive conceptions of history, it is the Western intellectual tradition that has come to define the prevailing readings of history and the accompanying understanding of the international order.[3] This raises an important question: If Western scholars are the primary generators and diffusers of norms and ideas in the world, including in the political arena, are others simply passive recipients of these ideas? Is there a role for non-Western as well as religious thought in reading and articulating the parameters of an emerging social order?[4]

Let us begin to answer this question by revisiting the first period of the BIC's engagement with the United Nations, starting with the founding of the United Nations in 1945. During this stage, in which the BIC relates to the United Nations as an "observer" NGO—a recognized international organization that can submit written contributions and participate in UN-hosted NGO conferences—we can discern how the BIC's conception of history shaped its interactions with the intergovernmental organization. The period concludes in 1970 when the BIC is granted the coveted "consultative status," which enables it to participate more fully in UN processes and deliberations. This shift to a qualitatively different kind of relationship with the United Nations marks the beginning of a new chapter in the unfolding narrative of BIC's engagement in the international arena.

Leading up to the United Nations' founding conference in San Francisco, there was great excitement within the Bahá'í community and civil society groups around the country. The aim of this historic conference was to finalize the structure and language of the new organization's Charter.[5] Many questions remained to be resolved: membership in the organization, the role of the General Assembly, the right of veto, self-defense, and the issue of human rights. The eyes of the world were on the historic, much anticipated, laboriously deliberated, and politically fraught developments leading up to the historic signing of the UN Charter on June 26, 1945.[6]

Shortly after plans for the conference were announced, the US Bahá'í community issued a letter to President Franklin D. Roosevelt (who died shortly before the opening of the conference) recognizing this "great turning-point in human history"[7] and expressing the hope that "the dire needs of humanity be met by the creation of a new world order through the efforts of the forthcoming conference in San Francisco."[8] What significance did Bahá'ís accord to the formation of the United Nations, and why?[9] What was the nature of the "new world order" to which they referred?

During this period, we will see in the BIC's statements and letters to various UN agencies and officials the unfolding of a particular view of history—one characterized by an evolutionary, developmental orientation, as initially outlined in the preceding chapter. We will see how such a view, in which a "long past interacts with an emerging present,"[10] became embodied in many facets of the BIC's efforts and how it generated a distinct narrative about the unfoldment of the international order.

A Long View of History

Recall from the discussion of the substrate that the Bahá'í conception of history—theorized in terms of progress through growing spheres of human solidarity and toward the emergence of a moral sensibility that encompasses all peoples and nations—casts the United Nations in a new light. The Bahá'í writings outline a millennia-long trajectory throughout which humanity has organized itself into increasingly larger and more complex social orders: from the "earliest beginnings in the birth of family life, its subsequent development in the achievement of tribal solidarity, leading in turn to the constitution of the city-state, and expanding later into the institution of independent and sovereign nations."[11] Such a progression is likened to the development of the life of an individual passing through stages of infancy, childhood, adolescence, adulthood, and maturity. Today, according to the Bahá'í Faith, humanity has reached the threshold of maturity—a stage marked by a growing consciousness of the oneness of humankind and the accompanying capacity to organize its life on a global scale.[12] We find this perspective echoed in a letter from the BIC's UN representative to National Spiritual Assemblies regarding the importance of gaining "a correct perspective on the UN":

> The UN is a mere beginning ... if Bahá'ís can view the United Nations as an expression of the power of unity released into the world by the Báb and Bahá'u'lláh ... they will see the UN in a different light. They can instead view it as evidence of the gradual awakening of man's consciousness to the essential need for the unity of mankind.[13]

We can contrast this with the more common presentist perspective that prevails at the United Nations, one that tends to examine reality in terms of its current state. Such a perspective brings to the fore the weaknesses and challenges of the organization: the imbalance of power among its member states; the lack of coherence across diverse agencies; the obstacles to multilateralism and collaboration; the inability to enforce international law; the failure to deliver on commitments; and so on. If we broaden our perspective to encompass the previous century, other realities become evident, such as the manner in which the United Nations addressed the challenges and shortcomings of earlier attempts at international collaboration (e.g., Council of Europe,[14] League of Nations). Extending the horizon further still, other civilizational perspectives come to light. As Acharya and Buzan point out, in the study of international relations it is not only Eurocentric but also generally limiting to ignore the longer, global

heritage of thought about historical processes and confine one's vision to ideas
generated in the last few hundred years.[15]

Two Parallel Processes: Integration and Disintegration

Another facet of the Bahá'í conception of history that shapes its engagement in
the international arena is the view of history in terms of two parallel and related
processes—one leading to greater degrees of social integration, the other leading
to demise and social disintegration. Processes bringing the world's people and
nations into unprecedented contact with one another have included advances in
communications technology and greater access to information; they have arisen,
too, from the tidal waves of migrations of the past several hundred years. Often
inextricably linked with great suffering and turmoil, these massive movements
of human populations brought into contact diverse peoples, with diverse
ways of knowing, thinking and being; for centuries, such exchanges unfolded
against a backdrop of exploitation and marginalization. At the same time, they
stimulated a questioning of established authority in fields as diverse as religion,
academia, government, commerce, and the media.[16] In the last century, the
rise of transnational networks and civil society organizations, the rise of global
agencies coordinating humanitarian, scientific, and economic activity; the rise of
international standards and legal frameworks, and the growing understanding of
the relationship between human activity and environmental degradation, among
others, have led to a heightened consciousness of our identity as members of one
human race, and the need for social institutions and approaches to social change
that extend the fruits of material and spiritual civilization to all peoples.

These processes have unfolded alongside processes those of social
disintegration, as described by the international governing body of the Bahá'í
community in terms of the

> vicissitudes that have afflicted time-honored institutions, in the impotence of
> leaders at all levels to mend the fractures appearing in the structure of society, in
> the dismantling of social norms that have long held in check unseemly passions,
> and in the despondency and indifference exhibited not only by individuals but
> also by entire societies that have lost any vital sense of purpose.[17]

But the processes are not working against one another; rather, they unfold in
tandem and carry humankind "each in its own way, along the path leading
towards its full maturity."[18] As such, the coming together of the nations of the

world in 1945 to create a new organization for the promotion of peace, formalize relationships that would enable the nations of the world to cooperate in matters of mutual interest, deliberate on issues of global concern, and articulate the moral, legal, and procedural norms for such an entity represented a milestone in the civilizational imperative toward greater international solidarity. We can appreciate, in this light, the civilizational significance of the period between 1945 and 1966, which saw the formation of the conceptual and legal framework for a new global community in the UN Charter, the Universal Declaration of Human Rights (UDHR), the International Covenant on Civil and Political Rights (ICCPR),[19] and the International Covenant on Economic, Social and Cultural Rights (ICESCR),[20] among others.

Viewed in light of the longer-term perspective and the imperative toward integration, we can appreciate that the Bahá'í community's desire to associate with the United Nations was not rooted in a naïve idealization of this nascent political entity but rather a desire to align itself "with the forces associated with the process of integration"[21] and to contribute its resources and ideas toward its advancement. It is in this spirit that the BIC addressed a letter to the United Nations' first secretary-general, Trygve Lie, stating that: "Baha'is wish to be associated with the consultative processes which have been adopted by United Nations for the evolution of world unity along social as well as political lines."[22]

Reading United Nations–Civil Society Relations

Through this lens, the emergence of civil society organizations as a source of influence on international policy and deliberations takes on additional significance. Their growing world-embracing networks were yet another expression of the spirit of solidarity that signaled the advancement of the processes of global integration as more and more individuals from all continents (though at the start it was primarily North America and Europe) began to collaborate on issues of common concern. Already, in 1945, no fewer than 1,200 voluntary organizations attended the founding conference of the United Nations.[23] Their presence was not merely symbolic or aspirational; they made major contributions throughout the conference process. These organizations played a key role in formulating the opening words of the Charter ("We the peoples of the United Nations") and lobbied for the inclusion of Article 71, which provides for "arrangements for consultation with civil society organizations."[24] While, at the time, the latter was seen as a very limited provision, it has in practice enabled "a very wide range of organizations to make their views known to the UN."[25] Furthermore, civil society organizations ensured the inclusion of human rights in the Charter.[26]

It would be another three decades before the voices of NGOs would become more influential in the international arena, but the parameters for their participation had been set[27] (see Figure 4.1). From a *realpolitik* perspective, in 1945, civil society did not represent a significant source of "soft" power, yet from a developmental view of history, one discerns in the formation of these organizations a significant trend toward new forms of collective enterprise and the emergence of a new kind of global polity.[28]

Reframing the Role of the Nation-State

In its contributions to the United Nations during this period, the BIC offered a distinct vision of the role of the nation-state in the modern order, rooted in its particular conception of history. Participating in the 1955 Charter Revision Conference, it notes that "real sovereignty is no longer vested in the institutions

Figure 4.1 The BIC's first representative to the United Nations, Ms. Mildred Mottahedeh (third from left), attending an NGO Conference on Technical Assistance held at UN Headquarters in New York, March 29, 1954. © Bahá'í World Centre.

of the national state because the nations have become interdependent."[29] Earlier, in its statement to the newly formed Commission on Human Rights, as it invited contributions from NGOs in the course of drafting the UDHR, the BIC suggested that while the "modern nation state came into existence as a unifier of diverse races and peoples," today it "has reached the limits of its development as an independent, self-directed social body."[30] The conceptualization of the nation-state, rooted in the centuries-old Treaty of Westphalia, needed to be rethought. In the 1930s, Shoghi Effendi asserts that "[n]ation-building has come to an end."[31] Indeed, the emergence of a "global imaginary" has become associated with modernity itself—the familiar concepts of community, society, and neighbor have come to encompass the whole world.[32] In its 1947 "Declaration of Human Obligations and Rights" addressed to the Commission on Human Rights, the BIC frames the role of the nation-state in the following terms:

> The true destiny of the national state is to build the bridge from local autonomy to world unity. It can preserve its moral heritage and function only as it contributes to the establishment of a sovereign world. Both state and people are needed to serve as the strong pillar supporting the new institutions reflecting the full and final expression of human relationships in an ordered society.

It is helpful to consider how much we take for granted the existence and nature of nation-states and, more generally, the structures and assumptions of the Western liberal order—to the point that we may not "notice" them at all.[33] In his study of non-Western thought about the international order, Acharya, for example, calls attention to conceptions of social order in other religions such as the Sikh *Khalsa Panth* or the Islamic *ummah*, which offer "more 'solidarist' conceptions of international society" than those inherent in Western readings of international relations. As Acharya and Buzan suggest, "Had [international relations] come out of Islamic history and political theory, it might well have been much more focused on world society rather than on a system of sovereign, territorial states."[34] We can hear the echoes of this sentiment in one of the BIC's first communications to the United Nations, a letter addressed to Secretary-General Trygve Lie stating:

> Every Baha'i is by moral conviction a world citizen, mindful of the teaching given by Baha'u'llah seventy-five years ago, "The world is one country and mankind its citizens ... Let not a man glory in that he loves his country; let him rather glory in this, that he loves his kind."[35]

The Direction of History and the Structures of a New Global Order

A theme that emerges from the BIC's contributions during this period is the sense of direction and imperative toward greater degrees of unity in humanity's ongoing efforts to construct a peaceful and sustainable social order. In its "Declaration of Human Obligations and Rights," the BIC writes:

> From the depths of man's divine endowment stirs response to the affirmation of oneness, which gives this age its central impetus and direction. Society is undergoing transformation, to effect a new order based on the wholeness of human relationships.[36]

Reflecting on the arena of human rights, the BIC explains that efforts to secure rights for the individual "record the most significant moral gains of the race in its incessant struggle to form a lasting society."[37] From a Bahá'í perspective, then, in the early twentieth century, humanity finds itself at the threshold of its collective maturity as it continues its long and turbulent transition from a world of sovereign states to a global community of nations.

Yet as Shoghi Effendi asserts in his correspondence to the Bahá'í community in the 1930s and 1940s, the idea must be incarnated in systems and institutions that can embody and give full expression to the reality of the profound relationship that binds all peoples and nations into one whole.[38] In their contributions to the United Nations, the BIC draws on the Bahá'í writings to convey the outlines and features of the institutions required to address the needs of the emerging world community:

> A world Super-State in whose favor all the nations of the world will have ceded every claim to make war, certain rights to impose taxation and all rights to maintain armaments, except for purposes of maintaining internal order within their respective dominions. This State will have to include an International Executive adequate to enforce supreme and unchallengeable authority on very recalcitrant member of the Commonwealth; a World Parliament whose members are elected by the peoples in their respective countries and whose election is confirmed by their respective governments: a Supreme Tribunal whose judgment has a binding effect even in cases where the parties concerned have not voluntarily agreed to submit their case to its consideration.[39]

Accompanying the broad outlines were specific recommendations for amendments to the UN Charter aimed at bringing its provisions in line with the exigencies of an evolving world community; among them: provisions for membership in the United Nations, freedom of discussion for the General Assembly, proportionate representation in the General Assembly, removal of term "enemy states," and compulsory jurisdiction of International Courts of Justice in all legal disputes between states, among others.[40]

In the early years of the United Nations, decades before the term "global governance" would enter common parlance, the BIC addressed skeptics by noting that, "[i]mpossible as the achievement of world order may appear to traditionalist or partisan, mankind is passing through a crucial stage likened to that of an individual entering maturity and using new powers and faculties beyond the grasp of irresponsible youth."[41] One can see in these statements what eminent peacebuilding scholar John Paul Lederach referred to as a "horizon of the future" that "points towards the possibilities of what could be constructed and built."[42] It is important to add here that the Bahá'í community was not at this time envisioning that a global government would come to be established in the near future. In the early days of its association, its aims were humble and circumscribed. In a 1947 letter, Shoghi Effendi notes that the primary reason for encouraging Bahá'í association with the United Nations was to acquaint the world with the Bahá'í community's aims of working for the "unification of the human family and permanent peace" and not because the Bahá'í community was "in a position to shape or influence directly the course of human affairs."[43]

For the purposes of this analysis, it is interesting to note the level of detail with which the Bahá'í writings engage with the history of the formation of the United Nations. The writings do not provide comment on the specific workings of the United Nations; rather, they contextualize a civilizational trajectory toward greater degrees of unity through the drama and turbulence of the twentieth century. In a 1947 letter to the American Bahá'í community, Shoghi Effendi situates the outbreak of the First World War and, in particular, the role of the United States within broader historical forces as they weave through successive efforts to articulate the outlines of a peaceful order among the nations of the world:

> the process dates back to the outbreak of the first World War that threw the great republic of the West [the United States] into the vortex of the first stage of a world upheaval. It received its initial impetus through the formulation of President Wilson's Fourteen Points, closely associating for the first time that republic with the fortunes of the Old World. It suffered its first setback through the dissociation of that republic from the newly born League of Nations … It acquired added momentum through the outbreak of the second World War, inflicting unprecedented suffering on that republic, and involving it still further

in the affairs of all the continents of the globe. It was further reinforced through the declaration embodied in the Atlantic Charter, as voiced by one of its chief progenitors, Franklin D. Roosevelt. It assumed a definite outline through the birth of the United Nations at the San Francisco Conference. It must, however long and tortuous the way, lead, through a series of victories and reverses, to the political unification of the Eastern and Western Hemispheres, to the emergence of a world government.[44]

Such commentary provided the Bahá'í community with a particular reading of the newly formed international organization, helping to conceive of it within the context of a much longer (and more difficult) trajectory of unifying the East and the West and establishing a system of governance whose jurisdiction would eventually encompass the nations of the world.

International Coordination in Principle and Practice

It is important to note that throughout all four historical periods covered in this volume, the BIC is not an isolated or autonomous NGO but rather an intrinsic part of a much larger global community. The concepts it presents to the United Nations are not abstractions or mere theories. Rather, the ideas put forward are intimately connected to the very practical exercise in which the entire Bahá'í world is engaged: the creation of communities that embody the principle of the oneness of humankind. The spirit that animates the desire to forge the machinery of universal international cooperation also finds expression in the daily life and social institutions gradually being established by Bahá'í communities around the world. A new global polity is coming into being.

The BIC, as an international NGO, was formed in 1948 when eight existing National Spiritual Assemblies (democratically elected nine-member governing bodies) were collectively recognized under the label of the "Bahá'í International Community." These included the National Spiritual Assemblies of: (1) the United States and Canada (one assembly)[45]; (2) the British Isles; (3) Germany and Austria (one assembly); (4) Egypt and Sudan (one assembly); (5) Iraq; (6) Iran; (7) India, Pakistan, and Burma (one assembly); and (8) Australia and New Zealand (one assembly).[46] By 1950, Bahá'ís had established communities in 100 countries,[47] but in order to be associated with the United Nations, a formal international structure was needed to demonstrate the international nature of the NGO. It would take eighteen years since the start of this period for the Bahá'í community to elect its first international governing body (the

Figure 4.2 United Nations Day Committee of Moulmein, Burma, October 24, 1957. © Bahá'í World Centre.

nine-member Universal House of Justice); as such, until that time, the National Spiritual Assembly (NSA) of the United States functioned as the representative of existing national communities in relation to the United Nations. As each new assembly came into being, it formally designated the assembly of the United States as its UN representative, and these authorizations were submitted to the United Nations to convey the international scope and structure of the organization.[48]

Early efforts at international coordination were evident in a number of ways. The BIC, along with many other UN-associated NGOs, worked hard to educate its community about the aims of the United Nations and its efforts in areas of peace, development, and human rights through the encouragement of observances of UN days. Informational materials were sent to numerous Bahá'í communities with accompanying instructions and recommendations for further actions (see Figure 4.2).

A prominent example of this cooperation was the BIC's endorsement of the Convention on the Prevention and Punishment of the Crime of Genocide ("Genocide Convention"), the first human rights treaty to be adopted by the UN General Assembly. Adopted on December 9, 1948, the convention was considered a crucial step in the development of modern international human rights and criminal law.[49] All existing National Spiritual Assemblies had confirmed to the BIC their endorsement of the convention. Borrah Kavelin, chairperson of the

Figure 4.3 Ambassador Ratnakirti Gunawardene (Ceylon's representative to the United Nations), president of the Human Rights Commission, receives representatives of the BIC on the occasion of presenting the Bahá'í endorsement of the Genocide Convention on April 10, 1959, at the UN Headquarters in New York. © Bahá'í World Centre.

NSA of the United States, formally presented the endorsement to the president of the Human Rights Commission, noting that the document represented an "act of conscience" of Bahá'ís from over eighty countries and territories and an expression of their "firmly held conviction of the oneness of mankind and of the human race"[50] (see Figure 4.3). He further states that:

> Nations, races and religious groups are called upon to enrich, through their own inherent gifts, the common treasury of civilization. Therefore, the destruction of any one of them impoverishes the whole human race. Upon the preservation of this basic noble principle depend all other efforts of the United Nations. By endorsing the Genocide Convention, the Baha'is express … the hope that all the nations of the world will rally around this great Convention.[51]

The president of the Commission, Ceylon's (now Sri Lanka) ambassador to the United Nations, Ratnakirti Gunewardene, replied by saying that the endorsement by Bahá'ís from all over the globe was a "most powerful expression of world opinion" and signaled that the work of the United Nations "is supported not only by the governments but by the people themselves."[52] "We now have in this Convention," he concludes, "a meaningful compact between East and West for the preservation of mankind."[53] The Convention entered into effect on January 12, 1951.

Bahá'í communities collaborated to take part in other UN initiatives. In preparation for the 1955 Charter Revision Conference, to which NGOs were invited to submit recommendations for revisions to the UN Charter, the BIC solicited each NSA for suggestions and input; comments were received from twelve assemblies from Asia, Europe, Africa, and North America.[54] In its cover letter to Secretary-General Hammarskjöld, the BIC notes that "the participation [of National Assemblies] unites a wide diversity of national, racial, and religious backgrounds in one common concept of the structure needed to establish justice and peace."[55] The practice of requesting endorsements from all existing NSAs for statements submitted to major UN bodies, such as the Commission on Human Rights, became commonplace. The significance of these actions was not only in the matter of their substantive engagement on the issues under consideration by the United Nations but in the practice of forging a unified peaceful community characterized by cultural and ethnic diversity. "The very existence of so widespread and varied a community," writes the BIC in a statement to the United Nations, "can serve the cause of human rights by demonstrating that under certain conditions the spirit of equality and cooperation can prevail."[56]

Another facet of the BIC's engagement during this time was the intentionally diverse constitution of the BIC's delegations to some of the earliest international conferences and gatherings organized by the United Nations. As early as 1949, the first representative of the BIC at the United Nations noted that in selecting delegates to international conferences, effort was made to include "as wide a range of racial and national backgrounds as possible."[57] That same year, the BIC delegation to the International Conference of International NGOs in Lake Success, New York, included citizens of China, Iran, Canada, and the United States (including an African-American delegate); it was "the most international of all the delegations"[58] (see Figure 4.4).

The point here is not to compete for "most international delegation" but to highlight that even the structure of delegations was an expression of a distinct rationality. The deliberately international character of the delegations served to embody the concept of the oneness of humankind—not only in outlook but also in representation. BIC reports from this period also note an intentional emphasis on including local delegates among representatives to international conferences. This ran counter to the usual practice, in these early years of NGO

Figure 4.4 Baháʼí delegates to the UN International Conference of NGOs, held at Lake Success, New York, April 4–9, 1949. Left to right: Amin Banani, Mildred Mottahedeh (principal representative), Hilda Yen, Matthew Bullock. © Baháʼí World Centre.

activity, of sending delegates mostly from Western Europe and the United States.[59] This measure not only was aimed at consciously building the capacity of local Baháʼí communities to engage more effectively in the public sphere, but it also was a deliberate move to convey Baháʼí efforts to construct a truly global community and bring new voices and perspectives to the table. Recognition of Baháʼí contributions at these early conferences was evident in repeated requests, by conference officials, for BIC representatives to chair various committees and lead efforts to carry out specific public information tasks.[60]

Attention to Process: Observing the Principle of Nonpartisanship

As noted in Chapter 1, one of the distinctive aspects of the Bahá'í community's engagement in the public sphere is its adherence to the principle of nonengagement in partisan politics. The Bahá'í writings state that Bahá'ís are to refrain from "interference in the political affairs of any particular government" and to rise above "all particularism and partisanship."[61] Throughout this period, we can see the manner in which Bahá'í representatives strove to engage with the United Nations without becoming enmeshed in partisan political issues. Early in this period, Bahá'í representatives were elected to leadership positions on various NGO committees and attended international conferences. In the guidelines issued in 1950, the BIC instructs its delegates: "We are absolutely forbidden to take part in any political dispute. You can sometimes wisely lead the discussion away from the political angle to a truly constructive point of action."[62] This stance becomes particularly relevant in light of NGO dynamics at the United Nations at that time. A BIC conference report notes that BIC delegates "felt that the tone of these International NGO Conferences had considerably deteriorated" from the noble aims expressed and evidenced at the 1948 conference: "The petty politics, the lobbying, the jockeying for power are reflected in the present political condition. Rivalries were intense and there was a sharp competition for leadership."[63] This same report notes that BIC delegates' efforts to be "constructive and non-political" came to be favorably recognized by other NGOs at the conference.[64] What emerges, even in the earliest years of engagement, is an emphasis on process—that in contending environments, where many good ideas and intentions may abound, the nature of the deliberations and the manner in which they unfold are as important as the ideas themselves. The historical imperative of unity entails modes of engagement suited to advancing this goal.

*

This analysis of the first of four periods of the BIC's involvement with the United Nations has shed light on the role that a conception of history has in the shaping of organizational rationality for engagement in the international arena. The Bahá'í understanding of history as a developmental and teleological process, unfolding over the millennia and advancing toward the formation of a global community of nations, casts the United Nations in a new light. Here, the United Nations is understood as a milestone in a millennia-long process, a major achievement by a beleaguered humanity emerging from two ruinous wars and endeavoring to put into place institutions and norms to prevent another global conflagration. The significance of the achievement aside, this view also engenders an awareness of the shortcomings and weaknesses of such an organization, one that expresses both the ideals of a new world order and the anxieties and mindsets of nation states seeking to preserve autonomy and status quo at all cost. In this period, then, the BIC strives to align itself with the forces of integration, of which it sees the United Nations as a major part. We also see distinct modes of engagement—such as the avoidance of partisanship and the inclusion of non-Western representatives in its delegations to international conferences—as a practical expression of the essential characteristics of the developing world order. What emerges is a new kind of agency—the religious organization not only as a passive consumer or recipient of knowledge about the international order, but one that generates a distinct view of international relations, the processes shaping relationships between member states, the forces leading to integration and disintegration, and the protagonists in the unfolding order.

Responding to Persecution and Mobilizing for Gender Equality: An Emerging Global Architecture of Diplomacy and Social Change (1970–1986)

Of the four periods examined in this study, this one would turn out to be the most dramatic for the Bahá'í community and, in many ways, the most challenging for the BIC. The years during this period would see the very existence of the Bahá'í community in Iran (the country of its birth), threatened by a government-backed campaign of violent, cruel, and systematic persecution aimed at exterminating it. With no recourse to justice in a country whose newly forged constitution accorded Bahá'ís no legal status, the community grounded its hope for justice and restitution in public awareness and the mechanisms of international law (which were still coming into being during this period). By the 1980s, the plight of the Bahá'í community in Iran would be recognized by the international community as one of the most severe cases of religious persecution.[1] In this dramatic unfolding of events, the BIC assumed the pivotal role of pursuing every possible avenue of legal recourse and means of raising awareness to stem the violence and destruction being unleashed on the Bahá'ís in Iran.

Parallel to these endeavors is the BIC's involvement with one of the United Nations' defining efforts during this period, the UN Decade for Women (1976–85). In support of the decade, the Universal House of Justice mobilized the worldwide Bahá'í community to focus on the cause of the advancement of women and girls; this unfolded through the building of the community's understanding of the Bahá'í principle of gender equality and how to express it more effectively in family and community life, as well as society as a whole. Guided by the Universal House of Justice, the BIC coordinated the engagement of national Bahá'í communities and played a pivotal role in the international NGO community working toward this end.

Together, the analysis of the BIC's response to persecution and its involvement in the UN Decade for Women brings to light the operation of the substrate and its embodiment in a distinct set of responses and approaches toward the pursuit of justice and social change in the international arena. I will consider these two major areas of engagement in turn.

The Historical and Political Context of the Persecution

In order to examine the role of the BIC vis-à-vis the Baháʼí community, it is important first to grasp the social, political, and historical context of the dire situation facing the Baháʼís during this period. The attacks on the Baháʼís date back to the mid-nineteenth century when its young leader, Mírzía Husayn-ʻAlí (1817–92), known by the name of Baháʼuʼlláh, was exiled by the Persian and Ottoman authorities for leading a religious movement whose teachings posed an ideological threat to the religious clerics of the day. Baháʼuʼlláh's predecessor, Siyyid ʻAlí Muhammad, known as the Herald of the Baháʼí Faith, or the Báb, was executed in 1850 by a government firing squad of 750 riflemen.[2] The attacks continued after the execution: waves of violent campaigns of torture, killings, imprisonment, and the damage and seizure of property—aimed at the complete destruction of the community. At the heart of the attacks on Iran's largest religious minority is Baháʼuʼlláh's teaching that religious revelation is continuous and progressive; that the line of divine messengers—among them, Abraham, Krishna, Zoroaster, Moses, Buddha, Jesus Christ, and Muhammad— does not end but continues to the present day (with the Báb and Baháʼuʼlláh) and into the future to provide guidance in accordance with the needs and exigencies of the time in which it is revealed. In the eyes of Iran's clerical leaders, the claim of a post-Islamic revelation is not only "heretical" but also a threat—in Cameron's words, "the clearest obstacle to the ideological unity in the clerics' project to fuse the state with a radical version of Shiʼa Islam."[3]

Amid revolutionary turmoil preceding the overthrow of the Pahlavi Regime in Iran, the 1970s saw a sharp rise in anti-Baháʼí propaganda. As early as 1971, Ayatollah Khomeini—the revolutionary cleric who would lead the 1979 Iranian Revolution—stoked resentment of Baháʼís, accusing them of being "centers of evil propaganda" and agents of Western powers. When asked directly whether Baháʼís would be granted freedom under the new Islamic government, he replied: "They are a political faction. They are harmful. They will not be accepted"; as for their freedom of religion, he simply answered, "No."[4] By 1979, leading the Iranian

Revolution that unseated Iran's pro-Western monarch, Shah Reza Pahlavi, Khomeini had risen to political power, and the situation for Bahá'ís continued to deteriorate. The newly adopted theocratic constitution accorded the Bahá'ís no rights as a religious minority.[5] As the emergent regime consolidated its power, religious minorities were portrayed as symbols of Western interference. Bahá'ís were accused of being spies for Israel; agents of American, British, or Russian imperialism; allied with communism; and the like.[6] The stage was set for "an orgy of retribution ... [and] vindictive justice."[7]

The campaign to extinguish the Bahá'í community was swift and brutal; it left in its wake the destruction of the holiest Bahá'í shrine in Iran; the expropriation of all private, community, and business properties; the dismissal of thousands of government employees; the cancellation of pensions; the denial of employment and exclusion of Bahá'ís from institutions of higher education; and the murder and execution of over 200 Bahá'ís, many of them elected leaders of the community.[8] Ensuing juridical decisions confirmed that killing a Bahá'í was not a crime. Furthermore, in 1984, the Iranian government declared membership in Bahá'í administrative institutions a criminal act. By the early 1980s, the oppression of Bahá'ís was generally recognized as a foremost example of religious persecution.[9]

The Bahá'í Community's Response to Persecution

When considering the BIC's response to the persecution, it is helpful to remember that the era of NGO advocacy was still in its infancy.[10] At the beginning of this period, the BIC had just been granted "consultative status" by the UN's Economic and Social Council, which elevated it from its "observer status" and afforded it privileges to participate and contribute to UN deliberations and conferences.[11] Of the 213 NGOs with consultative status in 1970, only 24 were religiously affiliated.[12] Moreover, the BIC was the first accredited NGO representing a tradition other than Christianity, Judaism, or Islam.[13] The involvement of NGOs on the world stage consisted mostly of attending major conferences, with NGOs often confined to venues removed from governmental deliberations. At the opening of this period, UN diplomats and representatives were largely unfamiliar with the Bahá'í Faith and its community.

By the late 1970s, as the perilous nature of the persecution in Iran became increasingly clear, the BIC began to send detailed information to UN authorities—particularly, Secretary-General U Thant and UN human rights organs—about the rapidly unfolding attacks. After the election of Kurt Waldheim as secretary-general, the BIC urged him to protect the lives of Bahá'í community members.[14] As Iran's revolutionary government took power, the BIC cabled Iranian Prime Minister Mehdi Bazargan to request full rights and protection for Bahá'ís under the new constitution; however, the rights were not granted. In addition, the BIC made appeals to Iran's Mission to the United Nations, urgently seeking appointments to address deteriorating circumstances, and yet despite assurances, deterioration and attacks continued. Following the destruction of the holiest Bahá'í shrine in Iran,[15] the BIC sent letters to UN ambassadors of 100 nations "conveying the shock and dismay" of the Bahá'í world.[16] As fanatical elements in Iran continued to operate unchecked, the BIC enlisted the help of prominent human rights organizations, including Amnesty International, the International League for Human Rights, and the International Commission of Jurists, to help raise public awareness of the situation.

When all appeals to Iranian authorities went unheeded, the Universal House of Justice directed the BIC to communicate with the United Nations' international human rights bodies.[17] The BIC submitted reports and updates

Figure 5.1 BIC representatives to the UN Commission on Human Rights, in Geneva, Switzerland, February 15, 1982. Left to right: Mrs. Machid Fatio, Mr. Gerald Knight. © Bahá'í World Centre.

to the Commission on Human Rights, the Sub-Commission on the Promotion and Protection of Human Rights,[18] and the Third Committee of the UN General Assembly.[19] The United Nations appointed special rapporteurs and experts to pursue in-depth investigations into Iran's human rights violations, and their reports played a critical role in the UN's examination into the Bahá'í situation in Iran. Appeals to the United Nations' human rights bodies were a "precarious business"[20] given the complexity and fluidity of their work, which involved focusing on a diverse range of issues, a constantly expanding mandate, reliance on inputs from NGOs, strongly contested majority voting, and a paucity of procedural frameworks in favor of an *ad hoc* approach to most situations.[21] The BIC faced challenging questions about the nature of the persecution: Was it a byproduct of revolutionary upheaval or was it specifically targeting Bahá'ís? Could it be considered "religious" persecution if the Bahá'ís were not recognized as a religious minority?[22] In both cases, the Sub-Commission concluded that the answer was in the affirmative and expressed "profound concern for the perilous situation facing this religious Community."[23] It ultimately determined that religious freedom should be granted to the Bahá'í community in Iran.

Despite concerted efforts by Canadian and European parliamentarians to bring attention to the persecution on the world stage, the kidnappings and executions continued. The Bahá'í community intensified its efforts, reporting immediately to the secretary-general, governments, and media correspondents each time a major incident occurred. At the same time, reports were published by the BIC to document the persecutions and counter the false charges leveled against the Bahá'ís, as well as to present an accurate account of the principles of the Bahá'í Faith.

In 1982, the Iranian delegation unfurled a vicious campaign of misinformation, circulating to UN representatives documents accusing Bahá'ís of being a political entity "created and nourished by anti-Islamic and colonial powers ... engaged in spying for other governments."[24] That same year, the BIC cabled Khomeini as well as the chief justice of the Supreme Court of Iran to protest the executions of eight elected leaders of Iran's Bahá'í community and to ask for evidence to support the charges of espionage. No such evidence came. Rather, it had been ascertained that in almost every case of execution, Iranians held out the promise of release in exchange for a recantation of the Bahá'í Faith.[25]

By 1986, at the close of this period, details about the persecution of Bahá'ís as well as accurate information about the community and its teachings had been conveyed to nearly every head of state, all UN ambassadors and countless diplomats, human rights officials, and NGO representatives. Over 100 national Baháʼí communities had taken steps to apprise their government representatives of the situation and ask for their support. In doing so, they brought the attention and censure of the international community to bear on Iran's efforts to eliminate the Baháʼí community from its midst. On December 13, 1985, in a historic resolution, the UN General Assembly identified Iran as a violator of human rights and called attention to the particular plight of the Baháʼís.[26] It was the first occasion on which a minority group suffering human rights violations had been specially named in a General Assembly resolution and only the fourth instance since 1945 that the General Assembly had adopted a resolution censuring the human rights record of a specific country.[27] After 1986, Iran's practice of executing Baháʼís, while not entirely halted, had considerably slowed, and its actions were laid bare and immediately reported to senior human rights officials, diplomats, and governments around the world.

The Distinctive Nature of the Baháʼí Community's Response

The above section provided a broad overview of actions taken, which we will now examine more closely in order to glean insights into the conceptual underpinnings of the response. First, an analysis of the expression of the substrate will illuminate the BIC's qualitatively different approach to involvement in the political arena. Second, it will clarify the operation of the BIC as part of a broader, global effort to lay the foundations for a more just and peaceful society. This is to say that the BIC, in its efforts to defend the beleaguered Baháʼí community, is not only trying to stem the persecution; it is also acting as an integral part of a worldwide community that is seeking to establish distinct patterns of relationships, including ones among communities and governing institutions. As the Universal House of Justice states, "The proper response to oppression is neither to succumb in resignation nor to take the characteristics of the oppressor."[28] An exploration of the substrate enables us to see that the diplomatic work emerges from the matrix of a dynamic, evolving community whose distinct epistemology and structure give rise to a distinctively global polity that offers an alternative model of pursuing social change in the international arena.

The Nature of the Struggle

The Baháʼí community's response to persecution can be considered as a reply to the following question: In what ways can a community struggle for change without reproducing the current patterns of antagonism and conflict—patterns that are ill-suited to the construction of a more just, united, and interdependent human society? The BIC's response to the persecution offers a critique of contemporary forms of politics—in particular, the practices associated with acrimonious "debate, propaganda, the adversarial method, [and] the entire apparatus of partisanship."[29] It brings to light, as political scientist Arash Abizadeh points out, the "long-standing tradition in the history of political thought that views politics essentially as a form of war."[30] But consider that the "oneness of humanity" element of the substrate is entirely anathema to the division of humanity "into essentially warring camps"[31] and endless variations of "us vs. them" constructions. This kind of theological underpinning, then, has potentially radical consequences for the nature of interaction in the political arena. In his analysis of Bahá'í political thought, Ulrich Gollmer differentiates between two prevalent types of social action: "strategic" and "communicative." While strategic action focuses above all on realizing stated goals (and often entails combative means), communicative action prioritizes the attainment of collective understanding about a given manner, coordinating action on the basis of this understanding.[32] The BIC's response during this period demonstrates a principled adherence to communicative action, fostering relationships of trust within the UN community, furnishing timely and factual accounts of the persecution and of the community in general, and working with a diversity of NGO, human rights, and diplomatic partners to build awareness of the extent and gravity of the threat to the Bahá'í community.[33]

The Bahá'í Community's Relationship to Government Authorities and the International Community

The Bahá'í community's relationship to government authorities and to the international community emerges as one of the salient features of its response to the persecution. As Ghanea notes in her analysis of the United Nations' response to the persecution of the Bahá'í community, "Bahá'ís do not demand self-determination, they hold obedience to government as one of their religious tenets and they have not taken the law into their own hands by engaging in any use of force to demand their rights."[34] In the face of the persecution, rather than mounting revolts against the actions of the government, the Bahá'í community, guided by the Universal House of Justice, used the available mechanisms of international law to seek redress for their mistreatment. In his analysis of the Bahá'í Refugee Resettlement Program (1981–9), which assisted governments with the resettlement of Iranian Bahá'ís rendered stateless by the Islamic

Republic of Iran, Cameron notes that the program "was not aimed at creating an alternative arena of action from the state. Rather, it validated state authority to oversee the process of refugee resettlement."[35] In a similar manner, the BIC used every possible legal means of redress available to it, beginning with awareness raising, peacefully communicating with Iranian state authorities, and supplying information to the UN human rights bodies and the office of the secretary-general, keeping UN ambassadors apprised of the situation.

What we see in the actions of the Bahá'í community is the steadfast pursuit of every legal, constructive channel to effect social change. With the lens of the historical impetus toward greater degrees of integration, Bahá'ís view social change in civilizational terms as well as more immediate terms. In terms of the latter, by supporting mechanisms and processes conducive to the exercise of justice and social order (e.g., international human rights mechanisms), the BIC sees itself as contributing, however modestly, to the collective long-term enterprise of strengthening the international community's capacity to exercise justice across various arenas of human endeavor.

This capacity was strengthened in a number of ways during this period. In 1981, the General Assembly adopted the Declaration on the Elimination of All Forms of Intolerance Based on Religion or Belief, considered one of the most important documents protecting religious freedom.[36] The declaration affirms the universal right to "freedom of thought, conscience and religion" and to "manifest [one's] religion or belief in worship, observance, practice and teaching," and further states that "[n]o one shall be subject to discrimination by any state, institution, group of persons or person on grounds of religion or other beliefs"[37]—marking a landmark consensus among the international community on this fundamental right. While not a legally binding document, the declaration set a clear standard for religious freedom. The international community's human rights machinery was further strengthened by the General Assembly's adoption of the Convention against Torture and Other Cruel, Inhuman or Degrading Treatment or Punishment, which states that "[n]o exceptional circumstances whatsoever, whether a state of war, internal political instability or any other public emergency, may be invoked as a justification of torture."[38] The BIC received permission from the Universal House of Justice to approach governments to seek support for the adoption of this convention.

The principle of obedience to government may appear counterproductive in the face of state-sponsored violence; some may wonder whether it perpetuates oppression at the hands of government authorities. And yet, Bahá'ís are exhorted to behave with "loyalty, honesty, and truthfulness" toward the government.[39]

We see this in the Bahá'í community's obedience to the Iranian government's ban on all Bahá'í administrative institutions and community activities, making membership in Bahá'í administrative institutions a crime. In 1982, at the height of the persecution of Iranian Bahá'ís, the Universal House of Justice exhorted the Bahá'í community to see the wave of persecution as an opportunity to "demonstrate their unity and fellowship before the eyes of a skeptical and declining world … to establish the reverence of our Faith for Islam … to assert the principles of noninterference in political activities and obedience to government, which stand at the very core of our Faith, and to provide comfort and solace to the breasts of the serene sufferers and steadfast heroes in the forefront of the persecuted community."[40] It is important to note here that the Universal House of Justice had, in an earlier letter, emphasized that the Bahá'í principle of loyalty to one's respective government did not imply agreement with or promotion of any particular "political principles or policies."[41] Neither should the principle of obedience to government be equated with passivity of any sort; the Universal House of Justice would later use the term "constructive resilience" to describe the nature of the beleaguered Iranian Bahá'í community's response to its ongoing struggle. A prominent example of this, for example, in response to the ban on Bahá'ís attending university in Iran, is the establishment of the Bahá'í Institute for Higher Education in Iran, an open educational program organized through online instruction and supplemented by in-person teaching, offering over 700 courses across fourteen undergraduate and three graduate degree programs with the support of approximately 275 faculty and staff.[42]

Building Institutional Capacity for International Collective Action

The Administrative Order, as an element of the substrate, comes to the fore during this period in which highly coordinated and swift international action is required, accurate information must be obtained and communicated to numerous diplomatic and decision-making entities in a timely manner, representatives of over 100 national Bahá'í communities need to make coordinated appeals to their respective governments, campaigns of misinformation must be addressed and corrected, and the lives and fates of the Iranian Bahá'í community hang in the balance. From a historical perspective, the 1970s and early 1980s are still the very early days of transnational civil society organizing, and the means of instant international electronic communication are at least a decade away.

While the BIC appears as a discrete diplomatic actor in the drama unfolding in this period, it in fact forms part of a complex matrix of an organically developing community, guided not only by a particular set of practices and beliefs but also by clearly defined institutions that operationalize the teachings in a global administrative order. What we learn from this example, as scholars have pointed out, is that religions are not only reacting to globalization but are active agents in its making.[43] Indeed, as Susanne Hoeber Rudolph identifies, religious communities are among the oldest "transnationals" whose broad geographic reach and coordination long predate that of the nation-state.[44] The example of the BIC and the worldwide Bahá'í community's involvement in the work to stem the persecution against Iranian Bahá'ís sheds light on the processes that give rise to a new global order. This is not to imply the existence of a single exclusive global order that vies for power and ascendancy with the international order of nation-states or the transnational patterns of NGO activity; rather, it points to one element of the more "complex geography" of global governance in which we see emerging myriad "global, regional, transnational systems of authoritative rule-making and implementation."[45] What is of particular interest is the operationalization of an order that develops from the teachings of a (relatively) recent religious tradition, and one that provides so explicitly for the pattern of social organization required to address the ills of fragmentation, injustice, and conflict in the modern world.

Shoghi Effendi elaborated the structures and processes of Bahá'í administration and worked arduously to raise up the pattern of local and national governance so as to pave the way for the election of its first global governing body, the Universal House of Justice, in 1963. As he states, the teachings of the Bahá'í Faith "can never permeate and exercise an abiding influence upon mankind unless and until it incarnates itself in a visible Order."[46] The analysis of institutional structures has not generally been a part of the study of religious formations. International relations scholars have generally approached religion as "a set of norms, a discourse, or a basis of individual or group identity."[47] However, one cannot understand the BIC's engagement in the international arena without an earnest consideration of the distinct institutional arrangements that permeate its very identity. We must then consider the organic and systematic unfoldment of the structures and mechanisms of global governance, even in their earliest forms, taking shape during this period. Figure 5.2 below outlines a selection of major developments in the global governing system of the Bahá'í community during this period.

The Bahá'í Administrative Order—most notably, the Universal House of Justice—provides the oversight of the BIC and guides the development of the wider Bahá'í community, whose national governing bodies are called upon to

Figure 5.2 Emerging elements of the Baháʼí system of global governance

Year(s)	Development	Significance
1963[48]	Election of the first nine-member global governing and legislative body of the Baháʼí community[49] (Universal House of Justice)	Members of fifty-six National and Regional Baháʼí Assemblies cast their votes to elect the first nine-member Universal House of Justice.[50] Two hundred eighty-eight Assembly delegates cast their votes in person. The Universal House of Justice assumes the oversight of the BIC in 1967.[51]
1971–1986	Number of National Spiritual Assemblies (NSAs) increases by 47 percent, from 101 to 148	As each National Assembly forms, it becomes an affiliate of the BIC, thus expanding the global representation of the BIC and growing the institutional resources necessary to support the defense of the Baháʼís in Iran.
		Capacity of National Assemblies to engage effectively with their respective governments expands.
		Growing understanding of the Administrative Order among NSAs and their role within an evolving global order; Universal House of Justice states, "Since the Baháʼí Community must operate as a cohesive entity, it is not conducive to its success for any single unit of that world-embracing organism to go off at a tangent in its reactions to the situation, as well-intentioned as that unit might be."[52]
1972	Constitution of the Universal House of Justice is adopted[53]	The Constitution elucidates the binding terms of reference[54] for the Universal House of Justice, its legislative authority.
		"Powers and duties" encompass doing "its utmost for the realization of greater cordiality and comity amongst the nations and for the attainment of universal peace"; "[safeguarding] the personal rights, freedom and initiative of individuals"; "[giving] attention … to the development of countries and the stability of states"; "safeguard[ing] the unity of its followers and maintain[ing] the integrity and flexibility of its teachings."[55]
1973	English publication of the codification of Baháʼí laws[56]	Availability of the laws to all members of the Baháʼí community (translations into many languages), clarification of norms in the Baháʼí community, and consolidation of the Baháʼí community.
1983	Completion of the Seat of the Universal House of Justice in Haifa, Israel	Further material consolidation and development of the Administrative Order.

respond to the persecution in their respective national contexts. The governing structure ensures the coherent development of a nascent polity whose capacity for coordinated diplomatic action—that adheres to the high standards of integrity and nonpartisanship set forth in the Bahá'í writings—must develop quickly to address the attacks on the Bahá'í community. What this type of guidance enables us to see is the centrality of the role of the Universal House of Justice in the defense of the Bahá'í community in Iran. During this time, the Bahá'í community is learning new patterns of interaction in the political arena and new modes of pursuing social change (within a global polity context), the efficacy of which may not be immediately apparent in a national context but which becomes apparent when considering the nature and complexity of the transnational diplomatic effort, guided by the House of Justice, to protect the Bahá'í community in Iran.

BIC Engagement in the UN Decade for Women: Fresh Perspectives on Advancing Gender Equality

In the second half of this chapter, I explore the influence of the substrate on the BIC's engagement with another defining area of the United Nations' activities during this period—the UN Decade for Women. The following analysis will reveal in particular the role of the Bahá'í Administrative Order, especially the Universal House of Justice, in providing authoritative guidance on the meaning and implications of gender equality and mobilizing and building the capacity of the worldwide Bahá'í community to enter this arena of action. This section will also demonstrate the role of the Administrative Order not only in clarifying the conceptual underpinnings of the Bahá'í understanding of gender equality, but also in helping to create the conditions and patterns of community life that support the full participation of women and men in all its facets.

In the period between 1970 and 1985, the international community witnessed major intellectual, institutional, and social advancements in the arena of gender equality. In 1972, fully twenty-seven years after the founding of the United Nations, the first woman was appointed to a top leadership position: Helvi Sipilä from Finland became the first female UN assistant secretary-general.[57] That same year, the General Assembly declared 1975 as International Women's Year. Following the ensuing first World Conference on Women, held in Mexico[58] in 1975, the United Nations formally declared 1976–85 as the UN Decade for

Women, suggesting that the question of women and their rights and needs would now be addressed across the entire UN system. This broad mandate "created enormous demands for information" and "produced an explosion of knowledge"[59] arising in part out of global reviews of the condition of women. Further developments included the creation of the first global UN institutions assigned to women,[60] major advancements in NGO networking and strategizing, as well as the creation of normative standards and mechanisms to identify and remedy discrimination, foremost among them the 1979 landmark Convention on the Elimination of All Forms of Discrimination against Women.[61] Whereas, in 1975, women were still portrayed as "passive victims of structures and practices"—as needing to be trained, integrated, or allowed to participate fully in political life[62]—by the end of the decade, the advancement of women was recognized as "a precondition for the establishment of a humane and progressive society";[63] in short, the advancement of women was now seen as central to the realization of the goals of the United Nations.

The Universal House of Justice: Authority, Mobilization, and Capacity Building

As mentioned earlier, the Universal House of Justice is the global governing body of the worldwide Bahá'í community, whose authority extends to legislation on matters that are not explicitly stated in the Bahá'í writings.[64] In this section, I explore its role along two dimensions: first, in deepening the community's understanding of the Bahá'í concept of gender equality; second, in mobilizing and guiding the community's involvement in the decade. What emerges, even during these earliest days of NGO organizing for gender equality, is the articulation of a distinct and evolving understanding of gender equality, the dynamic interaction between evolving human rights norms and religiously based understandings of gender equality, and the Bahá'í community's discovery of some of the enabling factors of gender equality within its communities. The analysis demonstrates the pivotal role of the Administrative Order in shaping the BIC's engagement with the international community.

The Idea of Gender Equality

The intersection of religion and questions of gender equality has often been associated with contentious debates, characterized by various permutations of "us versus them," liberal versus conservative, modern versus traditional, and an ethos of adversarialism and ideological gridlock, all of which tend to peak in relation to questions of sexual and reproductive health. As one UN agency noted, "conservative religious actors see religious moral principles as timeless and non-negotiable, while feminists and other human rights advocates argue for pluralist and rights-based alternatives."[65] The rise of religious extremism and fundamentalism has exacerbated the perception of utter incommensurability between "religious" and "progressive" or modern views of gender equality. Since the 1970s, a number of "feminist theologies" (or "religious feminisms") have emerged from within religious traditions, seeking to "[reinterpret] religions and the traditions that surround them in order to uncover and promote understandings of religions that are gender equal."[66]

What makes the BIC an interesting case study in this case is that the equality of women and men is a tenet of the Baháʼí Faith—one that its elected leaders, whether local, national or international, must observe and promote. "The world of humanity has two wings," state the Baháʼí writings, "one is women and the other men. Not until both wings are equally developed can the bird fly. Should one wing remain weak, flight is impossible."[67] However, in the early 1970s, the Baháʼí community was still quite small, the Universal House of Justice had been elected only seven years earlier, the Baháʼí writings had not yet been translated into many languages, and as such, not all Baháʼís had access to the teachings about gender equality. In light of these limiting factors, the BIC notes in its statement to the UN Economic and Social Council:

> It is inevitable at this time that there are wide differences in the [Baháʼí community's] understanding, as well as in the application, of these principles [including gender equality], and that the full appreciation of their significance, and its demonstration in action, are dependent upon many factors in the life of the individual and in society.[68]

Yet as the United Nations announced 1975 to be the International Women's Year (followed by the UN Decade for Women), the Universal House of Justice saw this as an opportunity for the Baháʼí world to deepen its understanding of this pivotal principle of the Baháʼí Faith, as well as its ability to contribute to the strengthening of family and community life and to work to raise consciousness of the importance of this tenet in the broader society. In a letter to national Baháʼí communities that year, the Universal House of Justice notes the designation of 1975 as "International Women's Year" and calls on eighty National Spiritual Assemblies (NSAs) to "initiate and implement programs which will stimulate and promote the full and equal participation of women in all aspects of Baháʼí community life."[69] Moreover, it asks Baháʼís to "demonstrate the distinction" of the Baháʼí Faith in this field of endeavor.

Baháʼí activities in this arena grew exponentially during this period: at the local level, communities around the world established programs to promote the advancement of women. National Baháʼí communities organized and sponsored conferences on women.[70] The BIC collaborated with NGOs and the United Nations in numerous (elected) roles such as chair of the NGO Committee on UNICEF, vice-chair of the Committee for the United Nations Decade for Women, secretary of the Sub-Committee on Women (Geneva Office), and chair of the Human Rights Committee, among others.[71] Leading up to the UN World Conference on Women, the BIC participated in and invited local delegates to attend preparatory conferences in Europe, Asia, Latin America, Africa, and the Pacific.[72] BIC and local delegates were present at the UN World Conferences on Women in Mexico (1975), Copenhagen (1980), and Nairobi (1985).[73]

The example brings to the fore the question of authority associated with the Universal House of Justice and the Baháʼí Administrative Order in general. While it is difficult to make a general statement about the status of women around the world in the 1970s, as progress (and understanding of gender equality) unfolded very differently in different places, it is reasonable to assume

Figure 5.3 The Baháʼí delegation to the World Conference to Review and Appraise the Achievements of the United Nations Decade for Women, held in July 1985. Left to right: Alberta Deas, Peter Vuyiya, Jane Faily, Magdalene Carney, Mary Sawicki, Ethel Martens, Shomais Afnan, Thelma Khelgati, Richard Mandara, Catherine M'boya. © Baháʼí World Centre.

a degree of resistance to inculcating this principle into family, community, and the functioning of society as a whole. It wasn't until 1979 that the United Nations General Assembly adopted the first international legally binding instrument to eliminate discrimination against women.[74]

Bahá'í efforts to advance gender equality go back to the turn of the century, when the community established schools for both girls and boys and were "at the forefront of the advances in education that were occurring in Iran" at the turn of the twentieth century.[75] By 1974, Bahá'í women in Iran under the age of forty had achieved 100 percent literacy in comparison to the national average of only 15 percent.[76] In response to the Bahá'í community's understanding of this principle at the time, the BIC, as guided by the Universal House of Justice, undertook to share with national Bahá'í communities compilations of authoritative Bahá'í teachings concerning gender equality as well as suggestions of additional resources so as to deepen their understanding of it. Of course, reading and embodying these principles in action are two very different things, and the BIC acknowledged this in its statement to the United Nations:

> Certainly the problems which individual Bahá'ís and local and national Bahá'í communities must face in gradually educating and raising themselves to the high standards inculcated in the Teachings of Bahá'u'lláh may be different; but the direction is determined. [...] A gradual but steady change in attitudes can be counted upon because of the roots from which such action springs."[77]

During this period, the Bahá'í community's understanding of the principle of gender equality and its application in community life continued to evolve. The United Nations, as well, was refining its understanding. The traditional approach of "formal or *de jure* equality, which involves simply 'adding women' to the existing paradigm," noted a human rights scholar, was an inadequate way to approach inequality.[78] The task before the United Nations was therefore a deeper rethinking of equality, which included "addressing the institutionalized nature of women's disadvantage and changing the cultural, religious, and traditional beliefs that typecast women as inferior to men."[79] The groundbreaking Convention on the Elimination of All Forms of Discrimination against Women (CEDAW) crystallized the concept of substantive equality, as opposed to the traditional model of "formal equality," showing "that women can be different from men but still equal to them."[80] In order to assist Bahá'í communities in cultivating a deeper understanding of the concept of gender equality, the BIC included in its mailings to over 100 national communities copies of key UN human rights documents and conventions related to gender equality.[81] We can see, therefore, a developmental approach taken by the Universal House of Justice to build the capacity of Bahá'í communities to be grounded in the spiritual dimensions of the teaching of gender equality, as well as the evolving legal and technical dimensions provided in the documents coming from the United Nations. This is perhaps best exemplified in the BIC's 1985 statement to the United Nations, which asserts:

> since equality is ... a religious obligation and the potential development of a spiritual equality is unlimited, practice of the equality of men and women must necessarily continue to evolve over time to accommodate the needs of an ever-advancing civilization, rather than terminate once certain minimal rights are achieved.[82]

Over the years, the BIC would introduce many concepts related to gender equality into the discourse at the United Nations, among them: women as protagonists of development, the spiritual dimensions of equality, the nature and purpose of education, gender equality as a prerequisite for peace, and gender equality as a component of the larger unity of the humankind.[83] Institutionally, the BIC would be elected to numerous leadership roles in the gender equality work at the United Nations, including positions on executive committees organizing the global conferences. For example, a BIC representative served as vice-chair of the Committee on the UN Decade for Women and as chair and vice-chair of the NGO Committee on the Status of Women.

Early Insights into the Relationship between the Administrative Order and Gender Equality

As mentioned in the opening of this section, as the United Nations embarked on the Decade for Women, it created a large demand for information about the status and condition of women on many fronts. Following suit, NGOs undertook to provide the United Nations with information about women in their respective communities. In a similar manner, the BIC sent a survey to over 100 NSAs that included questions about changing attitudes of both men and women, the influence of traditions and customs, participation of women in Bahá'í community life (e.g., administrative activities, elections, community deliberations, service on committees and elected bodies, teaching of Bahá'í classes), and questions relating to education. The replies received from eighty-two national communities provided important insight into the mechanisms and processes that were considered among the most conducive to the advancement of women.

According to the questionnaire results, the most frequently cited positive influence was the Bahá'í Administrative Order (which was at this time functioning in 140 countries).[84] In order not to confuse the reader, it is helpful to reiterate that the Administrative Order is among the elements of the substrate that shape the engagement of the BIC in the international arena. In the previous section about the persecution of the Bahá'í community, I focused on the particular approaches taken by the BIC and how these were shaped by the operation of the Administrative Order, especially the Universal House of Justice. In this specific example, a transformative and emancipatory dimension of the Administrative Order comes to light not in the actions of the BIC itself but in the observed patterns of community life as examined through the lens of gender equality. This is still relevant as we consider that the BIC is an integral part of the worldwide Bahá'í community, and it reflects and brings the insights from this community to bear on its involvement with the United Nations. Returning then to our discussion about the questionnaire results: In what way was the Administrative Order considered to facilitate greater measures of gender equality in many of the communities?

According to the results, communities reported that it was participation in the processes of Bahá'í community governance that had the strongest influence on the level of women's engagement in all facets of community life. Briefly, Bahá'í elections are characterized by the following: absence of campaigning or electioneering,[85] understanding of the spiritual nature of participation in elections ("sacred task"),[86] attitude of voters ("without the least trace of passion or prejudice"), encouragement of universal participation,[87] secret ballot, and principle-based criteria for leadership. Furthermore, elected bodies follow principles of Bahá'í consultation—principled deliberation and decision-making processes. Responses to the questionnaire observe the empowerment of women in the process:

> The very act of becoming a Bahá'í is the first major personal decision for most women in rural areas. Then, as they are deepened in the Bahá'í Teachings, and the role they are expected to play in Bahá'í administrative activity, they are changed from being passive members of an existing social order into dynamic members of a new order. Because of their functions in serving on administrative bodies and in voting and in being voted for and elected, women have made great strides in a largely male dominated society.[88]

As another country's representative notes, "Since many women are involved in all aspects of community administration and community life, this appears to be the area where the principle of equality bears the most fruit."[89]

What is interesting to note in the questionnaire results is that it is the governing structures and processes themselves that are conducive to the participation of women or, put differently, do not embody those elements that may (however unintentionally) exclude or hinder the participation of women. According to the survey, in all Bahá'í communities but one (of those reporting), women actively participated in voting for their local governing body ("Local Spiritual Assembly"). The report notes that even in communities where "acceptance of the equal status of women is underdeveloped," Bahá'í women vote in elections.[90] Sometimes, "this participation is their first attempt at freedom of expression," and "this activity [elections] has given women their first opportunity to take part in administrative affairs" in village and rural areas.[91] Even in countries "where tradition is strongly against the participation of women in community life," Bahá'í women are active in discussions and are often "a decisive factor in elections."[92] Other reporting communities noted that in countries where by tradition, women seldom speak in the presence of men, and where great discrimination exists, women are elected to Local Spiritual Assemblies. And further, in places where only men serve on village councils, women are elected to the Bahá'í assemblies, which suggests that some men's attitudes changed enough to make them consider a woman for a leadership position. According to the questionnaire, women were also elected to a majority of NSAs in Europe (88 percent), Africa (77 percent), Asia (60 percent), Americas (97 percent), and Australasia (90 percent).

The responses to the questionnaire, which the BIC shared with the UN Economic Social Council, highlight another facet of the operations of the Administrative Order—namely, the intimate relationship between the local and the global. What becomes apparent, particularly with an issue such as gender equality, is that engagement in the international arena at the level of contributions to discourses and policy-making and collaboration with civil society are part of a much larger, all-encompassing project of building new patterns of community life from the ground up. As the House of Justice writes to the worldwide Bahá'í community in 1985, on the eve of the third World Conference on Women in Nairobi, Kenya:

> The Bahá'í community will be strongly represented at the culminating event of the United Nations' Decade of Women in this same year … But it is in the local Bahá'í communities that the most widespread presentation of the Faith can take place. It is here that the real pattern of Bahá'í life can be seen. It is here that the

power of Bahá'u'lláh to organize human affairs on a basis of spiritual unity can be most apparent.[93]

*

In this chapter, we encounter two very different areas of BIC engagement: first, in coordinating the global response to the persecution of the Bahá'í community in Iran and, second, in overseeing the participation of the Bahá'í community in the United Nations' efforts to advance the status of women. In both cases, the role of the Bahá'í Administrative Order, as seen most clearly through the operation of the Universal House of Justice, brings into stark relief the unifying and coordinating power of this element of the substrate in the work of the BIC. In the human rights situation, the nascent Bahá'í community navigates a fraught political terrain to effect a global, principled, and urgent response to the attacks on their co-religionists in Iran. From a wider perspective, we come to see the emerging architecture of a global polity, the gradual strengthening of capacity for collective endeavor across nearly 150 national communities, the learning of new patterns of social action, and the rejection of partisanship and adversarialism as viable approaches to social change. In addition, the centrality of the Bahá'í Administrative Order to the BIC's engagement in gender equality yields two further insights. First, the Administrative Order itself, at the community level, restructures patterns of community life in a manner that facilitates a fuller participation of women in decision-making and in the governance of the community. As the BIC represents the Bahá'í community to the United Nations, it is through the channel of the Administrative Order that the principles of the Bahá'í Faith as a whole find expression in community life, and it from this place of lived experience and practice of the workings of a new social order that the BIC can convey a compelling vision and example to the United Nations. Furthermore, the generative and evolutionary dimensions of the substrate come to the fore as the Bahá'í community, across diverse national and sociocultural contexts, is guided to advance in its understanding of gender equality and to discover and refine its application in all facets of social life. While the lines between the BIC and the Bahá'í community may appear blurred in this chapter, that is because the two are intricately interwoven: in order to understand the work of the BIC, we must appreciate the authoritative, structuring, and unifying role of the Administrative Order.

Beyond Peace: The Greater Trajectory for Social Development (1986–2008)

To mark the fortieth anniversary of the United Nations, the General Assembly declared 1986 the International Year of Peace. The observance came in the midst of numerous upheavals and turning points in world politics. Indeed, the impetus for such a focus came, in part, as a response to the relentless tensions and conflicts threatening global security, the deterioration of economic and social conditions, as well as the growing loss of confidence in multilateralism.[1] In the six years that followed, the world witnessed the turbulence of the Chernobyl explosion (1986), perestroika (1987), the fall of the Berlin Wall (1989), the protests and massacre at Tiananmen Square (1989), the fall of the Soviet Union (1991), and the end of the Cold War (1992). During this same time, the stage was set for the flourishing of new social movements and the rise of civil society organizations around the world.[2] In the 1990s, UN global conferences brought together unprecedented numbers of heads of state and civil society representatives to deliberate on issues of global concern and, in 2000, to articulate a global development agenda (the Millennium Development Goals) to steer the international community for the first fifteen years of the new millennium. Such was the backdrop for the BIC's efforts in the arena of peace during this period.

A New Stage in the Development of the Bahá'í Community: The Emergence from Obscurity

The year 1986 marked a turning point for both the BIC and the Bahá'í community as a whole. In a letter to the worldwide Bahá'í community, the Universal House of Justice notes "a dramatic change in the status of the [Bahá'í] Faith"; "the great, the historic feature of this period," it writes, "is the emergence of the faith from obscurity."[3] In large part, the emergence was precipitated by forces outside the community—namely, the systemic and relentless persecution of the Bahá'í community in Iran, which accelerated in the 1970s and reached a dramatic peak in the early 1980s, as described in the previous chapter. In response to the violent persecution, the Bahá'í community, under the guidance of the Universal House of Justice, appealed to the highest levels of government and international law. Swift and widespread diplomatic efforts succeeded not only in containing the violence and persecution, but also in raising the consciousness of the majority of the world's governments about the existence of this religious community, its aims, and its plight under Iran's oppressive regime.[4]

Further contributing to its emergence from obscurity was the recognition of the Bahá'í Faith as an independent world religion in authoritative publications (such as the *Encyclopedia Britannica*), in court rulings,[5] and among government representatives.[6] The community had grown in size and geographic spread[7]; the 1988 edition of the *Encyclopedia Britannica* referenced the Bahá'í Faith as the second most geographically widespread religion in the world.[8]

In the context of these developments, the Universal House of Justice noted in 1986 that the BIC had reached a "new, potent stage in the development of the external affairs of the worldwide Bahá'í community."[9] Writing to this community, it states:

> The time has come for the Bahá'í community to become more involved in the life of the society around it, without in the least supporting any of the world's moribund and divisive concepts ... but rather, by association, exerting its influence towards unity, demonstrating its ability to settle differences by consultation rather than by confrontation, violence or schism.[10]

That same year, the Universal House of Justice launched a global six-year plan, the goals of which included "broadening the basis of international relations of the Bahá'í Faith" and "[fostering] association with organizations, prominent persons and those in authority concerning the promotion of peace, world order and allied objectives."[11] Under the auspices of the plan, the Universal House of Justice called on the BIC to be "the windows of the Bahá'í community to the world," displaying "ever more clearly the unifying principles, the hope, the promise, the majesty of the emerging order."[12]

A Focus on Peace

On the eve of the International Year of Peace—precisely on the fortieth anniversary of the United Nations on October 24, 1985—for the first time the

Universal House of Justice addressed a message to the peoples of the world. The message, titled "The Promise of World Peace," examined various social, economic, institutional, and spiritual dimensions of peace, and invited the generality of humankind to consider the outlines of a new social order, the glimmerings of which were already on the horizon. The creation of such an order would require not only spiritual and moral qualities but also the will to act, as well as the ability of world leaders to come together in a spirit of dispassionate, focused, and principled deliberation, animated by a consciousness of membership in an inextricably connected global community. The statement explores not only the pressing needs of a conflict-ridden global community, but the very concept of peace itself. It makes the following assertion:

> Permanent peace among nations is an essential stage, but not … the ultimate goal of the social development of humanity. Beyond the initial armistice forced upon the world by the fear of nuclear holocaust, beyond the political peace reluctantly entered into by suspicious rival nations, beyond pragmatic arrangements for security and coexistence, beyond even the many experiments in co-operation which these steps will make possible lies the crowning goal: the unification of all the peoples of the world in one universal family.[13]

In effect, the statement introduced a new narrative of social progress. Where such a narrative typically envisions "peace" as an end stage along a developmental trajectory, here the goal is shifted. It is reconstructed along a continuum of progress toward increasing spheres of unity, as it draws closer to the "crowning goal" of human social and spiritual evolution—the unification of the peoples of the world into "one universal family."

The statement and its wide-ranging analysis effectively set the agenda for the BIC's work with the United Nations during this period. Within several years, the message was translated into over seventy languages and presented to every head of state and UN mission, with over two million copies being distributed globally. National Spiritual Assemblies around the world, under the guidance of the Universal House of Justice, launched a myriad activities lifting up the pursuit of peace in their respective national contexts. That same year, UN Secretary-General Javier Pérez de Cuéllar designated five of the BIC's national affiliates (Australia, Belgium, Brazil, Kenya, and Lesotho) as "Peace Messengers,"[14] recognizing their efforts for the advancement of peace. The aim of this chapter is to examine how elements of the BIC's substrate give rise to a unique conception of peace. It is significant not only for its distinctiveness from the prevailing notions rooted in the Western liberal tradition, but also for

Figure 6.1 Baháʼís in Lesotho receive the UN "Peace Messengers Award" for the community's involvement in peace activities, September 15, 1987. © Baháʼí World Centre.

the manner in which it reframes the nature and goals of social progress and the very elements of human flourishing.

Conceptions of Peace

As some scholars have noted, the idea of peace is widely referred to but seldom defined.[15] It is too easy to assume that organizations working toward "peace" all have the same ends and conditions in mind, or to assume that civil society organizations, whether religious or secular, espouse the same conception of peace as is embodied in the UN Charter (although certainly they hold much in common). As Lederach asserts, religiously inspired peacebuilding "requires that we explore the understanding and perspectives that undergird the practices ... and meaning at a deeper level than the description of a particular technique."[16]

As I have acknowledged at the outset, the concept of peace is not a homogenous one; rather, it emerges from intellectual and philosophical traditions (e.g., democratic peace theory, realism, Marxist theory, social constructivism), which identify particular qualities of a desired state of social affairs.[17] Embedded within different constructs of peace are, among others, assumptions about the nature of the human being, the sources of conflict, requisite conditions for the flourishing of human society, and the means for attaining and sustaining these conditions. When we speak of peace in the Western liberal tradition, we must not assume that this idea maps perfectly onto concepts of peace emerging from other schools of thought. This is not to imply that we cannot work together toward peace as diverse peoples and nations but rather to highlight the need to be curious about and open to other perspectives on this long-sought ideal.

The concept of peace is, of course, foundational to the United Nations; indeed, the desire for peace among the nations is the reason for its existence. The preamble to the UN Charter opens with the words, "We the peoples of the United Nations determined to save succeeding generations from the scourge of war."[18] The Charter makes no less than fifty references to peace (most often in terms of "peace and security") and casts it largely in terms of an absence or prevention of threats, war, conflict, and aggression. The understanding of peace and its prerequisites has evolved through successive UN administrations and the organization's efforts to stem and address conflicts across the world. In 1992, UN Secretary-General Boutros Boutros-Ghali issued a seminal report introducing, among other things, the idea of "post-conflict peacebuilding," which centered on strengthening the structures of peace "in order to prevent a relapse into conflict."[19] Subsequent efforts—including the *Report of the Panel on UN Peace Operations* (2000), the International Decade for a Culture of Peace and Non-Violence (2001–10), and the creation of the Peacebuilding Commission (2005)—have further evolved the United Nations' understanding of peace and the mechanisms and processes for its promotion.[20]

While scholars have critiqued the Western liberal constructions of international peace as being conceived of largely as a Western activity "derived from war," and one understood in terms of a "liberal" peace,[21] the arena of peacebuilding has also seen a range of critical innovations. These have raised questions of methodology, epistemology, ontology, ways of "knowing peace," as well as related themes of emancipation, discourse, knowledge, power, and identity.[22] In a similar manner, each religious tradition has yielded a particular understanding and practice of peace.[23] Such an understanding bears directly on the work of religious NGOs, as well as faith-based organizations and religiously inspired social movements animated by particular conceptions of peace. As scholars of theology and peacebuilding Dubois and Hunter-Bowman point out, a "lack of deep appreciation for theologies—embodied as well as verbal—limits understanding of social change processes and skews interpretations of religious actors."[24] It is precisely with the aim of gaining a clearer understanding of the manner in which peace is conceived and pursued that a substrate-based analysis is applied to the study of the BIC's work in this arena during this period.

The Bahá'í Approach to Peace: A Focus on Unity, Evolutionary Processes, and Temporal Frames

The Bahá'í concept of peace encompasses both the transformation of the human being at the level of identity and orientation toward other human beings and, at the same time, the reform and reconstruction of the world's governing and social institutions. We can see Bahá'u'lláh's multifaceted approach to peace outlined in his letters to the rulers of the world, discussed in detail in Chapter 2. In these letters, he calls for collective security, democracy, the elimination of poverty, the cessation of the arms race, the eradication of all kinds of prejudice, the outlawing of slavery; he outlines concepts of freedom and unity in diversity; he rejects patriarchy; and calls for a culture of peace based on a redefined identity rooted in the consciousness of membership in a global community.[25] For our purposes, in order to continue the examination of how the BIC's distinct rationality (as rooted in the substrate) shapes its engagement in the international arena and specifically its pursuit of peace, I will focus on three elements of the BIC's construct of peace: the relationship between peace and unity, peace as evolutionary processes, and the temporal dimensions of peace.

Unity as a Foundational Element

The Bahá'í Faith asserts: "The well-being of mankind, its peace and security are unattainable, unless and until its unity is firmly established."[26] The establishment of unity among the peoples and nations of the world is put forward as the prerequisite for the attainment of peace and security. The concept of unity is intimately related to that of the oneness of humankind, a link demonstrated in the following excerpt from Shoghi Effendi:

> Far from aiming at the subversion of the existing foundations of society, [the oneness of humanity] seeks to broaden its basis, to remold its institutions in a manner consonant with the needs of an ever-changing world ... It does not ignore, nor does it attempt to suppress, the diversity of ethnical origins, of climate, of history, of language and tradition, of thought and habit, that differentiate the peoples and nations of the world. It calls for a wider loyalty, for a larger aspiration than any that has animated the human race. It insists

upon the subordination of national impulses and interests to the imperative claims of a unified world. It repudiates excessive centralization on one hand, and disclaims all attempts at uniformity on the other. Its watchword is unity in diversity.[27]

In this passage, Shoghi Effendi outlines the characteristics of the condition of "unity" that are required for the establishment of peace: (a) unity must be rooted in diversity and not uniformity;[28] (b) excessive centralization must be avoided; (c) unity must be embodied in the governing institutions of society; and (d) the functioning of the governing institutions must remain flexible enough to meet the needs of "an ever-changing world." What emerges is a conception of solidarity that transcends the "signifying divide of state and culture"[29] while at the same time acknowledging—and indeed, celebrating—the richness inherent in cultural diversity. 'Abdu'l-Bahá uses the analogy of a garden to convey the beauty and significance of diversity:

> Diversity of hues, form and shape enricheth and adorneth the garden ... In like manner, when divers shades of thought, temperament and character, are brought together under the power and influence of one central agency, the beauty and glory of human perfection will be revealed and made manifest.[30]

The Bahá'í writings, then, effectively shift the focus from peace as a social condition to a condition contingent on a particular kind of knowledge and orientation toward not only one's fellow man (in the spirit of the Golden Rule), but explicitly to humanity as a whole. It echoes the orientation of the Constitution of UNESCO, which states that "since wars begin in the minds of men, it is in the minds of men that the defences of peace must be constructed."[31]

If we consider the content of the seminal "Promise of World Peace" message through the lens of this orientation toward peace, we can see that the statement analyzes social ills in terms of the obstacles they pose to solidarity among the peoples and nations of the world, rather than as sources of conflict per se. Such barriers include the view of human nature as "incorrigibly selfish and aggressive," religious fanaticism, materialism, nuclear warfare, racism, extremes of wealth and poverty, unbridled nationalism, gender inequality, lack of universal education, and the lack of communication between peoples (due in part to the absence of a common language).[32]

The relationship between unity and justice is also fundamental and bears highlighting. Bahá'u'lláh states that "[t]he purpose of justice is the appearance of unity among men."[33] In one of the most widely cited statements disseminated by the BIC during this period, "The Prosperity of Humankind," justice is

Figure 6.2 The inauguration of the Peace Monument at the UN Conference for Environment and Development (Earth Summit). The sculpture, initiated by the Bahá'í community as a monument to the summit, today contains soil from over 150 countries, as a symbolic representation of the oneness of humanity. © Bahá'í World Centre.

described as the "power that can translate the consciousness of oneness into collective will," "the ruling principle of social organization," and the "practical expression of awareness" of the link between the individual and society.[34] It underscores the multivalent nature of the concept of unity and its implications for the notion of peace. The substrate, then, draws attention to the relational dimensions of peace—whether at the level of the family, community, nation, or the world. Disunity, whether inward (lack of consciousness of the oneness of humankind) or outward (inability to undertake collective action), is seen then as a fundamental driver of social distress in its many forms, one of which is war.

Peace as Process

The BIC's conception of peace is also shaped by the dimension of the substrate that views history in a developmental and evolutionary perspective. Peace is conceived of in the context of a broader civilizational trajectory, which, starting with the family, moves through progressively larger spheres of unity and human organization until it encompasses the nations of the world. The earlier stages of this vast historical process include prejudice, war, exploitation, and the "unavoidable tumult which marks [humanity's] collective coming of age."[35] The developmental dimension of the substrate enables us to discern that the processes associated with the establishment of peace are evolutionary in nature. In its statements during this period, the BIC makes frequent references to the evolution and direction of the international order and the need to examine social challenges in this light.[36]

The Bahá'í writings identify two stages of peace toward which society is advancing: the *Lesser Peace* and the *Most Great Peace*. The Lesser Peace denotes a political unity among nations, a condition to be established by the nations themselves. Responding to a question about the concept of the Lesser Peace, the BIC's Office of Public Information noted that this concept implies the achievement of a relationship among the nations of the world that enables them "to resolve questions of international import through consultation rather than war."[37] According to the 1994 External Affairs Strategy of the BIC (written under the auspices of the Universal House of Justice), "two entities will push for its [the Lesser Peace's] realization: the governments of the world, and the peoples of the world through the instrumentality of the organizations of civil society."[38] The strategy paper goes on to explain that the role of the Bahá'í community in that process, both as a religious community and as a member of civil society, is to "lend spiritual impetus to the momentum" on the trajectory toward the Lesser Peace.[39] The concept of the Lesser Peace takes on central importance during this period as it becomes a lens through which the Bahá'í community "reads" the events unfolding in the international arena, seeking in particular to discern and support processes that foster constructive consultation among the nations and peoples of the world.

Further along humanity's developmental trajectory lies the goal of the *Most Great Peace*, an objective that denotes a more complete and mature social condition—not merely a "peace" arising from political and legal agreements but one that embodies the inner spiritual principles outlined by Bahá'u'lláh, such as the elimination of all forms of prejudice and the consciousness of the oneness of humankind. As Shoghi Effendi describes, it is a peace that is the "practical consequence of the spiritualization of the world."[40]

One might also illustrate this inner/outer distinction with reference to the arena of human rights: the legal assurance of equal rights for all (as attained by the Lesser Peace) differs significantly from the eradication of racial, religious, and gender prejudice, which is seeded in the individual conscience, or one's moral framework.[41] The UNESCO Constitution echoes this distinction, declaring

> that a peace based exclusively upon the political and economic arrangements of governments would not be a peace which could secure the unanimous, lasting and sincere support of the peoples of the world, and that the peace must therefore be founded, if it is not to fail, upon the intellectual and moral solidarity of mankind.[42]

Conceptions of Time

The distinction between the Lesser Peace and the Most Great Peace draws our attention to temporal frames with respect to the advancement toward peace: the processes of peace unfold in what we might refer to as "political time" (associated with the election of new governments and administrations), and at the same time, these processes are part of a much longer historical, civilizational trajectory that extends far beyond our own lives, the fruits of which will be apparent long after our departure from this world. Many religious traditions, in fact, challenge a "singular, flat depiction" of time.[43] As Talal Asad points out, there exist in religious traditions "simultaneous temporalities [that] embrace both individuals and groups in complexities that imply more than a simple process of secular time."[44] Time, in fact, is seen as a "pivotal category" in the analysis of historical processes.[45] This was demonstrated in Chapter 4, which explores the BIC's understanding of the significance of the United Nations' formation in the context of processes dating back to the outbreak of the First World War and in terms of humanity's millennia-long journey toward social organization and cooperation on a global scale. It is in light of the parallel consideration of diverse temporal frames, in terms of both the more immediate "political time" and the longer-term civilizational-time perspective, that new dimensions of the significance of events and processes come to light.

What emerges from this analysis is a conception of peace shaped by the elements of the substrate. Without this dimension of analysis we may simply have contented ourselves with answering the question, "What does the BIC do to promote peace?" without doing the deeper and necessary work to unearth the dimensions of a new and distinct conception of peace. What continues to be important as we proceed on the journey through the seventy-five-year history of the BIC–UN relationship is the continual awareness of the influence of philosophical underpinnings that shape the constructs that we are seeking to explore (for example, religion, civil society, peace, international relations) and the ever-present necessity—and indeed, discipline—of being attentive to alternative foundations and epistemologies that enrich our capacity to both "read" and construct a better world.

Ends and Means: Substrate-Based Approaches to Advancing Peace

The conception of peace outlined above and pursued by the BIC was accompanied during this period by a distinct methodology for its advancement. In both concept and approach, we continue to see how the generative elements of the substrate continue to shape organizational norms and dispositions in the international arena. The 1994 External Affairs Strategy laid out the approach that was to be taken: the BIC was tasked with "[influencing] the processes toward world peace" by "coherently, comprehensively and continually imparting [its] ideas for the advancement of civilization."[46] This was to be done "through a unified voice" of a diverse community that "could come to be regarded as representative of the aspirations of the peoples of the world."[47] The BIC was asked to concentrate its efforts in the areas of human rights, gender equality, global prosperity, and moral development.[48] We discern in these guidelines the expression of the elements of the substrate: a developmental perspective, a focus on unity, and the implicit operation of a global system of administration through which a "unified voice" can emerge.

The remainder of the chapter explores three approaches used by the BIC to "influence the processes toward world peace": (a) widespread generation and dissemination of ideas related to the resolution of problems of global concern;

(b) fostering a culture of principled deliberation; and (c) building coherence and capacity for collective action among national affiliates. Of these approaches, the first two are outward-looking, seeking to effect positive change in the wider community; the third—building the Bahá'í community's capacity for collective action—focuses on developing its ability to promote unity and peace.

Influencing Ideas

From one perspective, it can be said that all NGOs and UN member states are engaged in a continual exchange of ideas about the creation of a more just and peaceful world; one could say that human rights and gender equality are two such "ideas," albeit in a process of continual refinement and clarification. As Jolly, Emmerij, and Weiss point out in their intellectual history of the United Nations, *UN Ideas That Changed the World*, "international organizations live or die by the quality and relevance of the policy ideas that they put forward and support."[49] At the same time, however, the predominant method of intervention used by NGOs in the political arena is one of lobbying—seeking to influence decision-makers to accept specific positions on issues under consideration. An NGO might lobby for more funding for specific social needs, for new stricter laws, for attention to underserved populations, and so on. In these cases, a "position" is being advanced and used to push for changes in policy and practice. This approach, of course, has been fruitful in many cases; NGOs have successfully influenced legislation on countless issues. It is, however, a different orientation from that of generating and sharing ideas and recognizing the evolving panoply of ideas that exists in relation to any matter under consideration by the United Nations. The latter represents an intervention at the broader level of thought and discourse—it seeks to shape the manner that issues are understood and conceived.[50]

One of the most fertile and dynamic settings for the dissemination of ideas during this period was the historic UN global conferences and summits of the 1990s, bringing together record numbers of heads of state and civil society organizations (each one surpassing the record set by the previous conference) to consider issues ranging from gender equality, social integration, health, employment, education, the environment, and population, to human rights, finance, and governance.[51] The summits were

> agenda setters, dealing with the desperately unfinished business of the twentieth century and bringing up the curtain on the twenty-first. The world community looked to them as occasions to frame emerging global issues

Figure 6.3 The BIC's contributions to three major world conferences

Conference	Significance and output	BIC's major contributions
UN Conference for Environment and Development— "Earth Summit" (1992)[53]	• Agenda 21: comprehensive plan of action adopted by all participating nations; unprecedented global partnership to reverse environmental degradation of the planet.[54] • 108 heads of state; 172 nations represented • 2,400 NGO representatives • 17,000 NGO representatives at the parallel NGO Forum • 10,000 journalists • Climate Change Convention led to the adoption of Kyoto Protocol	• Statements: oral statement to conference plenary,[55] 16 written and 7 oral statements, 10 joint statements with NGOs and UN agencies • Leadership role in Earth Charter negotiations[56] • Spearheaded construction of Peace Monument (see Figure 6.2)[57] • Hundreds of thousands of statements distributed
UN Fourth World Conference on Women (1995)[58]	• Beijing Platform for Action signed by 189 countries: most progressive blueprint for advancing women's rights[59] • 30,000+ women from 189 countries attend the parallel NGO Forum • 12,000 people attend official conference (4,030 NGO representatives)	• 10 written statements • 1 oral presentation (on Youth Day) • BIC gave up coveted plenary spot to another NGO[60] • 20,000–25,000 statements distributed
UN World Summit for Social Development (1995)	• Copenhagen Declaration and Programme of Action adopted by 117 countries: "For the first time in history … we gather as heads of State and Government to recognize the significance of social development and human well-being for all and to give to these goals the highest priority"[61] • Largest gathering of world leaders at the time: 117 heads of state	• Oral statement to the plenary[62] • 2+ written statements • 3 joint NGO declarations • 40,000+ statements distributed

and mobilize political will …. [Civil society organizations] were attracted to the summits by the spaces they opened up and the opportunities they offered both to influence the substance of the discussions and the decision-making processes.[52]

Figure 6.5 below examines three of the major UN conferences in which the BIC was involved during this period—the Earth Summit (1992), the World

Figure 6.4 Rúhíyyih Rabbani, the widow of Shoghi Effendi, presenting the Baháʼí community's "Promise of World Peace" statement to UN Secretary-General Javier Pérez de Cuéllar in 1985. © Baháʼí International Community.

Summit for Social Development (1995), and the Fourth World Conference on Women (1995)—from the perspective of their global significance and the BIC's contributions in terms of content. Participation involved months and years of preparatory meetings (not only for the BIC but for hundreds of NGOs), thousands of volunteer hours, the dissemination of thousands of statements, coordination across many national communities, and collaboration with hundreds of like-minded NGOs, as well as UN agency representatives. The conferences gave rise to new modalities and unprecedented scales of international deliberation and cooperation.

This brief overview illuminates the degree to which the above conferences (along with other major international gatherings at this time) set the agenda for deliberation and policy-making in the realm of social development and protection of the environment. From the perspective of the BIC, the conference processes had a greater significance, as the BIC reported in 1995:

These conference processes—important pieces of the mosaic of the Lesser Peace—have contributed substantively to "an emerging unity of thought in world undertakings," the realization of which our sacred scriptures describe as one of the lights of unity that will illumine the path to peace.[63]

In a similar manner, we can underscore the significance of the UN Millennium Summit in 2000, which brought together over 150 world leaders (making it the largest gathering of heads of state and government to date), along with some 1,350 NGO representatives, to discuss the role of the United Nations at the turn of the twenty-first century. As co-chair of the Millennium Forum (organized by NGOs and held in advance of the summit), BIC representative Techeste Ahderom was invited to address world leaders gathered at the summit on behalf of civil society (see Figure 6.7).[64] Nearly three decades on, we may take these gatherings for granted, but during their time they were unprecedented, attracting record numbers of heads of state and civil society representatives. It is in this dynamic and fertile arena of the generation, sharing, and development of ideas—major milestones in the processes advancing world peace in the eyes of the Bahá'í community—that the BIC made its multifaceted contributions.

Let us consider more deeply the content of the statements themselves. Between 1986 and 2008, the BIC issued over 320 formal oral and written statements to the United Nations, as this was one of the common ways for civil society to insert ideas, commentaries, and proposals into the UN system. Figure 6.5 shows the wide-ranging themes addressed in the statements.[65]

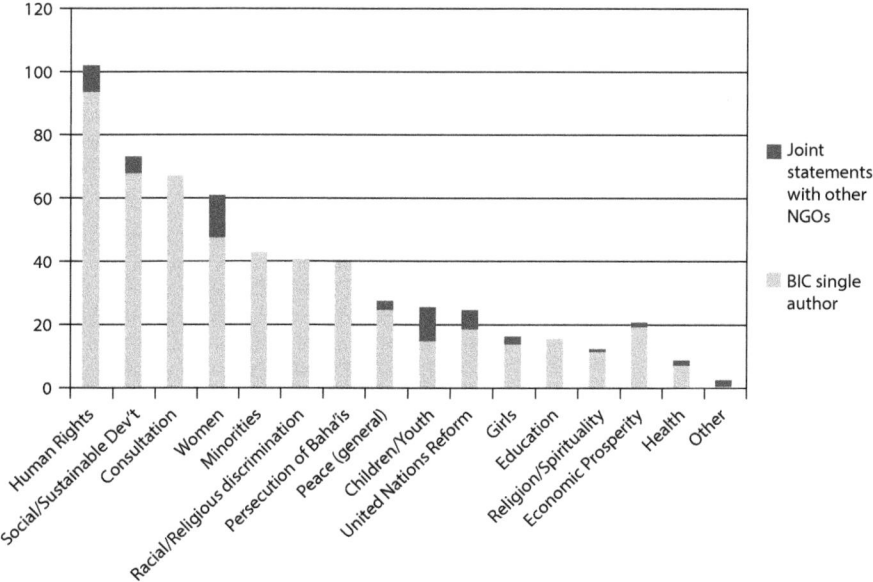

Figure 6.5 Key themes addressed in BIC statements to the United Nations (1986–2008)[66]

In order to explore the main ideas being shared by the BIC within the broader context of advancing the processes toward peace, I selected ten statements issued during this period that, given their dissemination, strategic importance, and the breadth of issues being addressed, can be considered seminal.[67] From the analysis of these and other related statements, six major themes emerge; these are presented in Figure 6.6 below, with accompanying excerpts from the statements themselves. Taken together, we can see the contours of a multifaceted construct of unity and its intimate association with the related concept of peace. Specifically, we can see how each concept is refracted in the imperative of progression toward solidarity among all peoples and nations.

Figure 6.6 Key concepts in BIC statements to the United Nations (1986–2008)

Category	Key Concept	Excerpt from Statement
Unit of analysis	Social issues are to be considered from a global perspective	As the integration of humanity gains momentum, those who are selected to take collective decisions on behalf of society will increasingly have to see all their efforts in a global perspective. Not only at the national, but also at the local level, the elected governors of human affairs should … consider themselves responsible for the welfare of all of humankind.[68]
Ontology	Relationships at all levels must be redefined in order to support human flourishing in the context of interdependence	[T]he emergence of a peaceful and just social order … is contingent upon a fundamental redefinition of all human relationships— among individuals themselves, between human society and the natural world, between the individual and the community, and between individual citizens and their governing institutions … Outmoded notions of power and authority need to be recast.[69]
	Assumptions about human nature must be rethought	… uncritical assent is given to the proposition that human beings are incorrigibly selfish and aggressive and thus incapable of erecting a social system at once progressive and peaceful … Dispassionately examined, the evidence reveals that such conduct, far from expressing man's true self, represents a distortion of the human spirit.[70]
	Spiritual dimension of human life plays a central role in establishing peace	The essence of any program of social change is the understanding that the individual has a spiritual or moral dimension. This shapes their understanding of their life's purpose, their responsibilities towards the family, the community and the world.[71]

Collective decision-making	Statements introduce "consultation" as principle-based method of collective deliberation and decision-making	Improvement in the ability of all members of the community to consult is a primary measure of success in every Bahá'í development project ... The ability of people to come together in these new and constructive patterns of participation and interaction is, in some respects, a more important outcome ... than the quantifiable goals traditionally associated with development projects.[72]
Human rights	Concern for human rights must be animated by, and expressed within, the context of the recognition of the oneness of humanity	Concern that each human being should enjoy the freedom of thought and action conducive to his or her personal growth does not justify devotion to the cult of individualism that so deeply corrupts many areas of contemporary life. Nor does concern to ensure the welfare of society as a whole require a deification of the state as the supposed source of humanity's well-being ... Only in a consultative framework made possible by the consciousness of the organic unity of humankind can all aspects of the concern for human rights find legitimate and creative expression.[73]
Justice	Justice and unity are inextricably linked	At the group level, a concern for justice is the indispensable compass in collective decision-making because it is the only means by which unity of thought and action can be achieved ... justice is the practical expression of awareness that, in the achievement of human progress, the interests of the individual and those of society are inextricably linked.[74]
Agency	The protagonists of change will be the people themselves, animated by the consciousness of solidarity in building a new social order; capacities must be developed to allow the expression of this role	If it is true that the governments of the world are striving through the medium of the United Nations system to construct a new global order, it is equally true that the peoples of the world are galvanized by this same vision ... The transformation in the way that great numbers of ordinary people are coming to see themselves ... raises fundamental questions about the role assigned to the general body of humanity in the planning of our planet's future.[75]
	Gender equality must be understood and pursued in the context of advancing the oneness of humanity	If the Platform for Action is to win the worldwide support it requires ... the principle on which it is founded ... needs to be understood as an essential aspect of an even broader principle: the oneness of humanity.[76]

What emerges from this examination is a distinct epistemology of peace: peace is advanced in part by supporting and promoting structures, processes, practices, attitudes, and norms that build humanity's capacity for collective deliberation and collective action in a manner that responds to the exigencies and imperatives of humanity's interdependence. The capacity for collective action, when illuminated by the consciousness of the oneness of humanity, provides resilience against the myriad social forces that undermine humanity's ability to come together in the face of collective ills and leave communities vulnerable to all forms of social distress—including, of course, outbreaks of war and violence.[77]

Figure 6.7 Techeste Ahderom, (then) principal representative of the BIC to the United Nations, speaking before the Millennium Summit, September 2001, in his capacity as co-chairman of the Millennium Forum. © Bahá'í International Community.

In addition to a focus on the interdependence of humanity and its implications for structural, institutional, and legal dimensions of international life, BIC statements conveyed a developmental view of history and an evolutionary perspective with regard to international norms. "An evolutionary mindset," the BIC writes, "implies the ability to envision an institution over a long timeframe perceiving its inherent potential for development, identifying the fundamental principles governing its growth."[78] Clarifying the manner of interpreting the tumult of the present-day, "The Promise of World Peace" states:

> prejudice, war and exploitation have been the expression of immature stages in a vast historical process and that the human race is today experiencing the unavoidable tumult which marks its collective coming of age is not a reason for despair but a prerequisite to undertaking the stupendous enterprise of building a peaceful world.[79]

"We are witnessing the beginning of the history of humankind," writes the BIC at the turn of the millennium, "the history of a human race conscious of its own oneness."[80]

Fostering Unity and Building Internal Capacity for Collective Action

In the BIC's pursuit of peace, the dissemination of ideas was accompanied by conscious and coordinated efforts to shape the processes and culture of deliberation itself. The approach used by the BIC sought to harmonize ends and means: if the aim was to unify, then the means themselves must be unifying as well. This quality takes on a particular significance during this period, which sees a rapid expansion in the number of NGOs and civil society organizations and the related emergence of more complex patterns of international organizing and cooperation among civil society. NGOs learned to work together in new configurations and coalitions and in ways that sought to exert greater influence on international policy and decision-making. Let us examine, then, two approaches taken by the BIC—one outwardly and one inwardly focused—to "influence processes towards the lesser peace" in the international arena: efforts to foster principle-based collective deliberation among NGOs (thus building capacity for collective action) and to build the capacity of the international Bahá'í community for collective action in the international public arena.[81]

In its engagement with the United Nations and NGO community, as well as in its work in various committees[82] and initiatives, the BIC sought to consistently apply the methods of Bahá'í "consultation"—a principle-based approach to collective deliberation, rooted in the Bahá'í writings, that is intended to be unifying rather than divisive. The method seeks to shift the dynamics of deliberation away from a focus on competing interests to one of the ethical and spiritual principles underlying the issues under consideration. The aim is to foster a moral and intellectual environment in which collective goals and courses of action can surface and be acted upon. Participants are encouraged to express themselves freely, albeit courteously, enabling a rich diversity of perspectives to come to light. This approach was noted in a 2002 research report by a Catholic agency studying RNGOs at the United Nations; the report recognizes Quakers and Bahá'ís as "key religious actors" at the United Nations, ones that were held in "high regard in UN circles" for seeking to build consensus on issues by engaging all concerned parties.[83] Furthermore, the report notes that "both [organizations] operate as facilitators rather than partisan advocates."[84] Again, what is significant in this approach is that it represents a methodology rooted in the substrate (oriented toward unity and rooted in the Bahá'í writings) and is applied consciously and intentionally by the Bahá'í community in an effort to foster capacity for collective decision-making and action, with an understanding that such a capacity represents an essential precondition of the Lesser Peace and progress toward the Most Great Peace.[85]

In the UN arena—often challenged by an oppositional dynamic, entrenched positions, and competition to secure advantage, access, or material resources—the BIC endeavored to put into practice the principles of consultation. During this period, BIC representatives were elected by their peers into various positions of leadership on key NGO committees.[86] Such positions included: co-chair of the UN Millennium Forum, which convened, for the first time, over 1,000 NGOs from over 100 countries to discuss the entire global agenda; member of the International Steering Committee of the Beijing (Fourth World Conference on Women) NGO Forum;[87] chair of the NGO Committee on the Status of Women;[88] vice-president (1986–8) and secretary (1988–91) of the Conference of NGOs in Consultative Relationship with the UN (CONGO);[89] co-chair of Global Forum of NGO Committee on UNICEF, and others.[90] These roles are not highlighted to suggest that the BIC was in any way superior to its NGO counterparts; rather, they are mentioned to demonstrate a particular type of contribution in supporting efforts toward peace. We might also infer—given the multiple facilitative and convening roles to which the BIC was elected—that its orientation toward nonpartisanship and principled deliberation was valued and effective in the NGO community.

The practice of consultation is also intimately related to the concept of nonengagement in partisan politics, a concept asserted unequivocally by Shoghi Effendi in his guidance to the Bahá'í community and specifically in his 1947 letter to the UN Special Committee on Palestine. It may appear as though adherence to this principle would be particularly challenging given some of the dynamics of civil society deliberations and organizing in the international arena. As international relations scholar Jeffrey Haynes points out:

> what often seems to divide FBOs [faith-based organizations] … in a quite fundamental way, is the extent to which they are prepared to follow what I have referred to as "politicized" paths to achieve their objectives … To what extent are FBOs prepared to cut deals, be pragmatic, build coalitions, and, in short, use a variety of means to achieve the progress they require to reach their objectives?[91]

And indeed this can be very challenging. In a report detailing the BIC's participation in the UN Fourth World Conference on Women and the processes leading up to it, the head of BIC's delegation and member of the International Planning Committee for the conference describes the challenges of seeking to remain neutral and principled when discussions became politicized, extreme, or radicalized, or when tensions arose between NGOs and the organizers of the conference.[92] Yet the faithful—if at times difficult—adherence to the modes of nonpartisanship and consultation challenge the idea that NGOs are forced to compromise norms and beliefs and to adopt the ways of the United Nations in order to exert influence. As the Universal House of Justice states, "It is not possible to build enduring unity through endeavors that require contention or assume that an inherent conflict of interests underlies all human interactions, however subtly."[93] The BIC's record demonstrates that it *is* possible for RNGOs to operate in a manner consistent with the organizational substrate and, at the same time, exercise influence within UN and civil society fora.

Reflecting on engagement in the UN conferences of the 1990s, a former BIC representative notes: "A very significant part we played was in bringing NGOs together, in helping them to achieve a unity of purpose."[94] This was a conscious, deliberate, and often challenging practice that served to build consensus, bring underrepresented voices to the table, and foster processes of deliberation that were in themselves unifying and, as such, considered by the Baháʼí community as building blocks of peace.

Building Internal Capacity to Promote Peace

When analyzing the manner in which an organization exerts influence in a particular environment or on a particular issue, it is important to distinguish between influence that results in outwardly visible change (such as policy changes and the adoption of new methods) and influence that builds capacity to carry out specific actions. In this final section, I explore the BIC's efforts to influence the processes of world peace by building the capacity of its national affiliates for collective action such that the unified voice of the community could come to be regarded as "representative of the aspirations of the peoples of the world."[95] In these efforts, we discern the influence and outworking of the structural dimension of the substrate.

During this period, BIC endeavors not only to advance sound and timely ideas, but also to demonstrate the qualities of a global community whose structure, beliefs, and practices manifest the efficacy and transformative potential of the ideas being shared. The ideas and the community seeking to give them expression are inextricably linked. One of the seminal BIC statements from this period expresses this in the following way:

> Composed of individuals from virtually every national, ethnic, and religious background … the worldwide Baháʼí community is nevertheless firmly united by a common commitment to a global program for moral, spiritual, and social progress. This program is characterized by support for … the elimination of all forms of prejudice; full equality between the sexes; the elimination of the extremes of poverty and wealth … universal education … and the establishment of a world federal system based on collective security and world citizenship. Taken as a whole, the worldwide Baháʼí community, in its day-to-day life, commitment to common principles, and activities aimed as assisting the whole of humanity, stands as a uniquely global organization with a broad and relevant reservoir of experience at building social cohesion."[96]

The 1994 External Affairs Strategy had set out a new role for the BIC: to guide and coordinate the efforts of the National Spiritual Assemblies in relation to their governments. In order to achieve a "coherent pattern" in its diplomatic activities worldwide, it asked the BIC to "give direction to [external affairs] activities in the form of information, materials, ideas and advice," as well as different forms of training.[97] The UN global conferences, as well as their preparatory processes, provided important opportunities to develop the Baháʼí community's capacity for coordinated action in the field of external affairs, and specifically their contributions to advancing processes associated with world peace.[98] At the Earth Summit in 1992, four National Spiritual Assemblies were officially represented at the conference (Brazil, Iceland, Singapore, and the United States), and the BIC drew on over 10,000 volunteer hours committed at international, national, and local levels in preparation for the conference. Twenty-four National Spiritual Assemblies were officially represented at the World Summit for Social Development of 1995, guided by the BIC, while a total of over 250 Bahá'ís from some forty countries attended the conference. Over 500 Bahá'ís, women and men, from over sixty nations participated in the Fourth World Conference on Women in 1995, and numerous national Offices for the Advancement of Women were created during this time. Bahá'ís constituted the largest delegation (eleven countries) to the UN Conference on Human Settlements of 1996.[99]

Extensive training opportunities and materials were created and conducted years in advance to prepare representatives of national Bahá'í communities to participate coherently in these global processes, interact with the media, effectively convey ideas and recommendations, and translate the representatives' experience into the development of their respective external affairs offices. At the core of the Bahá'í strategy to contribute ideas to the conference and to build relationships was an orientation to familiarize people with the nature of the Bahá'í community as one of the most diverse on the planet and, at the same time, one characterized by unity. In this sense, the contribution of the BIC and of the National Assemblies—in addition to the statements and the consultative processes—was the presentation of a community that, against all of the forces of disintegration and separation, had constituted itself as a diverse, unified entity. It was a practical and living expression of the organizational substrate that oriented all efforts in the direction of fostering conditions for social cohesion, solidarity, and unity in diversity.

By 1997, the BIC launched its first global external affairs training effort, aimed at building the capacity of nearly 100 National Spiritual Assemblies to engage with their government representatives. The theme of the campaign was carefully selected in light of the diverse national political climates and circumstances within which Bahá'í communities would engage. Given the formation of new National Spiritual Assemblies following the collapse of the Soviet Union (in the newly independent states of Kazakhstan, Kyrgyzstan, Tajikistan, Uzbekistan, Belarus, Georgia, and Armenia), as well as other newly formed Assemblies (such as Cambodia, Mongolia, and Eritrea), the settings for diplomatic relations couldn't have been more different. In consideration of the recently launched UN Decade for Human Rights Education (1995–2004), the growing experience of the Bahá'í community in the field of education and the call for the Bahá'í community to speak in a unified voice, the theme of "Human Rights Education"—rather than the more politically sensitive theme of human rights—was selected as the focus of the campaign.[100]

*

While much has been written about the contributions of religious organizations to the pursuit of peace—in its various dimensions of conflict resolution, peacemaking, peacebuilding, and reconciliation—this chapter has introduced the unique conception of peace pursued by the BIC. What emerges from this period is an understanding of peace in terms of processes that advance humanity's capacity for collective action and that are guided by a consciousness of the interdependence and oneness of humankind. The inextricable relationship between unity and peace provides a new lens for reading society, namely in terms of its capacity for social cohesion and collaboration on a global scale. The BIC's extensive participation in the UN global conferences attests to the significance accorded to these record-setting global gatherings, as milestones in humanity's growing capacity to come together on issues of global concern and, as such, "important pieces of the mosaic of the Lesser Peace." The growing momentum of civil society, as well as the challenges and accomplishments of the international community, is seen in light of humanity's progress toward the Lesser Peace, denoted by political unity among the nations, and the Most Great Peace, in which the spiritual and material requirements of human flourishing find their full expression. A distinct agency of the religious NGO comes to light, one which enriches prevailing Western liberal conceptions of peace and offers a unique epistemology of progress and human flourishing. In this way, religious NGOs enrich the lexicon, vocabulary, and the epistemology of the construct of peace—a fact that merits greater attention and consideration as we recognize the limitations of prevailing approaches and earnestly consider insights from diverse communities of belief and practice.

Beyond Pluralism: A New Framework for Constructive Engagement (2008–2020)

One of the central themes of the first three historical chapters has been a keen attentiveness to questions of process and approach, the *means* by which work in the international arena is carried out. The chapters have sought to highlight not only the crucial importance of the alignment of means and ends, but also the conditions of possibility that arise through adherence to modes of interaction that foster growing spheres of consensus and solidarity, rather than adversarialism and partisanship. This has reflected the imperative embodied in the substrate of the BIC, one that seeks not simply to promote cooperation among people and nations but rather calls for a "complete reconceptualization of the relationships that sustain society."[1]

During the final period in our study, encompassing the years 2008–20, the relationship between the BIC and the international community was itself reconceptualized under the guidance of the Universal House of Justice, which articulated the BIC's engagement in terms of "participation in the discourses of society." The word *discourse* suggests a "weightiness": "the theme is of the moment and consequence ... it is well established; it is of lasting importance, and it is meaningful in part because it repeatedly imposes itself on the public mind ... it commands general interest."[2] In a 2014 document outlining the vision for the external affairs work of the BIC, the Universal House of Justice elaborated further the new orientation:

> The purpose of such efforts is not to press others to accept a specific Baháʼí proposal ... nor should activities be conceived as part of a public relations or academic exercise. Rather, those involved ... are to adopt a posture of learning, seeking to stimulate a consultative process by engaging in genuine conversations in a range of social spaces, standing shoulder to shoulder with others and offering insights drawn from the Baháʼí writings and from the community's growing experience in applying them.[3]

This orientation echoed the directive in the Baháʼí writings that exhorts Baháʼís to focus their attention on the needs of society: "Be anxiously concerned with the needs of the age ye live in and centre your deliberations on its exigencies and requirements."[4]

The deliberate framing of engagement in terms of participation in the prevalent discourses in the international arena, while subtle in some ways, was very significant, as it shed new light on long-standing assumptions and questions about the dynamics of civil society and religious engagement in international affairs. This shift in orientation embodies an epistemology rooted in the elements of the substrate that has been examined in the three preceding chapters. An orientation toward *participation in discourses* situates the BIC as a contributor to evolutionary, dynamic processes by means of which thinking about issues of global import evolves and takes form in policy and practice. Furthermore, it highlights the collective dimension of the generation of insights and knowledge and the advancement of thought. As this chapter will demonstrate, it is an orientation that focuses on both substance and form, on the ideas and the discursive culture in which such ideas are generated. As such, it constitutes a new and distinct expression of the elements of the substrate.

Foucault, whose work is perhaps most closely associated with the concept of discourse, describes discourses as "practices that systematically form the objects of which they speak."[5] We can think of discourses as being "generative"— they give rise to new ways of thinking, doing, and being. The basic premise of discourse theory, which emerged from Foucault's pioneering work, is that "the ways we think and talk about a subject influence and reflect the ways we act in relation to that subject."[6] In one of his best-known treatises, he demonstrates the power of discourse in shaping conceptions of "madness" and "rationality" in Europe from the Middle Ages to the eighteenth century and explains how the embodiment of these conceptions in institutional structures (hospitals for the mentally "insane," for instance) and practices further perpetuated these conceptions.[7] Foucault shed light on the patterns of thought underlying social reality. Using a similar logic, the BIC notes in a 2013 report to the United Nations:

> Attitudes, thoughts, and conceptions of fundamental issues need to be reshaped as a truly global community emerges and develops in its understanding of the nature of human flourishing as well as the social and material conditions required for such flourishing. We believe, then, that a key part of the transformation that is required must occur at the level of thought.[8]

It is toward these patterns of thought—which are embodied in norms, laws, and institutions—that the BIC turned its attention in a very intentional manner during this period.

The introduction of the new framing should not suggest that the Baháʼí community had not been contributing its ideas about the betterment of society prior to this time; indeed, the community has continually drawn on insights from its scriptures and from its experience in applying the principles contained therein in its efforts to promote social justice. In fact, an NGO's consultative status with the United Nations implies that contributions will be made to discourses and deliberations on various areas within the NGO's expertise. What is significant is the conscious adoption by a religious community of a particular mode of engagement and the degree of emphasis placed on the manner of engagement, not just the substance of the contributions and policy proposals. It reflects a deeper conviction about the nature of social change—namely, that change springs not from the ideological victory of certain positions over others but is driven by *growing consensus about the underlying assumptions about the very nature of progress and the roles of various actors in the betterment of society.*

Before proceeding to discuss the manner and significance of operationalizing the orientation toward discourse, it is important to highlight a seminal 2013 letter from the Universal House of Justice that elaborated the "essential elements of the framework that shapes the Baháʼí approach to politics."[9] In the spirit of the progressively unfolding articulation of Baháʼí principles, in light of growing experience, the framework addresses the realities of "a world where nations and tribes are pitted one against the other"; it states its aims in terms of "[guarding] against competing interests of nations and political parties" and building the Baháʼí community's "capacity to contribute to processes that promote peace and unity."[10] The elements of the framework encompass:

> [t]he conviction of the Baháʼí community that humanity, having passed through earlier stages of social evolution, stands at the threshold of its collective maturity; its belief that the principle of the oneness of humankind, the hallmark of the age of maturity, implies a change in the very structure of society; its dedication to a learning process that, animated by this principle, explores the workings of a new set of relationships among the individual, the community and the institutions of society, the three protagonists in the advancement of civilization; its confidence that a revised conception of power, freed from the notion of dominance with the accompanying ideas of contest, contention, division and superiority, underlies the desired set of relationships; its commitment to a vision of a world that, benefitting from humanity's rich cultural diversity, abides no lines of separation.[11]

While the conceptual threads of the substrate explored in this book are carried forward, the statement of the Universal House of Justice elaborates a more expansive framework and introduces additional concepts: a "learning process" that explores new relationships among the individual, the community, and the institutions of society; the elaboration of these as the "protagonists in the advancement of civilization"; and a "revised conception of power." On their own, the concepts were not new to the Bahá'í community in 2013; what was new was their articulation in the context of a framework, which highlighted their interconnectedness and centrality to questions of political order.

In effect, the framework constituted an evolution of the substrate that I have been exploring throughout this book. It is helpful to recall that one of the defining elements of the substrate is that it is dynamic and generative; it evolves and is progressively clarified in light of the community's experience in applying its principles in varying contexts. Through the authoritative statements of the Universal House of Justice, the framework is made explicit; it is known and can be consciously acted upon by the community. Thus, going forward, scholars examining the work of the BIC and the interactions of the Bahá'í community in the political arena will be able to draw on this conceptual framework and, in turn, contribute to its further refinement.

Reframing the Terms of Engagement: Rethinking Oppositional Dynamics and Harnessing Diversity

I return now to the framing of BIC's engagement in the international arena in terms of "participation in the discourses of society," which sheds light on a number of questions within the study of religious NGOs in the international arena: questions of co-optation, oppositional dynamics between religious and secular actors, and the management of diversity.

Co-optation

Overall, the engagement of RNGOs in international affairs has been characterized by ongoing struggles among opposing parties, each trying to secure for themselves a greater share of power and resources. One such narrative and set of questions concern the question of co-optation. RNGOs who are perceived to be effective players and influencers in the international arena are seen as having been "co-opted" by governments or international agencies and are therefore no longer faithful to their original religious/faith-based mission. According to some, this leaves religious groups with only two viable options: "adapt to the liberal political-normative environment of the United Nations or remain on the margins of the organization."[12] In his study of Muslim discourse at the United Nations, Turan Kayaoğlu argues that the adoption of a "liberal discourse" by the Organization for Islamic Cooperation has left it vulnerable to co-optation[13] and observes that the United Nations has "successfully molded [religious voices] into a liberal framework."[14] Kerstin Martens raises a similar question: Does a consultative relationship with the United Nations compromise the ability of a civil society organization to advocate effectively for the interests it represents?[15] This leaves us then with a puzzle: If an RNGO's access to the United Nations depends on its strict adherence to UN-mandated criteria, how does the RNGO stay faithful to its mission, particularly if part of that mission is to challenge some of the values on which the United Nations is based? Similarly, if the RNGO follows the rules put in place by the United Nations, does that imply that the organization has been co-opted, that its mission is compromised, or that it is less "religious"?

There are no simple answers. The questions themselves point to underlying assumptions that give rise to an "us vs. them" and "zero-sum" way of conceiving of the UN–NGO relationship. This chapter explores how an orientation toward "participation in discourses" eschews this way of thinking and embodies a different set of assumptions—shaped by the substrate—that give rise to different patterns of interaction.

The BIC's description of its work in a 2012 report to the United Nations[16] provides an example of an RNGO negotiating the UN development framework while remaining faithful to its vision and priorities. To contextualize the excerpted portion: between 2000 and 2015, all NGOs were required to report to the United Nations the manner in which their work advanced the Millennium Development Goals (MDGs).[17] The rubric allowed for responses to be framed only in terms of material and technical contributions (e.g., number of schools built, volume of food distributed). While the BIC adhered to the rubric in its previous report, in 2012 it described its contributions in the following manner:

> While members of the Bahá'í community, in their respective cities, towns and villages cooperate with others to improve the social and material well-being of their communities, the Bahá'í International Community's contributions to the UN cannot be easily quantified according to the MDG rubric.

We believe that our collective advancement towards a more just and peaceful society requires profound alterations of social structures and a broadening of existing foundations of society … We believe, then, that a key part of the transformation that is required must occur at the level of thought …

We see ourselves as part of a discourse among the community of nations and seek to contribute to this discourse by offering new ways of approaching issues of global concern, by re-framing the way that certain problems are understood, by identifying assumptions and mental models underlying the understanding of reality and by drawing on insights from the fields of science as well as religion.[18]

In this excerpt, the BIC introduces a distinct element of its development framework in a manner that both responds to the question of the United Nations and introduces categories and rationale faithful to the vision and approach of the BIC.

During this period, UN agencies also began to give attention to the specific parameters for their collaboration with NGOs (and faith-based organizations in particular) and articulated new terms of engagement.[19] The guidelines that emerged from these efforts focused on building partnerships that combined "complementary strengths and contributions" of both entities in order to "achieve greater impact and synergy than when operating separately."[20] In its own

Figure 7.1 UN Climate Change Conference (COP21), Paris, December 2015. Panel, "Community resilience in the face of climate-driven extreme events." Left to right: Janot Medler de Suarez (technical advisor to the Red Cross/Red Crescent Climate Centre), Serik Tokbolat (BIC), and Temily Tavangar, University of Hong Kong. © Bahá'í International Community.

way, each set of guidelines recognized the diverse perspectives and experience that faith-based organizations brought to the partnership, while at the same time asserting that humanitarian principles and human rights instruments were fundamental elements of the United Nations' framework for action. Recognizing the tension that can arise from interpretations that place human rights frameworks in opposition to religious frameworks, UNICEF stressed the importance of building bridges across perceived differences:

> without listening to and then aligning the language of rights with the articulation of deeply held socio-cultural and religious values and beliefs, there can be a perception of alienation and imposition of foreign ideas despite the fact that the human rights framework is inherently based on these deeper values. Thus, language and approach are critical elements in the process of establishing and building meaningful partnerships.[21]

Similarly, the UN Population Fund noted that while the partnerships with faith-based organizations were centered on objectives identified by the International Conference on Population and Development and the Millennium Development Goals, faith-based organizations were free to use their own "language, networks and modus operandi" in working toward these objectives.[22] There was also an emerging openness to engagement at a deeper conceptual level and recognition that UN–RNGO partnerships would, in some way, "fundamentally alter the human development paradigms themselves."[23]

Reframing the "Clash of Civilizations"

Another prevalent narrative in the study of RNGOs in the international arena is that it belies a "clash of civilizations" reading of society, in which religious and cultural identities are viewed primarily as sources of conflict. Studies of RNGOs continue to highlight the perceived incompatibility between religious and secular frameworks. In order for RNGOs to influence UN debates and policy, the argument goes, they have to adopt the United Nations' "liberal-secular ethos, code and modus operandi [as well as] UN sanctioned language, concepts and modes of engagement."[24] It has been argued that the "liberal mold" of UN discourse—with its emphasis on individualism, a framework of human rights, and a belief in rational and scientific progress—clashes with agendas of religious NGOs, which tend to "value the community over the individual, duties over rights, and tradition over progress."[25] Others have noted that faith-based organizations "must accord with the UN's secular, liberal and irreligious values and this is obviously a problem for entities whose very raison d'être has its foundation in religious values."[26]

The human rights discourse is one that has at times been polarizing, bringing to the forefront the sharp philosophical distinctions between Western notions of individualism and more traditional emphases on collectivism and community. The human rights framework constitutes the normative and legal foundations for the work of the United Nations; all NGOs in consultative status with the United Nations, religious and secular alike, must operate within this framework and the broader goals of the UN Charter. Yet this structural reality does not necessarily imply a clash between the religious and the secular. The work of the BIC and others provides an example of how adversarial modes of functioning can be avoided entirely. On the one hand, the BIC works actively with civil society and UN bodies to strengthen existing human rights mechanisms and procedures.[27] The BIC recognizes that these mechanisms, while not perfect, represent the consensus of the international community regarding the dignity of the human being and the responsibilities of nation states to safeguard this dignity. Indeed, it is through appeals to international human rights mechanisms that the BIC has taken steps to defend the Bahá'í community from intense government-sponsored persecution. To support the development of human rights mechanisms is not to be co-opted or to stray from a faith-based mission but rather to recognize the current stage in the development of the international community's capacity to conceptualize and protect the dignity of the human being.

Yet contentious issues abound, and few have been more polarizing than that of gender equality, particularly concerning the family, sexual health, and reproductive rights. As I have elsewhere pointed out, "much of the discourse on gender equality is characterized by frameworks that reinforce a binary view of reality—such as secular vs. religious, modern vs. traditional, conservative vs. liberal, Western vs. non-Western, north vs. south, and the like."[28] The picture that emerges is that religion, writ large, is cast in opposition to conceptions of progress and modernity. A similar conclusion emerges from studies such as Clarke and Jennings's typology of faith-based public engagement, which found that the more an organization was guided by its faith, the more it tended toward fundamentalism, exclusion, and even violence.[29]

The framing of "participation in discourses" prefigures the important role of cultural differences and experiences in contributing to the evolution of thought; it focuses on the fluidity and civilizational trajectory of processes by which ideas are shaped, refined, and clarified over time. This is not to naïvely suggest that the challenges and differences of experience, perspective, and approach that arise are not very real and, at times, seemingly intractable. The discursive framing negotiates some of the deeply rooted assumptions about religion and modernity and orients itself toward the evolution of ideas, norms, and practices that give rise to expanded notions of modernity. Furthermore, the framing eschews the oppositional dynamic inherent in many facets of the relationship between governments and civil society and recognizes the evolutionary dimension of the fruits of this kind of engagement. Such an approach is embodied in the context of a BIC-hosted discussion at the Brussels office exploring the role of religion in Europe.[30] "The European Union is a secular political entity," notes a guest scholar and member of the Bahá'í community,

> but what precisely this secularity means is not fixed in stone …. It rather evolves alongside the understanding of decision-makers, thought leaders, civil society actors and citizens. Accordingly, one of the major tasks that stands before all involved parties is to creatively re-imagine what secularism can mean so that the ideal can best serve the whole of European society today.[31]

The aim of this and related gatherings and initiatives of the BIC is not to debate a secular versus religious logic but to create conditions conducive to understanding and collaboration among diverse individuals, groups, and communities.

Harnessing Diversity

The orientation toward participation in discourses also signals a larger enterprise, namely one of intentional engagement with diversity. The encounter with difference and the search for ways to reconcile the imperatives of unity and diversity have indeed been among the central preoccupations of modernity. It is interesting to consider how this dynamic played out in the UN arena during this period. As a UN annual report notes, the decade leading up to 2016 was one in which the voice of civil society was "resoundingly heard in global affairs."[32] It was a period marked by the rise of social media. The number of civil society organizations associated with the United Nations surpassed 4,000, and "interactive hearings" with NGO representatives had become a well-established practice during all major UN conferences. In September 2015, the universal adoption of "Agenda 2030," which established a global framework for sustainable development efforts, set a high-water mark for global civil society participation and was hailed as "one of the most inclusive and holistic processes in United Nations history."[33]

The manner of civil society engagement in the international arena became particularly salient during this period as the governments of the world and its peoples struggled to keep up with the rapidly accelerated and increasingly complex pace of change. Secretary-General Ban Ki-moon describes the decade between 2007 and 2016 as one of "tectonic turbulence and exponential change"[34] in which "the status quo was irrevocably weakened and the contours of a new world began to emerge."[35] Many of these contours—in the form of global agreements, commitments, and international strategies—were shaped by the diverse voices of civil society on issues such as climate change, health, disarmament, and terrorism.

One of the central questions in political processes in which the elements of the social order are being negotiated and refined is the encounter with difference. Indeed, it is that spirit of exchange and knowledge-sharing that underlies the United Nations' formal engagement with civil society in the form of consultative status. How diversity is conceptualized by a given NGO, then, becomes critically important when we seek to understand the manner in which it engages in the arena of public policy and international norm setting. It is helpful to consider participation in discourses alongside other approaches to the negotiation of difference. In *Edgework: Critical Essays on Knowledge and Politics*, Wendy Brown provides a lucid analysis of such approaches:

> Late modernity has revealed the limits in most of the usual models for holding together two or more truths. The many inflections of *dialectic* bear a common dependence on ... a construction of the formulations at stake *as* opposites ... *paradox* tends to be anti-political in the mutual undoing ... of the truths it addresses, *contradiction* [implies] mutual cancellation ... *Pluralism* capitulates to relativism ... without giving us a clue about how to weigh or navigate [multiple truths]. *Integration* always entails the high price of assimilation; invariably, one side normatively governs and incorporates the other.[36]

Brown also notes that none of the above approaches allows "several truths" to be "enriched even as they are offset by each other"[37]; none allows the "truths to be dynamic and the proliferation of truth itself to be part of the dynamism."[38] I posit that the "participation in discourses" approach sets the stage for encounters in which various perspectives (or "truths," as Brown refers to them) can be enriched and, as a result, for new understandings (new "truths") to emerge from this evolving process.

During this period, BIC representatives were invited to serve in a number of key "penholder" roles—preparing initial drafts of collective declarations, including most recently the People's Declaration on the seventy-fifth anniversary of the United Nations.[39] This has presented opportunities for the BIC to build its capacity to communicate ideas in a way that harmonizes and faithfully represents the insights and aspirations of diverse communities and organizations.

Orientation toward Learning

The theme running through many BIC contributions during this time, as well as throughout its history, has been a vision of an emerging global community, one whose contours are only gradually coming into view. There is a challenge in conveying a vision of something that has never existed in human history— patterns of collective life that have yet to be built. Looking specifically at the concept of gender equality, this challenge is aptly captured by one of the BIC's representatives:

> We must acknowledge that none of us—no group, no individual, no country, no leader—actually knows what a society that is truly based on the principles of gender equality looks like. Such a society has never existed. Therefore, while we may be able to identify some of the obstacles stymying gender equality in our current paradigm, we have to learn our way towards a new paradigm where gender equality is the norm. The path forward may not be entirely clear, but a path forward is urgently needed. The great enterprise of ensuring human rights for all people, and of bringing about gender equality, in this light, can be understood as an urgently-needed learning process.[40]

As the Universal House of Justice points out, the Bahá'í principle of the oneness of humankind "asks not merely for cooperation among people and nations"; rather, "it calls for a complete reconceptualization of the relationships that sustain society"[41]—relationships among individuals, communities, and institutions of governance. The task then is a deeply creative one that cannot be carried out by one group of people on behalf of another; it must be carried out by the generality of humankind. The process that corresponds to this civilizational and developmental narrative is not one of trying to press others to accept a particular position but rather one of learning—one in which insights and knowledge emerge from diverse populations is shared and serves to illuminate deliberations and decisions focused on the flourishing of all.

An orientation toward learning has raised a number of questions that the BIC continues to explore: How do we reinforce inclinations toward learning among civil society, and with member states? How can we move past the fear of failure that paralyzes action and constrains experimentation with promising approaches? What is the role of civil society in fostering an ethic of learning? Further structural questions emerge as well: Do the structures and deliberative process of the United Nations provide an environment in which thinking can evolve at the level of conceptual foundations and not just operations? What conditions foster the evolution of thought on the core issues before the United Nations? Consider that UN diplomatic staff are directed what to say by their respective capitals, or that civil society organizations are similarly guided by their respective headquarters. If the United Nations is effectively a forum for the exchange of positions by representatives from respective countries and organizations, where are the possibilities for real change? Furthermore, the continuous rotation of diplomatic staff and restructuring of UN agencies are a challenge to sustained collective exploration. In what ways can individuals be brought together to explore questions more deeply, as individuals rather than representatives, with the freedom to voice their opinions and consider the perspectives of others?

Creating New Spaces for Deliberation

The United Nations is a world of ideas in which discourses concerning countless social and economic issues are continually evolving. Although far from perfect, or perfectly representative of the peoples of the world, it is not lacking in ideas and ideals. Yet the modes of deliberation and exchange of ideas leave much to be desired. Prompted by the Universal House of Justice to "remain acutely aware of the inadequacies of current modes of thinking and doing,"[42] the BIC explored how it could contribute to the promotion of a more constructive culture of discourse at the United Nations. The BIC noted a number of challenges plaguing modes of deliberation in the international community, among them: a culture characterized by adversarial and positional debates; a tendency to dichotomize issues; an emphasis on technique over substance; a preoccupation with short-term outcomes; and a fragmented, siloed approach to problem-solving.[43] Accordingly, it sought to promote the idea that "progress is not contingent on technique but rather unity of thought, consistent action and dedication to learning."[44] While much has been written about the importance of ideas themselves, we can take this one step further to say that the *framework* within which these ideas are shared and explored matters as well. Ideas introduced in a partisan setting may never emerge from the gridlock, and if they do and are implemented they may soon be undermined when an opposing group comes to power. Therefore, ideas matter *and* the culture of deliberation matters.

One of the United Nations' areas of focus during this period was the articulation of a new set of international development goals to succeed the Millennium Development Goals, which had been providing a focus for the international development efforts from 2000 to 2015. As mentioned earlier, in the years leading up to 2015, the nations of the world, with an unprecedented level of engagement from civil society and NGOs worldwide, negotiated "Agenda 2030." While far from perfect, the agenda is the product of one of the most inclusive processes in UN history; it seeks to "leave no one behind" and to embody the "global vision of the world we want to live in."[45] As the BIC began to engage in preparatory processes, it found itself drawn into "one of the most extensive discourse networks at the UN," including numerous UN agencies, member states, and civil society organizations.[46] What quickly became apparent was the absence of a cross-institutional exchange allowing for communication and reflection on issues of common concern: UN agencies, member states, and civil society organizations did not have a space to come together to discuss issues related to "Agenda 2030." The BIC, along with ATD Fourth World, initiated a series of "Informal Breakfast Meetings" to create such a space. As word quickly spread about the utility of these gatherings, many became regular attendees, with forty to seventy people participating on any given month. Different participants were invited to give framing remarks at the opening of each gathering, depending on their area of expertise, after which the discussion was opened to all. Participants were encouraged to speak freely, not necessarily "on behalf" of their respective organization but rather as individuals engaged in a common exploration (Chatham House rules were assured[47]).

Between July 2012 and July 2020, nearly sixty-five such meetings were held, each exploring a different theme related to the parallel UN negotiations on "Agenda 2030."[48] The BIC also began to bring together colleagues from both the United Nations and civil society to read together various working documents and discussion pieces that it had drafted on themes pertaining to matters under UN consideration. This approach sought to experiment with a small-group discursive approach, with a focus on in-depth consultation and collective exploration of issues on the UN agenda. The approach resembles the "quiet diplomacy" strategy used by the Quaker UN Office to bring together UN personnel and civil society representatives for off-the-record meetings. In

Figure 7.2 NGO and UN representatives engage in discussions, held at the BIC Office in New York, about "Fostering the Enabling Conditions of Peaceful, Just and Inclusive Societies," as part of the UN High Level Political Forum, July 11, 2019. © Bahá'í International Community.

those settings, "issues can be explored, ideas exchanged, perceptions changed, directions set."[49] Similar to the BIC approach, Quaker representatives explain that their focus has been on process rather than positions: "We have felt the real show is not winning on particular issues here, but rather strengthening the capacity of the institution to resolve the kinds of problems that need to be resolved if the world community is to be a community."[50]

Bridging Divides: Bringing Together Religious and Secular Actors to Work toward Gender Equality

One of the policy discourses in which the BIC has played a leading role for many years is that of gender equality. In fact, one of the BIC's first statements to the United Nations concerned the advancement of women and girls. Throughout its history with the United Nations, BIC representatives were consistently elected to leadership positions on major committees addressing gender equality.[51] In addition to working closely with NGOs and UN agencies to implement the goals of the Beijing Platform for Action,[52] adopted by member states at the historic 1995 UN Fourth World Conference on Women, the BIC sought to bridge the religious–secular divide, which kept like-minded

Figure 7.3 The BIC contributed to the discourse on the advancement of women during the sixtieth Session of the UN Commission on the Status of Women in March 2016. Pictured third from the right in the front row is Bani Dugal, principal representative of the BIC. © Bahá'í International Community.

civil society organizations from working together toward gender equality. We can observe this effort in the BIC's role on the civil society committee[53] that led the campaign to create a new, consolidated, and stronger UN agency to address gender-based disparities and discrimination. The Gender Equality Architecture Reform campaign, known as GEAR, mobilized over 300 religious and secular organizations (including human rights, development, and women's organizations) and focused its attention on the consolidation of four disparate UN agencies[54] that worked on different but overlapping facets of the gender equality agenda, though taken individually, each entity lacked the resources and representation to influence UN decision-making at the highest levels. After four years of civil society-led efforts, in 2010 the United Nations announced the creation of the United Nations Entity for Gender Equality and the Empowerment of Women, also known as UN Women. With an under-secretary-general at its helm, the entity would ensure that for the first time in UN history, issues of gender equality would be represented at the highest level of decision-making within the UN secretariat.

One can also discern an orientation toward bringing together religious and secular civil society organizations in the BIC's leading role in creating the Working Group on Faith and Feminism at the United Nations. Formed in 2015, with the encouragement of UN Women and the United Nations Population Fund (UNFPA), the group focuses on, among other things, developing a multireligious narrative for gender equality; fostering a constructive and collaborative discourse between faith-based, feminist, secular, and social justice organizations; and enlarging the national-level democratic space for civil society organizations and organizations concerned with gender equality in particular.[55] In its official statement to the sixty-first Session of the Commission on the Status of Women, the Working Group asserted the need to replace the "confrontational dynamic between secular and faith-based proponents of gender equality" and stated that "religious and secular actors [need] to work together, to create a narrative that encompasses the ideals inherent in respective worldviews—a narrative that focuses on our common humanity, on justice and the establishment of a prosperous and peaceful world civilization for all."[56] We can see in this orientation the outworking of a consultative epistemology animated by a commitment to the promotion of the oneness of humanity and evolutionary processes.

Contributing Ideas to Prevalent Discourses at the United Nations

Alongside its focus on fostering a culture of deliberation, the BIC contributed insights from the Bahá'í Faith from its efforts to apply Bahá'í teachings at the community level. These also demonstrate various facets of an epistemology and outlook rooted in an orientation toward unity and a long-term view of social evolution and the advancement of civilization. The following excerpts from various BIC statements to the United Nations provide a sample of the BIC's conceptual contributions to various policy discourses during this period. While each statement puts forward policy recommendations concerning an issue under consideration (e.g. gender equality, human rights, eradication of poverty, education, role of youth, etc.), it also—as highlighted in Figure 7.4—delves more deeply into the assumptions and patterns of thought shaping the questions at hand. In this way, the excerpts demonstrate the BIC's understanding of its work at the United Nations during this period: seeking to contribute to key discourses by

> offering new ways of approaching issues of global concern, by re-framing the way that certain problems are understood, by identifying assumptions and mental models underlying the understanding of reality and by drawing on insights from the fields of science as well as religion.[57]

Figure 7.4 Selected concepts in BIC statements to the United Nations (2008–2020)

Empowerment	[I]individual and collective empowerment can be conceived as the expansion of vision, capacity, and volition necessary for people to act as effective agents of human well-being and prosperity.[58] … the path from doubt to self-confidence, from silence to voice, from passivity to action, cannot be understood only in terms of entering the labour market or integrating into a global production chain of one kind or another. The development of capacity must concern itself with all aspects of human existence—economic as well as social, intellectual, cultural, spiritual, and moral.[59] … the sense of collective vision and volition inhabitants are developing gives them greater capacity to absorb external assistance in ways that strengthen local ownership and agency, rather than undermining or replacing them.[60]
Conceptions of the "other"	Is a conception of society without an "other" even possible? We propose that not only is it possible, timely and practical but … essential to the maturation of the human race. Humanity is experiencing a transition that can be described as the passage from a collective childhood to our collective maturity …. Characterizing this transition is the redefinition of human relationships within the context of a single social body, animated by bonds of mutualism and reciprocity. Such a transition calls for an organic change in the structure of society on an unprecedented scale. It requires that the oneness of humanity become the operating principle of our collective life.[61]
Development	… poverty reflects not simply a scarcity of material resources, but a deficiency in the way human beings perceive, relate to, and value one another.[62] In the context of more traditional development efforts, the spirit nurtured by communal prayer also helps protect a community against reductionist views of human nature that collapse life down to its most materialistic elements alone. It imparts a growing awareness of the transcendent and non-material aspects of human well-being, and invites exploration of how these vital aspects of individual and social life can be strengthened.[63] … financial capacity is not synonymous with the human capacity needed to advance constructive social transformation. Those with limited material means far outnumber those living in abundance, and no longer can it be realistically imagined that a small segment of humanity should, drawing on its own resources and according to its own views, bring about the advancement of all the rest.[64]

Capacity building	Some [capacities] will pertain primarily to intellectual, technical, and scientific pursuits. Others will be more social in nature, focused on strengthening and refining patterns of interaction, association, and relationship among inhabitants. Still others will focus on the moral and normative aspects of collective life, drawing on the religious heritage of humankind to address foundational issues of meaning, higher motivation, and moral purpose. Due attention must be given to the development of all these capacities, if ... pitfalls such as narrow materialism, social fragmentation, selfishness, and passivity are to be avoided.[65]
Human rights	A balance must be struck between the preservation of individual freedom and the promotion of the collective good ... concern that each human being should enjoy the freedom of expression and freedom from want does not justify ... support for unbridled individualism ... At the same time, concern for the welfare of society does not require a deification of the state as the only source of human well-being. An equilibrium of responsibilities is implied—responsibilities shared by individuals, communities and their social institutions. Human rights, then, achieve their highest expression when understood in the context of relationships, at the local, national and international levels.[66]

What also emerges from these statements is a sense of encouragement and the recognition of what is going well, of what elements are showing promise—however small or slow to emerge. This reflects an appreciation of the developmental and evolutionary nature of processes and attention to trends and progress over longer periods of time—elements that may be nearly invisible when assessed on the basis of a shorter time frame and therefore can lead to a lot of frustration.

An orientation toward contributing to discourses also requires the capacity to discern in which discourses it is most fruitful to engage.[67] The 2014 External Affairs Strategy, prepared under the guidance of the Universal House of Justice, advocates for the selection of discourses that "have a real bearing on the course of humanity's advancement toward its maturity"[68]; further, it cautions against involvement in areas "so controversial that consensus appears beyond reach."[69] In its 2012 Annual Report, the BIC reflected on the process of selecting discourses in which meaningful contributions can be made:

we may want to revisit our decisions to not participate in certain particularly contentious and dichotomized discourses (e.g. racism, right to development) and consider ways in which we could make a meaningful contribution. We may consider framing these discourses in a different, less confrontational way, and inviting organizations to explore these themes with us. Our involvement in the discourse on indigenous issues, for example, is teaching us how to offer contributions in an environment that is at once unified and contentious.[70]

The criteria for engagement in a particular discourse arise not only from the particular concerns of an NGO, or its specific area of expertise, but, as in this case, from a desire to contribute to broader civilizational processes that help humanity to advance toward greater degrees of unity and consensus on a range of issues.

The ability to draw on examples of growing spheres of unity and collective endeavors from the Bahá'í community highlights a narrative that is often neglected in the media—a narrative that brings attention to the capacity for not only peaceful co-existence but also systematic co-construction of patterns of community life, attitudes, and profound shifts at the level of thought that are occurring in tens of thousands of communities around the world. Alongside the fragilities that threaten society are strengths whose impact is equally real.

As Bahá'í communities around the world have continued to grow, develop, and mature, they have helped generate further examples of the on-the-ground operation of principles and approaches shared in BIC contributions to the United Nations. Examples of the application of the principle of gender equality, for instance, have drawn on experience from communities around the world in refashioning the conception of relationships between women and men, with the broader goal of enabling women and men to work shoulder-to-shoulder in constructing more equitable patterns of life and helping to raise the institutional structures to support such a vision.[71] On this theme, a series of articles feature examples of how the principles of gender equality, as outlined in the Beijing Declaration and Platform for Action,[72] have begun to take form in neighborhoods and villages around the world. Interviews with communities in Mwinilunga (Zambia), Kejau (Malaysia), Hasankheda (India), and Riohacha (Colombia) reveal the practical and profound aspects of reshaping patterns of interaction between women and men, girls and boys, such as: family-level decision-making; fostering educational programs that develop orientation toward community service; building capacity for equitable decision-making within the community; prioritizing the education of girls; and exploring practices of early marriage and relationship choices in light of the exigencies of education, universal participation in community life, and the recognition of the inherent nobility of every human being.[73]

Other contributions explore the role of young people in shaping new ways of thinking and behavior by addressing prevailing normative ideologies targeting youth, such as rampant materialism and exaggerated individualism. A series of educational programs developed by the Bahá'í community and offered to communities at large builds the capacity of young people to recognize the cultural forces shaping their lives and develop the tools to become, alongside others, protagonists of change, recognizing both the material and spiritual dimensions of the challenges facing contemporary society.[74] As has been mentioned throughout this book, what comes into sharper relief through these examples is the interconnectedness between the BIC and the wider community of practice of Bahá'ís learning to apply the principles in the Bahá'í writings. The growing and maturing experience of the community enriches its understanding of the concepts themselves and, in turn, the depth and breadth of insights that it is able to share in international fora.

Language and Mode of Communication

The new framework for action also prompted the BIC to rethink both the mode and the language used to describe its communication with the United Nations. While NGOs generally refer to the formal documents they issue as "statements," the BIC began to use terms such as "contribution," "initial reflections," and "initial considerations" in the titles of its formal documents.[75] Reflecting on this conscious change in language and approach, the BIC notes in its annual report:

> we began to move away from a focus on sharing "statements" to creating spaces for genuine conversations in which insights, including those of the Bahá'í community, could emerge and collective understanding could be advanced. This led to a number of small-group discussions with members of civil society, Member States, and UN agencies that were exploratory in nature and centered on a brief document or thought piece developed by our Office. We also invited [colleagues] from outside of our Office to facilitate these sessions.[76]

While the difference between a "statement" and a "contribution" may appear subtle, for the BIC it embodied a shift in perspective about the kind of enterprise in which it was involved. The making of (formal) statements to the United Nations implies a certain kind of relationship between two entities, one akin to position-taking and imparting of information by one entity to another. The term "contribution," on the other hand, implies involvement in a collective process; it is not a rigid, final statement of truth, nor a ready-made solution to the problem at hand. It conveys an appreciation of the insights possessed by other contributors to a given discourse. Similarly, to be engaged in a discourse is different than making a statement: a discourse evolves, changes through experience, and generates insights as it unfolds. This approach was openly conveyed in various

BIC contributions during this period, such as a document produced for the 2010 Session of the UN Commission on Sustainable Development:

> We invite others actively working to promote sustainable consumption and production to engage with us in dialogue ... in order to learn from each other's perspectives and experiences and to collectively advance efforts to build a just and sustainable society.[77]

The BIC experimented with different modes of communication so as to bring them in line with the orientation toward discourse rather than statement-making. One such mode was publishing "Perspective Pieces" on the BIC's website authored by its representatives. These were less formal in nature than official statements and offered a more agile platform for contributing to various discourses in a timely, more conversational manner.[78] Other approaches to fostering more dynamic modes of communication and featuring diverse perspectives on issues under consideration at the United Nations were the use of interviews with Bahá'í delegates to UN commissions and colleagues from civil society organizations and the United Nations.[79] In March 2008, the BIC created a BIC YouTube channel, which, along with its growing presence on Facebook, enlarged its communicative repertoire.

In developing the statements, the BIC was attentive to the manner in which specific terms were used, being careful not to unwittingly reproduce implicit assumptions in the way that it described particular social issues. For example, in its 2013 Annual Report, the BIC explains that in drafting a discussion paper

Figure 7.5 Selected appointed and elected leadership roles held by BIC representatives in the New York office (2008–20)[83]

Faith and Feminism Working Group to the United Nations,[84] Convener
Inter-Agency Network on Youth Development, Civil society representative
Multifaith Advisory Council to the UN Inter-Agency Task Force on Religion and Development, Co-Chair
NGO Committee on the Status for Women, Executive Committee
NGO Committee on the Status of Women—Young Professionals, Co-Chair
NGO Committee on UNICEF, Executive Committee
NGO Committee on UNIFEM,[85] Executive Board
NGO Forum (for the UN Commission on the Status of Women) Planning Committee, Co-Chair[86]
NGO Major Group,[87] Global Organizing Partner
NGO Committee for Social Development, Chair
NGO Working Group on the Security Council, Co-Chair
Working Group on Girls to the United Nations,[88] Chair
World Council of Religions for Peace, Co-President and Member
66th UN Department of Public Information-NGO Conference—Youth Steering Committee, Co-Chair

---

exploring the role of religion in society, it tried to use language "that did not give rise to either/or dichotomies such as secular vs. religious, material vs. spiritual, and public vs. private" and that conveyed an "understanding of reality as a coherent whole."[80] The BIC also notes its efforts to build capacity to "integrate the language of social analysis and critique with that of spiritual principles."[81] Moreover, the 2014 External Affairs Strategy called attention to specific terms, such as "diplomatic," asking the BIC to exercise care when using this term so as not to give the impression, particularly among Bahá'í representatives at a national level, that the Bahá'ís were an *external* group (as the term conveys something of an insider–outsider distinction). Rather, the BIC (as well as Bahá'í representatives at national levels) is asked to "work with a wide range of like-minded individuals" for the progress of their country or of humanity as a whole.[82]

During this period, the BIC continued to be appointed and elected to serve in a variety of convening, facilitative, and leadership roles. I list a selection of these roles here to provide a sense of the breadth of spaces and discourses in which BIC representatives were actively engaged:

*

A review of seventy-five years of the Bahá'í community's engagement in the international arena has echoed the earliest measures taken by its founder and early leaders to bring into the world a vision of the emerging global order. In his earliest letters to the kings and rulers of the world, penned in the 1860s and 1870s, Bahá'u'lláh calls on them to adhere to the highest principles in human and international relations and to come together in a commonwealth of nations; 'Abdu'l-Bahá carried forward these efforts throughout his travels to the West and his exposition on themes concerning the prerequisites of peace and the role of religion in the modern world. Finally, Shoghi Effendi nurtured the rise of the Bahá'í Administrative Order, which would provide the structure by which the spirit and principles of the Bahá'í Faith could find expression in communities and nations throughout the world. We can view the seven decades examined in this book as the continuation—in the international arena—of a gradual, deliberate, and methodical unfolding of the vision, structures, and processes of a new world order. Such an unfolding has not arrived as a "clash of civilizations" or revolution in the traditional sense of the word, but rather as a body of ideas and practices rooted in the awareness of the exigencies of the historical moment and the imperative of giving full expression of the oneness of humankind—the inescapable interdependence of the peoples of the world—in the structures and practices of international affairs.

Rethinking Religion and Social Transformation in the Modern World

This book has focused on the Bahá'í International Community (BIC) in order to examine how a religious community that emerges in the modern era addresses itself to questions of modernity and the international order, and how its interactions in the international arena embody a distinct rationale and approach to social transformation. In this final chapter, I bring together insights from the exploration of the BIC's seventy-five-year engagement with the United Nations in order to shed light on the central questions of the book: How can we study the rationality that drives and shapes the engagement of RNGOs in the international arena? How does this rationality shape engagement across different historical contexts? In what ways does it challenge or enrich our understanding of the philosophical foundations of the present-day social order? What insights can we glean about the changing role of religion in the modern world?

Religion, Rationality, and Reimagining Modernity

By delving into the inner world of a religious NGO, this book has sought to highlight the distinct manner in which a religious community participates in the creation of the modern world. It endeavored to illuminate distinct understandings of progress, human flourishing, the means of social transformation, and religion itself, in order to demonstrate an important role that religion plays in the modern world. We might think of this in terms of providing us with new "conditions of possibility"[1]—illuminating new ways of seeing the world and of being in it. The book's contribution is not only one of revealing something new, but one that invites and stirs reflection on the liberal ideologies underpinning the structures, institutions, and processes that characterize our modern world. Furthermore, it has raised questions about the manner in which the category of religion/religious—a category often set in opposition to concepts of progress and modernity—is applied to ways of being in the world. What emerges from the study of the BIC's relationship with the United Nations is a role for religion and religious organizations in the construction of modernity—as an active participant in humanity's collective efforts to articulate the nature of human flourishing and related concepts of justice and peace, as well as the nature of an international order needed to foster such flourishing.

To make this assertion is not to overlook the less constructive—or outright destructive and violent—ways in which religious communities have sought to impose their view of the "good" and the "right" on the wider community. These examples have received much attention and have been the focus of the research agenda for the past several decades. Yet this disproportionate focus on the combination of violence and religion has also fed a distrust of initiatives motivated by and rooted in religion, leading to conclusions suggesting that the more deeply organizational motives are rooted in religion, the more likely they are to be fundamentalist or to resort to violence. This study is an effort to contribute to scholarship that turns its attention to the nonviolent and non-adversarial ways by which religious organizations challenge the status quo. It brings to the fore the operation of a rationality that eschews partisanship and adversarialism of any kind—not in the narrow sense of simply "avoiding conflict" but out of a conviction that unifying and consensus-building measures and processes are, in the long run, more powerful mechanisms for social transformation and human progress. While it may appear that such a stance renders engagement in political processes of any kind impossible, this study suggests that this is not so; that actors on the political stage—particularly the civil society organizations that are the focus of this study—can choose to align themselves either with those processes that build consensus or with those characterized by adversarialism and partisanship. To choose the former is not to flee from the most contentious social issues that must be addressed by communities and nations, but rather to identify and engage in social spaces, processes, and discourses from which growing degrees of consensus and constructive action can emerge.

The book also reveals the Bahá'í community's engagement with the category of religion. Religion is redefined in terms of a single, continuously unfolding process by means of which God intervenes in human history, through the teachings of the great prophets (or "Manifestations of God" in Bahá'í terminology), to cultivate humanity's spiritual and intellectual qualities. In this light, religion is not set apart or in conflict with the forces of modernity, it *is* one of the vital social forces contributing to the shaping of modernity; each successive revelation from God (with the Bahá'í Faith being the most recent, but not the last) addresses itself to the specific needs, exigencies, and capacities of the historical period in which it appears. The conception of religion as "vitalized, moving, progressive"—as something responsive to historical circumstances rather than absolute—calls for analytical tools suited to the dynamic and organic nature of the phenomenon at hand.

Methodology: Approaching "Religion"

This study offered the concept of the *substrate* as a way of studying the religious dimensions of engagement in the international arena. As methodologies arise from some prior understanding of the phenomenon being studied, this methodology responded to a view of religion as a living, organic phenomenon, in contrast with conceptions of religion as a set of beliefs, rituals, and forms of worship. In that sense, I have approached religion not as a set of laws and ordinances but as a generative epistemological foundation that gives rise to distinct ways of knowing, being, and doing. This has enabled me to examine the expression of certain concepts (elements of the substrate) over time to see how they shaped behavior across different sociopolitical circumstances—in this case, across seventy-five years of history with the United Nations. Of course, we cannot essentialize religion, point to a particular concept and say "here's the religion," and then link it directly to a particular behavior. A historical study, however, makes it possible to examine how over longer time periods, certain concepts, and orientations incline the organization toward a set of behaviors in the international arena, giving rise to a particular way of reading social events and prompting a specific way of being in and responding to the world.

Furthermore, a historical perspective allows the generative nature of the substrate to be more apparent. Simply put, the distinct rationality of the BIC gives rise to a multitude of different approaches and initiatives as the organization responds to sociohistorical exigencies and opportunities—behaviors that might have been impossible to envision or foreshadow in earlier stages of the life of the organization. I posit that the generativity of religious constructs is one of the most important features of religion in modernity, particularly in the context of the rapidly changing circumstances of modernity. Therefore, the ability to study change, innovation, evolution, and adaptation of RNGOs is a critical dimension of the study of religion in modernity.

The substrate also enables the study of the RNGO as a *religious* actor, rather than exclusively as a social or political actor—though the designations are not mutually exclusive. It has brought to the fore understandings of a distinct teleology, ontology, authority, and approaches to social transformation that emerge from the teachings of a particular tradition; in brief, it has revealed a different way of knowing—in this case, specifically, a different way of "knowing the international." In addition, the substrate makes explicit the concepts and assumptions that very often remain hidden in the study of civil society engagement in the international arena. This is a significant advance, as it disturbs a certain complacency toward, or perhaps resignation to, the prevailing structures and assumptions shaping our international order, when, in fact, such an order rests on beliefs and ideals that human beings have themselves constructed. The study of the substrate, then, brings our attention to new conditions of possibility that emerge from a different figuration of time, history, the human being, and ways of knowing and organizing human society.

The use of the substrate also highlights the importance of attending to the particularism of the tradition being studied, studying the tradition on its own terms, and being faithful to the perspective and experience of those who practice it. In a very deliberate way, it raises the researcher's consciousness of the intellectual history and assumptions underpinning particular methods and terminologies that may obscure the richness of the tradition being studied.[2]

Agency and Social Transformation

The study of the BIC's relationship with the United Nations expands the understanding of what some scholars have referred to as the *emancipatory* dimension of civil society. In addition to its well-recognized role in fostering the "associational" fabric of society as well as its deliberative dimension (such as helping to articulate common ideals and values), the role of civil society has been associated with "liberation from political, social and cultural oppression."[3] The capacity to imagine and work toward the construction of a more just social order has been a key feature of civil society movements. Yet as some scholars have shown, this "moral imagination appears confined to Western liberal democracy as the normative standard for emancipation."[4] Through the close examination of the rationality underpinning the BIC's engagement in the international arena, we encounter a different conception of social order—one that broadly incorporates the democratic, participatory dimensions of liberal democracy but eschews its competitive and partisan dimensions. My point is not to cast the BIC's work in terms of a critique of the problematic dimensions of liberal democracy but rather to highlight that its rationality and involvement bring forward a distinct social imaginary characterized by a social order rooted in non-adversarial modes of social transformation. What makes the BIC example particularly relevant for study is its deep theological engagement with questions of international order, pluralism, and diversity; its reconfiguration of conceptions of solidarity; and its adherence to a mode of functioning that harnesses diversity and avoids adversarial and partisan methods. Beyond this theological engagement, it is an important example of solidarity rooted in both a unified vision and rich cultural diversity, as the Bahá'í community is a unified social structure spread across over 100,000 localities throughout the world.

This study also reveals the agency of religious actors in conceptualizing the terms of international relations. In that sense, it responds to the important and timely question raised by political scientists Acharya and Buzan: Are non-Western as well as religious actors simply the recipients of norms and ideas generated in the West?[5] Is it possible that they too are "producers" of knowledge rather than "passive recipients" of theories and knowledge claims generated by Western (predominantly European) scholars? Whereas Western international relations thought and practice have been drawn more toward "sovereignty, territoriality, international anarchy, war and international society,"[6] examples drawn from Chinese theory focus on unity and hierarchy, while Islamic history and theory prioritize "world society" rather than a system of territorial states. The experience of the BIC brings attention to different rationalities, theories, approaches, and ways of understanding history; it provides an example of a tradition whose engagement with questions of international order is rooted in its scriptures and in the actions of its founder and early leaders of the community. Most importantly, perhaps, as we see in the work of the BIC is its rootedness and attentiveness to the particular exigencies of modernity and the evolution of the modern international order.

This book also brings the study of RNGOs into close association with scholarship about epistemic communities, which comprise individuals bound together by a "shared belief or faith in the verity and applicability of particular forms of knowledge or specific truths."[7] Conceiving of RNGOs in terms of epistemic communities has implications for scholarship that examines the "potential for religion and for [faith-based organizations] to fundamentally challenge, from a multiplicity of theological and political standpoints, the way that contemporary society operates, to confront and alter values that drive it."[8]

The BIC emerges as an epistemic community whose structures of knowledge and convictions give rise to distinct framings of social issues, readings of social ills, understanding of modernity, and conceptions of the means of social transformation.

Finally, in addition to the emancipatory and epistemic dimensions of the BIC's engagement, there is a *constructive* dimension as well—what we might call "constructive agency." In this sense, the BIC, as an RNGO, is part of the larger enterprise of constructing a global community whose characteristics align with the elements of the BIC's substrate. On one level, this kind of "construction" takes place within the UN context, as the BIC seeks to create new kinds of social spaces that encourage collective (interagency, intergovernmental, and/or intersectoral) deliberation and action on issues of common concern and, at the same time, foster a culture of deliberation and nonpartisanship. On another level, however, the BIC draws on (and shares in UN contexts) the experience of the global Bahá'í community in its efforts to foster new patterns of community life that advance the equality of women and men, strive to eradicate the extremes of poverty and wealth, that support constructive relationships among individuals, communities, and governing institutions, and that foster a sustainable relationship between humanity and the environment. Such efforts are rooted in the recognition of the need for "a complete reconceptualization of the relationships that sustain society" and "an organic change in the very structure of society."[9] The Bahá'í Administrative Order, an element of the substrate, provides the framework and the indispensable link between the work carried out in international fora and the larger, practical and spiritual enterprise of fostering local and national communities that embody the teachings of the Bahá'í Faith.

A Matter of Time

This study has brought to the fore the importance of the category of time, and the associated matter of the reading of history, as a key element—one often entirely hidden from view—for understanding the nature of RNGO political engagement. While the element of time will not play the same role in the rationality of all organizations, religious or, otherwise, this study has shown the implications of different conceptions of time structuring particular rationalities and modes of engagement. In this sense, the findings have supported the work of scholars highlighting different conceptions of time[10] and developed further the understanding of the implications of such conceptions for the engagement of

RNGOs in the political arena.[11] The study has demonstrated that different time frames give rise to different lenses for the reading of history; for understanding patterns, processes, and the nature of the present. As Brown asserts, "potential political critique must know what time it is—in short, it must grasp the age."[12] In the case of the BIC, the Universal House of Justice and the writings of the Bahá'í Faith respond unequivocally: "The human race ... has passed through evolutionary stages analogous to the stages of infancy and childhood ... and is now in the culminating period of its turbulent adolescence approaching its long-awaited coming of age."[13]

Religious communities and NGOs are particularly noteworthy in this respect when one considers that every major world religion has introduced its own calendar, thereby providing a new way of experiencing, marking, and understanding the passage of time. Given that many religious communities have existed for centuries, and some for millennia, this lends a distinct element to the conception of time as compared to modern-day international relations, which tends to conceive of processes in terms of decades, and possibly centuries (as scholars trace the roots of modern international relations to the early nineteenth century). We can see this in the BIC's understanding of the United Nations as a "mere beginning" in the "gradual awakening of man's consciousness to the essential need for the unity of mankind."[14] The sense of "beginning" focuses on the potential inherent in a given entity rather than its flaws at any given moment. This is not to say that there is one correct way of viewing the United Nations or international relations in general, but simply that from the perspective of longer time frames, different patterns and processes come to light, ones that might appear entirely different, or not at all, when viewed through the lens of a shorter period of time. As Acharya and Buzan point out, it is not just "Eurocentric but absurdly limiting for IR/World Politics to ignore its global heritage and confine itself to events and ideas from the last hundred years."[15]

We learn from the BIC's example the manner in which it understands its work in terms of advancement toward the Lesser Peace and, eventually, the Most Great Peace. In this sense, progress is discerned in the growing capacity of humanity to undertake constructive collective action, deliberate peacefully and effectively on matters of global concern, erect institutions capable of implementing the outcomes of such decisions, and build capacity among peoples and nations (including civil society and governments) to come together in such a manner locally, nationally, and at the global level. This also brings to light the significance of processes that may appear to be inconsequential when assessed through the lens of *realpolitik*. The coming together of thousands of civil society organizations around a common cause might not immediately achieve desired policy outcomes, but the mere fact of cooperation, organization, and advocacy on a global scale around a given set of social issues is a sign of an emerging capacity that is critical for social change and transformation efforts.[16] In this light, the global conferences of the 1990s not only generated norms, commitments, and plans for action, but, equally importantly, created spaces for unprecedented levels of international collaboration, as a result of which the capacity of the world's people (as represented, albeit imperfectly, through the voices of civil society) to come together across geopolitical, cultural, and socioeconomic divides expanded tremendously.

An Orientation toward Unity:
Implications for Politics and Social Change

The idea of the oneness of humankind—one of the elements of the substrate explored in this book—appears at first deceptively simple. On an ideological level, the concept is easy to grasp; in practice, it proves much more challenging. The political landscape we see around us today is fraught with division and divisiveness—to the point of gridlock. Whereas multilateralism has made substantial progress since the end of the Second World War, waves of nationalism, factionalism, and extremism have been steadily undermining the ability of nations to come together around issues of common concern.

What makes the study of the BIC, then, particularly relevant for our time is that the principles of unity and the oneness of humankind—as the developmental imperatives of humanity in this age—are fundamental to its engagement in the political arena and have profound implications for all facets of social behavior. As Shoghi Effendi cautions, the oneness of humankind is not to be mistaken for "ignorant emotionalism" or "vague and pious hope," nor is it merely an attempt at "fostering harmonious cooperation among individual peoples and nations."[17] Rather, the oneness of humankind concerns itself primarily with the relationships binding states and nations and calls for

> the reconstruction and the demilitarization of the whole civilized world—a world organically unified in all the essential aspects of its life, its political machinery, its spiritual aspiration, its trade and finance, its script and language, and yet infinite in the diversity of the national characteristics of its federated units.[18]

When considered through the lens of Western liberal democracy, this appears to be a radical proposition. Consider that our system of democratic governance is structured on competitive and oppositional processes; it is based on the premise of individual and group competition for political power, the most recognizable form of which is the party system.[19] Without a deeper examination of the rationality underpinning current structures of governance, one may assume that political parties are natural, normal, and perhaps even inevitable components of a system of governance. As Karlberg argues, the formation of political parties "results in the artificial construction of oppositional identity camps that become increasingly entrenched … over time."[20] The underlying assumption is that the "best way to organize governance is through interest group competition."[21] The examination of the BIC's substrate enables us to analyze behavior shaped by a rationality that eschews all forms of partisanship and adversarialism and by the conviction that processes that set groups of individuals in opposition to one another, however subtly, undermine the potential for constructive and sustained social action, which can emerge only from conditions of unity.

Throughout its history of association with the United Nations, the BIC gives as much attention to the means and principles of deliberation as to the subject matter itself. In the committees in which it participates, the coalitions it chairs, the meetings it organizes, and the processes it facilitates, the mode of deliberation is conscious and intentional: all forms of partisanship and competition are assiduously avoided. Freedom from such modes of engagement allows the richness and diversity of perspectives to give rise to new insights and to be detached from the individuals offering the perspectives such that they become the property of the collective. This, in turn, can lead to higher levels of consensus, clarity in decision-making, and a strengthening of the bonds of association between those consulting together. In short, great attention is given to the culture of deliberation, with the understanding that divisive patterns of interaction, language, and rhetoric limit the potential for the generation of new knowledge and collective insights that arise from unifying modes of interaction. While this may seem overly idealistic to some, the proof of the value and practicability of this approach lies in the countless positions of leadership to which BIC representatives have been elected (without self-nomination), recognizing their ability to create and foster spaces for constructive deliberation and decision-making.

We find the idea of the oneness of humanity expressed in the conceptualization of peace, justice, progress, and human flourishing; in the analysis and framing of social ills and challenges; in the structure of contributions of its delegations.

We can find this expression in the BIC's efforts to open the way for greater civil society participation, in the content of the statements and messages to the United Nations, and in the way it strives to bring together disparate voices and perspectives to find common ground on issues of mutual concern.

Reconfiguring the "Other"

The spirit of voluntary association and cooperation toward common ends is at the heart of civil society. As scholars have observed, the "social capital" generated by the relationships arising from such association is critical to the functioning of a healthy society.[22] The concept of the oneness of humanity reconfigures the collective; in this construct, there is no cultural "other" against which to define a collective. The developmental reading of history, constitutive of the substrate of the BIC, further underlines that it is the collective "we" of humanity that has reached a new stage of development and must now respond to the imperative of putting in place norms, structures, and practices that embody this reality. This response operates on both a practical and spiritual level. On a practical level, most of the problems we face are global in nature (climate change, disease, economic inequality, etc.) and require robust mechanisms of global coordination and decision-making; on a spiritual level, the interconnectedness of humanity provides the moral foundation for mutual accountability and care: because we are connected, we are responsible for one another and to one another. While these assertions may not appear radical, they have not yet been able to find full expression in our political processes.

Authority: Integrity and Flexibility

The third element of the substrate examined in this book is the Administrative Order of the Bahá'í community—a system of institutions at the local, national, and global levels that not only administers the internal aspects of Bahá'í community life, but is also envisioned to serve as "a pattern and a nucleus" of a future "world commonwealth."[23] It may seem out of place to include a structural element in the analysis of the rationality of an organization, as it is in some ways qualitatively different from the concept of the oneness of humanity and a developmental view of history. Yet in the spirit of attending to the particularism of the tradition being studied, it is important to recognize that the Administrative Order is inseparable from the principle of the oneness of humanity. In that sense, it is helpful to recall

Byrd's analogy in his study of 300 years of Quaker engagement in international affairs. He writes:

> No important religious movement can maintain its vitality and spirituality without a body of cohesive principles which form the central structure—the invisible skeleton—of its life.[24]

In the case of the BIC, the Administrative Order, along with a developmental view of history and the oneness of humankind, constitutes its deep organizational structure. It is a structure that oriented towards fostering "the kind of relationships that must come to bind together and sustain society as humanity moves towards collective maturity."[25]

What makes this element of the substrate so compelling for study—particularly in the context of an RNGO–UN relationship—is that it provides an alternative model of organizing society, from the local level to the global. It is a model that emerges directly from the teachings of a religious tradition and whose unfoldment is contemporary with the rise of the international order. While it is distinct from any of the recognized systems of government (whether democratic, autocratic, republican, or monarchist), Shoghi Effendi notes that it "nevertheless embodies, reconciles and assimilates within its framework such wholesome elements as are to be found in each one of them."[26] What this study has endeavored to demonstrate is how the existence and operation of this element of the substrate shapes the BIC's work in a context defined by a different international order, by its own rationality, and by its own terms of engagement for working with RNGOs. This study challenges long-held assumptions about the incommensurability and incompatibility of "secular" and "religious" frameworks, a clash-of-civilizations dynamic, and the inevitability of co-optation of the RNGO by the dominant structures of the international order. While some argue that the BIC–UN compatibility is a function of the small size of the Bahá'í community (which limits its capacity to significantly upset the status quo) and not an attribute of its structure or principles, one cannot so easily discount the existence of a global community spread out over 180 nations, with local and national councils democratically elected by all adult members of the community, as well as a democratically elected global governing body that oversees its development and functioning.

This study also reveals the operation and significance of two facets of the Administrative Order that are at the heart of the conversation about religion and modernity—namely, integrity and flexibility. On the one hand, religious civil society organizations represent moral resources: the ability to convey and embody their vision and ideas gives them their soft power and legitimacy. RNGOs often bowing to different pressures may find their message or aims diluted, distorted, or perhaps co-opted and eventually losing clarity, vigor, and focus. The question of flexibility introduces equally significant challenges: How, in the face of rapidly shifting social, technological, intellectual, and geopolitical currents, do religious organizations remain relevant to the most pressing needs and questions of the day? And further, how do they do this without splintering into factions, when every challenge results in divergent viewpoints and interpretations of doctrine? The examination of the substrate across seventy-five years of the BIC–UN relationship reveals an approach to this in the functioning of the Universal House of Justice, whose constitution stipulates that it is to "ensure the continuity of divinely-appointed authority … and to maintain the integrity and flexibility of its teachings."[27] Through its guidance to the BIC, attentive to the stage of development of the Bahá'í community and the BIC itself, it has increased the ability of the BIC to be a more effective contributor in the international arena in terms of both substance (evolving understanding of Bahá'í concepts) and method (for example, nonpartisanship and universal participation). Furthermore, the Universal House of Justice has fostered coherence between the development of the worldwide Bahá'í community and its contributions in the global arena, ensuring that relevant insights and knowledge generated at the grassroots level about issues of global concern are shared in global fora. In doing so, it has shaped the emergence of a new epistemic community, whose contributions in international settings have been rooted in a distinct understanding of the most pressing challenges facing humanity and the required approaches to social transformation.

Emerging Paths of Inquiry

This study is, in many ways, only a beginning. It identifies three elements of what I have referred to as the substrate of the BIC's engagement in the international arena; but certainly there are others, which future scholars will identify as they continue to refine our understanding of this distinct rationality and method of engagement. They may wish to examine more directly the conceptions of power inherent in the BIC's orientation and how they shape engagement—a question that, though not explicitly addressed here, was explored indirectly through discussions about the Administrative Order and approaches to social transformation, among others. They may also wish to explore how the Bahá'í view of human nature relates to the BIC's goals and approaches. While both of these elements are addressed indirectly throughout the historical analysis, a deeper examination would further illuminate the distinctive elements of the BIC's approach in the arena of politics.

Future scholars may also look more closely at the other major areas of the BIC's work—namely, defending the human rights of the Bahá'ís persecuted in their respective countries, most notably Iran. Whereas this study focuses on the BIC's engagement in New York, it is the BIC's Office in Geneva that deals primarily with issues concerning human rights.[28] Given the highly sensitive nature of much of this work, it was not possible to address it in detail in the context of this study.[29] An exploration of the BIC's long engagement in the arena of human rights, including its defense of the Bahá'í community in countries where it is persecuted, as well as its contributions to international deliberations concerning freedom of religion, freedom of expression, and human rights norms and mechanisms, would shed light on faith-based contributions to the discourse and practice of international human rights (a discourse associated with secular–religious polarization).[30]

While the study focuses on the work of the BIC Offices in New York, there are other, more recently established regional offices, whose work would be worthwhile to examine in the sociopolitical contexts of their geographic region. These include the Brussels Office, which operates at the European level and engages with the European Union, the Council of Europe, and the Organization for Security and Co-operation in Europe; the Addis Ababa Office, which works in collaboration with governmental, intergovernmental, and non-governmental agencies in Africa; and the Jakarta Office, which works with intergovernmental associations (e.g. ASEAN), governmental agencies, civil society organizations, and research institutes in Southeast Asia. Further examination of the work of these offices could explore how the BIC's rationality finds expression in religiously, culturally, and geopolitically diverse settings.

In addition to the above, it will be useful to examine more closely the substrate and the rationality of other RNGOs and members of civil society in order to see how alternate ways of knowing, being, and doing are shaping engagement in international affairs and toward what end. For those studying civil society organizations on a more operational level, it may be fruitful to give attention to these underlying and often hidden dimensions of engagement so as to acknowledge the diversity of perspectives and epistemologies shaping their work.

Most of all, this book is an invitation to go deeper, beyond the surface of protests, lobbying, position-taking, deliberating, consensus-building, associating, movement-building, vision-setting, and idea-generating work that characterizes civil society engagement in politics. It is an invitation to explore often hidden structures of thought and rationality that expand our understanding of the social order, its constructedness, and the associated possibility for reconstruction. In these hidden structures and diverse rationalities, new conditions of possibility present themselves and bear the fruit of new modalities of engagement, new forms of agency, and new kinds of polities. In the seeming chaos and disorder of our time, a new modernity is being born.

Notes

Chapter 1

1   Victor Hugo, "The History of a Crime: The Testimony of an Eye-Witness," trans. T. H. Joyce and Arthur Locker (1877), retrieved from http://www.gutenberg.org/files/10381/10381-h/10381-h.htm.

2   Catholic social teaching encompasses Catholic doctrines on matters of human dignity and the common good. Among its foundational documents are Pope Leo XIII's encyclical *Rerum Novarum* (1891) on the theme of capital and labor, which some consider the "most serious political statement of the nineteenth century." (Michael Jon Kessler, *Political Theology for a Plural Age* Oxford, UK: Oxford University Press, 2013, 25.) An extensive body of literature has arisen to document the transformative influence of the Second Vatican Council ("Vatican II," 1962–5), on the Catholic Church's involvement in society, including the rise of Christian and Catholic NGOs. Other key papal encyclicals include: *Pacem in Terris* (1963), *Gaudium et Spes* (1965), and *Laudato Si* (2015).

3   See, for example, Mary McClintock Fulkerson and Sheila Briggs, eds., *The Oxford Handbook of Feminist Theology* (Oxford, UK: Oxford University Press, 2012).

4   R. Scott Appleby, *The Ambivalence of the Sacred: Religion, Violence, and Reconciliation* (Oxford, UK: Rowman & Littlefield, 2000); Bruce Hoffman, "'Holy Terror': The Implications of Terrorism Motivated by a Religious Imperative," *Studies in Conflict and Terrorism* 18 (1995): 271–84; Mark Juergensmeyer, *Terror in the Mind of God: The Global Rise of Religious Violence*, 4th ed. (Berkeley, CA: University of California Press, 2017); Mark Juergensmeyer, Margo Kitts, and Michael Jerryson, eds., *The Oxford Handbook of Religion and Violence* (Oxford, UK: Oxford University Press, 2015). Because expressions of "religiously motivated" violence have represented a security threat and profoundly impacted American and European geopolitics, this issue has received much attention from governments, think tanks, and academia, thus driving a particular research agenda.

5   Friedrich Nietzsche, *The Gay Science: With a Prelude in Rhymes and an Appendix of Songs*, trans. Walter Kaufmann (New York: Vintage, 1974), 181.

6   Peter L. Berger, *Sacred Canopy: Elements of a Sociological Theory of Religion* (New York: Random House, 1990), 107.

7   Peter L. Berger, "Secularism in Retreat," *The National Interest* 46 (1996/97): 3.

8   For example: Islamic movements demanding the promotion of Islamic law around the world, the Catholic Church's embrace of human rights and mobilization against

autocratic regimes, the emergence of "Engaged Buddhism" and the activism of the Dalai Lama of Tibet, the rise of the Moral Majority and the Christian Coalition in the United States, and the proliferation of religious NGOs and faith-based organizations advocating for social justice.

9 Monica Duffy Toft, Daniel Philpott, and Timothy Samuel Shah, *God's Century: Resurgent Religion and Global Politics*, the Norton Series in World Politics (New York: W. W. Norton, 2011), 7.

10 Timothy Samuel Shah, Alfred Stepan, and Monica Duffy Toft, eds., *Rethinking Religion in World Affairs* (Oxford, UK: Oxford University Press, 2012), 3.

11 See, for example, Karl Jaspers, *The Origin and Goal of History*, Routledge Revivals (London: Routledge, 1953); John D. Boy and John Torpey, "Inventing the Axial Age: The Origins and Uses of a Historical Concept," *Theory and Society* 42, no. 3 (2013): 241–59.

12 Shmuel Noah Eisenstadt, "Multiple Modernities in an Age of Globalization," *The Canadian Journal of Sociology* 24, no. 2 (1999): 283–95.

13 Benjamin Schewel identifies seven narrative frameworks that underpin contemporary academic discourse on religion: (1) subtraction, (2) renewal, (3) transsecular, (4) postnaturalist, (5) construct, (6) perennial, (7) and developmental narratives. (Benjamin Schewel, *Seven Ways of Looking at Religion: The Major Narratives* [New Haven, CT: Yale University Press, 2017], 3–6.)

14 Joseph A. Camilleri, "Postsecularist Discourse in an 'Age of Transition,'" *Review of International Studies* 38, no. 5 (2012): 1020.

15 Gerard Clarke and Michael Jennings, "Introduction," in *Development, Civil Society and Faith-Based Organizations: Bridging the Sacred and the Secular*, ed. Gerard Clarke and Michael Jennings (New York: Palgrave, 2008), 32–3.

16 Some of the world's largest humanitarian and relief organizations self-identify as religious organizations, for example, World Vision, Caritas Internationalis, Lutheran World Federation, Lutheran World Relief, and Catholic Relief Services.

17 Ruth Braunstein, Todd Nicholas Fuist, and Rhys Williams, eds., *Religion and Progressive Activism: New Stories about Faith and Politics*, Religion and Social Transformation (New York: New York University Press, 2017), 232.

18 Arie Molendijk, Justin Beaumont, and Christoph Jedan, eds., *Exploring the Postsecular: The Religious, the Political, and the Urban* (Leiden, the Netherlands: Brill, 2010), 210.

19 Ibid., 30.

20 Amitav Acharya, *Rethinking Power, Institutions and Ideas in World Politics: Whose IR?* (Abingdon, Oxon, UK: Routledge, 2014), 1.

21 Luca Mavelli and Fabio Petito, "The Postsecular in International Relations: An Overview," *Review of International Studies* 38, no. 5 (2012): 5.

22 Mavelli and Petito, "Postsecular," 8. As Helene Slessarev-Jamir points out, "religious commitments create possibilities for people to act in ways that defy the dominant

models of rational, self-interested actors found in most current theories of political behavior …. [T]his brand of activism has the power to create ethical foundations for solidarity between the politically marginalized and those with privileged access to political power" (*Prophetic Activism: Progressive Religious Justice Movements in Contemporary America* [New York: New York University Press, 2011], 7).

23 Bahá'u'lláh, in Arabic, means "Glory of God."

24 Geoffrey Cameron and Nazila Ghanea, "Bahá'ís in the Middle East," in *Routledge Handbook of Minorities in the Middle East*, ed. Paul S. Rowe (Abingdon, Oxon, UK: Routledge, 2018), 170–1.

25 Ibid., 170.

26 The Bahá'í use of the term "new world order" predates Wilson's use of the term in his "Fourteen Points" speech in 1918 by about sixty years. Bahá'u'lláh states, "The world's equilibrium hath been upset through the vibrating influence of this most great, this new World Order. Mankind's ordered life hath been revolutionized through the agency of this unique, this wondrous System—the like of which mortal eyes have never witnessed" (Bahá'u'lláh, *Proclamation of Bahá'u'lláh* [Wilmette, IL: US Bahá'í Publishing Trust, 1978]).

27 Bahá'u'lláh, *Gleanings from the Writings of Bahá'u'lláh* (Wilmette, IL: US Bahá'í Publishing Trust, 1990), 213.

28 In a 2002 report, *Religion and Public Policy at the UN*, interviewees identify the Quakers and the Bahá'ís as "two religious NGOs often praised for UN work" ([n.p.: Religion Counts, 2002], 14). The report further notes: "These faiths share some common traits that may explain their high regard in UN circles. Both hold basic tenets consistent with UN ideals—for Quakers an end to war and conflict, for Bahá'ís the establishment of a peaceful and equitable world. Both seek to build consensus on issues by engaging all concerned parties … both operate as facilitators rather than partisan advocates" (37). See other committee roles.

29 The BIC was granted consultative status (Category II) with the United Nations Economic and Social Council (ECOSOC) in 1970. The organization also has consultative status with the United Nations Children's Fund (UNICEF), as well as accreditation with the United Nations Environmental Programme (UNEP) and the United Nations Department of Public Information (DPI). The BIC maintains United Nations offices in New York and Geneva, as well as regional offices in Addis Ababa, Brussels, and Jakarta.

30 Zheng Xuan Wu, "The Bahá'í International Community in Global Governance," PhD diss., Fudan University, Shanghai, China, 2012. Further, Nazila Ghanea's *Human Rights, the U.N. and the Bahá'ís in Iran* (Oxford, UK: George Ronald, 2003) examined specifically the contribution of the United Nations to the human rights situation of the Bahá'ís in Iran.

31 See Abbas Amanat, *Resurrection and Renewal: The Making of the Babi Movement in Iran, 1844–1850* (Ithaca, NY: Cornell University Press, 1989); Soli Shahvar, *The Forgotten Schools: The Bahá'ís and Modern Education in Iran, 1899–1934*, International Library of Iranian Studies (London: I.B. Tauris, 2009); Moshe Sharon, ed., *Studies in Modern Religions, Religions, Religious Movements and the Babi-Bahá'í Faiths*, Studies in the History of Religions (The Netherlands: Brill, 2004); Peter Smith, *The Babi and Bahá'í Religions: From Messianic Shi'ism to a World Religion* (Cambridge, UK: Cambridge University Press, 1987).

32 See Nader Saiedi, *Logos and Civilization: Spirit, History, and Order in the Writings of Bahá'u'lláh* (Bethesda: University Press of Maryland/CDL Press, 2000); Nader Saiedi, *Gate of the Heart: Understanding the Writings of the Báb* (Waterloo, Ontario, CA: Wilfrid Laurier University Press, 2008); Udo Schaefer, *Bahá'í Ethics in Light of Scripture*, 2 vols., trans. Geraldine Schuckelt and Gerald Keil (Oxford, UK: George Ronald, 2007–2009); Roshan Danesh, *Dimensions of Bahá'í Law* (Wilmette, IL: US Bahá'í Publishing Trust, 2019).

33 See Will C. van den Hoonaard, *The Origins of the Bahá'í Community of Canada, 1898–1948* (Waterloo, Ontario, CA: Wilfrid Laurier University Press, 1996); Michael McMullen, *The Bahá'í: The Religious Construction of a Global Identity* (Piscataway, NJ: Rutgers University Press, 2000); Robert H. Stockman, *The Bahá'í Faith in America: Origins, 1892–1900* (Wilmette, IL: US Bahá'í Publishing Trust, 1985); Louis Venters, *No Jim Crow Church: The Origins of South Carolina's Bahá'í Community* (Gainesville, FL: University Press of Florida, 2015).

34 See Ghanea, *Human Rights*; Michael Karlberg, "Constructive Resilience: The Bahá'í Response to Oppression," *Peace & Change* 35, no. 2 (2010): 222–57; Gundula Negele, "Engagement for Religious Freedom at the United Nations: The Contribution of the Bahá'ís," in *Human Rights and Religion in Educational Contexts*, ed. Manfred L. Pirner, Johannes Lähnemann, and Heiner Bielefeldt, Interdisciplinary Studies in Human Rights (Switzerland: Springer, 2016), 91–103.

35 For example, see Janet A. Khan and Peter Khan, *Advancement of Women: A Bahá'í Perspective* (Wilmette, IL: US Bahá'í Publishing Trust, 2003); Erin Murphy-Graham, *Opening Minds, Improving Lives: Education and Women's Empowerment in Honduras* (Nashville, TN: Vanderbilt University Press, 2012).

36 Sona Farid-Arbab, *Moral Empowerment: In Quest of a Pedagogy* (Wilmette, IL: Bahá'í Publishing, 2016).

37 See, for example, Babak Bahador and Nazila Ghanea, *Processes of the Lesser Peace* (Abingdon, UK: George Ronald, 2003); Michael Karlberg, *Beyond the Culture of Contest* (Oxford, UK: George Ronald, 2004); Brian D. Lepard, *Rethinking Humanitarian Intervention: A Fresh Legal Approach Based on Fundamental Ethical Principles in International Law and World Religions* (University Park, PA:

Pennsylvania State University Press, 2002); Sovaida Ma'ani Ewing, *Collective Security within Reach* (Oxford, UK: George Ronald, 2007).

38 Geoffrey Cameron and Benjamin Schewel, eds., *Religion and Public Discourse in an Age of Global Transition: Reflections on Bahá'í Practice and Thought* (Waterloo, Ontario, Canada: Wilfrid Laurier University Press, 2018); Schewel, *Seven Ways*.

39 Richard King, *Orientalism and Religion: Postcolonial Theory, India, and "The Mythic East"* (London: Routledge, 1999), 40.

40 Bahá'í World Centre, *One Common Faith* (Haifa, Israel: Bahá'í World Centre, 2005), 23.

41 Shahriar Razavi, "Bahá'í Participation in Public Discourse: Some Considerations Related to History, Concepts, and Approaches," in *Religion and Public Discourse in an Age of Transition: Reflections on Bahá'í Thought and Practice*, ed. Geoffrey Cameron and Benjamin Schewel (Waterloo, Ontario, CA: Wilfrid Laurier University Press, 2018), 73.

42 Ulrich Golmer, "Bahá'í Political Thought," in *Making the Crooked Straight: A Contribution to Bahá'í Apologetics*, ed. Udo Schaefer, Nicola Towfigh, and Ulrich Golmer, trans. Geraldine Schuckelt (Oxford, UK: George Ronald, 2000), 466.

43 'Abdu'l-Bahá, *Paris Talks*, 11th ed. (London: UK Bahá'í Publishing Trust, 1972), 130.

44 Four popes have addressed the UN General Assembly: Paul VI (October 4, 1965), John Paul II (October 2, 1979, and October 5, 1995), Benedict XVI (April 18, 2008), and Francis (September 25, 2015).

45 A non-derogable right is one that may not be violated under any circumstances.

46 In a dramatic gesture, in August 2000, the UN General Assembly Hall hosted over 2,000 of the world's religious and spiritual leaders gathered together for the World Peace Summit to demonstrate their willingness to work together to eliminate their causes of war.

47 Article 71 of the UN Charter lays the groundwork for UN consultation with non-governmental organizations. Today, the relationship between the United Nations and NGOs is governed by Resolution 1996/31 of the Economic and Social Council (ECOSOC). International, regional, and national NGOs, as well as nonprofit public or voluntary organizations, are eligible for consultative status. The three categories of status are general, special, and roster consultative status. As of September 2016, over 4,500 NGOs have been accorded consultative status by the United Nations (United Nations Economic and Social Council, *List of Non-Governmental Organizations in Consultative Status with the Economic and Social Council as of 1 September 2016* [December 29, 2016], https://digitallibrary.un.org/record/1286140?ln=en).

48 For more about religious NGOs at the United Nations, see Julia Berger, "Religious Nongovernmental Organizations: An Exploratory Analysis," *Voluntas: International*

Journal of Voluntary and Nonprofit Organizations 14 (2003): 15–39; Marie Juul
Petersen, "International Religious NGOs at the United Nations: A Study of a Group
of Religious Organizations," *The Journal of Humanitarian Assistance* (November 17,
2010), https://sites.tufts.edu/jha/archives/847; Karsten Lehmann, *Religious NGOs
in International Relations: The Construction of "the Religious" and "the Secular*,*"*
Routledge Studies in Religion and Politics (New York: Routledge, 2016); Joseph S.
Rossi, *Uncharted Territory: The American Catholic Church at the United Nations,
1946–1972* (Washington, DC: The Catholic University of America Press, 2006);
Josef Boehle, "Religious NGOs at the UN and the Millennium Development Goals:
An Introduction," *Global Change, Peace & Security* 22, no. 3 (2010): 275–96; Josef
Boehle, "The UN System and Religious Actors in the Context of Global Change,"
CrossCurrents 60, no. 3 (2010): 383–401; Religion Counts. *Religion and Public
Policy at the UN.* Observatory on the Universality of Rights. April 2002. https://
www.oursplatform.org/wp-content/uploads/Catholics-for-Choice-Religion-
Counts-Religion-and-Public-Policy-at-the-UN-1.pdf; Matthew Weiner, "Religion
and the United Nations: Introduction," *CrossCurrents* 60, no. 3 (2010): 292–6. Case
studies include David Atwood, *From the Inside Out: Observations on Quaker Work
at the United Nations* (Australia: The Religious Society of Friends, 2012); Verena
Beittinger-Lee and Hugh Miall, "Islam, the OIC, and the Defamation of Religions
Controversy," in *Religion, NGOs and the United Nations: Visible and Invisible
Actors in Power*, ed. Jeremy Carrette and Hugh Miall (London: Bloomsbury, 2017),
155–75; Verena Beittinger-Lee, "Catholicism at the United Nations in New York,"
in *Religion, NGOs and the United Nations: Visible and Invisible Actors in Power*,
ed. Jeremy Carrette and Hugh Miall (London: Bloomsbury, 2017), 177–94; Jeremy
Carrette, "The Paradox of Globalization: Quakers, Religious NGOs and the United
Nations," in *Religions in Movement: The Local and the Global in Contemporary Faith
Traditions*, ed. Robert W. Hefner et al., Routledge Studies in Religion (London:
Routledge, 2013), 37–56; Jeremy Carrette and Hugh Miall, eds., *Religion, NGOs
and the United Nations: Visible and Invisible Actors in Power* (London: Bloomsbury,
2017); Turan Kayaoğlu, "Islam in the United Nations: The Liberal Limits of
Post-secularism," paper presented at "The Post-secular in International Politics,"
University of Sussex, October 27–28, 2011.

49   The following UN agencies developed frameworks for engagement with RNGOs:
the United Nations Population Fund (*Guidelines for Engaging Faith-Based
Organizations as Agents of Change*), the Joint United Nations Programme on HIV/
AIDS (*Partnership with Faith-Based Organizations UNAIDS Strategic Framework*),
the United Nations Children's Fund (*Partnering with Religious Communities for
Children*), the United Nations Development Programme (*UNDP Guidelines on
Engaging with Faith-Based Organizations and Religious Leaders*), and the UN
Refugee Agency (*Partnership Note*).

50 The term "faith-based" has been preferred by entities that do not readily identify with the term "religion" (such as Hindu or Buddhist organizations, for instance) and generally encompasses humanitarian and relief organizations. The term "NGO" is often applied to and used by organizations concerned with advocacy and government-facing activities.

51 United Nations Entity for Gender Equality and the Empowerment of Women, "In Brief: Policies and Practice: A Guide for Gender-Responsive Implementation of the Global Compact for Migration" (n.p.: UN Women, 2019), 2, https://www.unwomen.org/-/media/headquarters/attachments/sections/library/publications/2018/guide-for-gender-responsive-implementation-of-the-global-compact-for-migration-en.pdf?la=en&vs=5533.

52 Rossi, *Uncharted Territory*, 42.

53 Pope Paul VI, "Address of the Holy Father Paul VI to the United Nations Organization," October 4, 1965, https://holyseemission.org/contents/statements/address-of-the-holy-father-paul-vi-to-the-united-nations-organization.php.

54 Lehmann, *Religious NGOs*, 7. His research examines two agencies: the Commission of Churches on International Affairs and Pax Romana.

55 Robert O. Byrd, *Quaker Ways in Foreign Policy* (Toronto: University of Toronto Press, 1960), xv.

56 Ibid.

57 *Oxford English Dictionary*, "Substrate," n.p.

58 Ibid.

59 Ibid. Related concepts include the *neural substrate*, which refers to brain structures that underlie specific behaviors or psychological states; in a similar manner, soil constitutes the *substrate* of most seed plants.

60 William E. Connolly, "Biology, Politics, Creativity," *Perspectives on Politics* 11, no. 2 (2013): 508.

61 Michel Foucault, *The Order of Things: An Archaeology of the Human Sciences* (Reprint, New York: Vintage, 1994 [1970]), 168.

62 Byrd, *Quaker Ways*, 110.

63 Shoghi Effendi, *The Promised Day Is Come*, rev. ed. (Wilmette, IL: US Baháʼí Publishing Trust, 1980), 45.

64 Baháʼí International Community, *Baháʼí International Community's Quadrennial Report (2010–2013)* (New York: Baháʼí International Community, 2014), 6–7.

Chapter 2

1 The Báb (1819–50) was the Herald of Baháʼu'lláh, a role similar to that of John the Baptist in Christianity. According to Baháʼí scripture, he was also an independent

Prophet or "Manifestation of God." For details about his life and teachings, see Saiedi, *Gate of the Heart*.

2   Jürgen Osterhammel, *The Transformation of the World: A Global History of the Nineteenth Century*, America in the World (Princeton, NJ: Princeton University Press, 2014), 392, 421, 514, 571.

3   See Mark Mazower, *Governing the World: The History of an Idea, 1815 to the Present* (New York: Penguin, 2013).

4   See Wolfram Siemann, *Metternich: Strategist and Visionary* (Cambridge, MA: Harvard University Press, 2019).

5   Osterhammel, *Transformation*, 406.

6   Ibid., 393.

7   For a historical overview of Bahá'u'lláh's life, see Hasan Balyuzi, *Bahá'u'lláh: The King of Glory* (Oxford, UK: George Ronald, 1991); Adib Taherzadeh, *The Revelation of Bahá'u'lláh*, 4 vols. (Oxford, UK: George Ronald, 1974–87).

8   Ninian Smart, *Worldviews: Crosscultural Explorations of Human Beliefs*, 3rd ed. (New York: Scribner's, 1983).

9   The Báb, meaning "the Gate" in Arabic (given name was Ali Muhammad), was the Herald of the Bahá'í Faith. He foretold that his own Revelation would be succeeded by the appearance of a promised "Manifestation of God"—a divinely inspired Educator who would fulfill the promise of every religion, a role publicly claimed by Baha'u'llah in 1863.

10 Bahá'u'lláh, *The Hidden Words of Bahá'u'lláh*, trans. Shoghi Effendi (Wilmette, IL: US Bahá'í Publishing Trust, 1985), Arabic no. 67.

11 A number of scholars (such as Georg Wilhelm Friedrich Hegel and Robert Bellah) have proposed what Schewel refers to as a "developmental narrative" of religion, which claims that religion, as a unified construct, has proceeded through several stages of historical development (Benjamin Schewel, "Religion in an Age of Transition," in *Religion and Discourse in an Age of Transition: Reflections on Bahá'í Practice and Thought*, ed. Geoffrey Cameron and Benjamin Schewel [Waterloo, Ontario, CA: Wilfrid Laurier University Press, 2018], 26). Furthermore, German philosopher Karl Jaspers has advanced the thesis of an "axial age," which reconceptualizes religious traditions as the expression of a "unified process of civilizational development" (Jaspers, *Origin and Goal of History*).

12 Bahá'u'lláh, *Proclamation*, 116.

13 Bahá'u'lláh, *Gleanings*, 250.

14 Ibid., 213.

15 The letters are published together in Bahá'u'lláh, *The Summons of the Lord of Hosts* (Haifa, Israel: Bahá'í World Centre, 2002), http://bahai-library.com/bahaullah_summons_lord_hosts.

16 In his letter to Queen Victoria, who ruled from 1837–1901, Bahá'u'lláh commends the monarch for abolishing slavery, congratulates her on the British system

of parliamentary governance, and calls upon parliamentarians worldwide to undertake measures to bring about justice in their nations and the world. Specifically, he warns against ruinous arms races and over-taxation and emphasizes the need for a system of collective security (Bahá'u'lláh, *Summons*, 89–96).

17 While the letter is addressed specifically to the pontiff, Bahá'u'lláh implies that these words are meant for the followers of all religions (Bahá'u'lláh, *Summons*, 55–67).

18 For example, Bahá'u'lláh states: "The Sun of vicegerency hath dawned, the Point of knowledge and wisdom hath been made plain, and the Testimony of God, the Almighty, the All-Wise, hath been made manifest. Say: The Moon of eternity hath risen in the midmost heaven, and its light hath illumined the dwellers of the realms above. My face hath come forth from the veils, and shed its radiance upon all that is in heaven and on earth" (Bahá'u'lláh, *Summons*, 233).

19 Shoghi Effendi, *Promised Day*, 45.

20 Bahá'u'lláh, *Summons*, 30.

21 Universal House of Justice, "Introduction," in *The Summons of the Lord of Hosts* (Haifa, Israel: Bahá'í World Centre, 2002), ii.

22 Bahá'u'lláh, *Summons*, 84.

23 Bahá'u'lláh praises Queen Victoria for having "entrusted the reins of counsel into the hands of the representatives of the people" (Bahá'u'lláh, *Summons*, 90).

24 The Bahá'í writings state that "conflict and contention are categorically forbidden" (Bahá'u'lláh, *Tablets of Baha'u'llah Revealed after the Kitáb-i-Aqdas*, comp. the Research Department of the Universal House of Justice, trans. Habib Taherzadeh et al. [Haifa, Israel: Bahá'í World Centre, 1982], 221).

25 'Abdu'l-Baha's birth name was Abbas; he took the title 'Abdu'l-Bahá, which means "Servant of Bahá."

26 An English translation of Bahá'u'lláh's will and testament is included in the *Tablets of Bahá'u'lláh Revealed after the Kitáb-i-Aqdas*, published in 1978.

27 See Mina Yazdani, "'Abdu'l-Bahá and the Iranian Constitutional Revolution: Embracing Principles while Disapproving Methodologies," *Journal of Bahá'í Studies* 24, no. 1–2 (2014): 47–82. See also Nader Sohrabi, "Historicizing Revolutions: Constitutional Revolutions in the Ottoman Empire, Iran, and Russia, 1905–1908," *American Journal of Sociology* 100, no. 6 (1995): 1383–447.

28 Yazdani, "'Abdu'l-Bahá," 49.

29 'Abdu'l-Bahá, *The Secret of Divine Civilization* (Wilmette, IL: US Bahá'í Publishing Trust, 1957), 23.

30 Yazdani, "'Abdu'l-Bahá," 74.

31 This was the Second Hague Peace Conference, known for issuing the first formal statement of the laws of war and war crimes in the body of secular international law (Osterhammel, *Transformation*, 469).

32 For detailed accounts of 'Abdu'l-Bahá's travels in America, see Robert H. Stockman, *'Abdu'l-Bahá in America* (Wilmette, IL: US Bahá'í Publishing Trust, 2012); for talks delivered during his stay in Paris, see 'Abdu'l-Bahá, *Paris Talks*; for talks delivered during his travels in America, see 'Abdu'l-Bahá, *The Promulgation of Universal Peace*, 2nd ed. (Wilmette, IL: US Bahá'í Publishing Trust, 1982).

33 'Abdu'l-Bahá, *Selections from the Writings of 'Abdu'l-Bahá* (Haifa, Israel: Bahá'í World Centre, 1982), 297.

34 Ibid., 304.

35 'Abdu'l-Bahá, *Promulgation*, 265.

36 Ibid., 230.

37 The Central Organization for a Durable Peace was established at The Hague in the Netherlands in April 1915. Its members represented nine European nations and the United States and called for a "new diplomacy," willing to accept military sanctions against aggressive countries. For more details, refer to Fannie Fern Andrews, "The Central Organization for a Durable Peace," *The Annals of the American Academy of Political and Social Science* 66, no. 1 (1916): 16–21, https://doi.org/10.1177/000271621606600104.

38 'Abdu'l-Bahá, *Selections*, 299.

39 Ibid.

40 Bahá'í World Centre, *One Common Faith*, 23.

41 Bahá'u'lláh, *Gleanings*, 286.

42 'Abdu'l-Bahá, *Paris Talks*, 130.

43 'Abdu'l-Bahá notes that "although the League of Nations has been brought into existence, yet it is incapable of establishing Universal Peace" ('Abdu'l-Bahá, *Selections*, 306).

44 Chris Hedges, "What Every Person Should Know about War (Excerpt)," *The New York Times*, July 6, 2003, http://www.nytimes.com/2003/07/06/books/chapters/what-every-person-should-know-about-war.html.

45 See, for instance, Martin Gilbert, *A History of the Twentieth Century: The Concise Edition of the Acclaimed World History* (New York: HarperCollins, 2001) and Michael D. Richards and Paul R. Waibel, *Twentieth-Century Europe: A Brief History, 1900 to the Present*, 3rd ed. (Malden, MA: Wiley, 2014).

46 'Abdu'l-Bahá, *Selections*, 35.

47 Foucault, *Order of Things*, xxiii–iv.

48 'Abdu'l-Bahá, *The Will and Testament of 'Abdu'l-Bahá* (Wilmette, IL: US Bahá'í Publishing Trust, 1990). In his will, 'Abdu'l-Bahá appointed "twin successors": his eldest grandson, Shoghi Effendi, to the position of "Guardian" of the Faith and the institution of the Universal House of Justice to be elected in the future.

49 Universal House of Justice, *Ministry of the Custodians: An Account of the Stewardship of the Hands of the Cause 1957–1963* (Haifa, Israel: Bahá'í World

Centre, 1992), 35. Almost, 2 countries opened to the Faith in the years between 1844 and 1853; 13 more opened during the ministry of Bahá'u'lláh (1853–92); 20 more opened during the ministry of 'Abdu'l-Bahá (1892–1921); 93 more opened during Shoghi Effendi's ministry (1921–57); 131 more opened in the years between Shoghi Effendi's passing in 1957 and the election of the first Universal House of Justice in 1963. For detailed statistics about the growth of the Bahá'í community during these years, please see Shoghi Effendi, *The Bahá'í Faith: 1844–1952* (Wilmette, IL: Bahá'í Publishing Committee, 1953) and Hands of the Cause of God Residing in the Holy Land, ed., *The Bahá'í Faith, 1844–1963: Information and Statistical Comparison*, vol. 128 (Ramat Gan, Peli: PEC Printing Works, 1963).

50 *The Bahá'í World, 1930–1932*, vol. 4 (New York: J. J. Little and Ives, 1933), 257–61.

51 Shoghi Effendi, *God Passes By* (Wilmette, IL: US Bahá'í Publishing Trust, 1979), 342.

52 For a brief biography and overview of Shoghi Effendi's writings see Bahá'í World Centre, "The Life and Work of Shoghi Effendi," *Bahá'í.org*, Bahá'í International Community, http://www.bahai.org/shoghi-effendi/life-work-shoghi-effendi.

53 Shoghi Effendi, *The World Order of Bahá'u'lláh* (Wilmette, IL: Bahá'í Publishing Trust, 1991), 42–3.

54 Shoghi Effendi, *Promised Day*, 114.

55 See *The Bahá'í World, 1944–1946*, vol. 10 (Wilmette, IL: Bahá'í Publishing Committee, 1948) and *The Bahá'í World, 1979–1983*, vol. 18 (Haifa, Israel: Bahá'í World Centre, 1986).

56 'Abdu'l-Bahá, *Promulgation*, 36.

57 Ibid., 125.

Chapter 3

1 In general, studies of religious organizations pay little attention to the belief system shaping organizational behavior—making only passing references to religious laws and observances and how they shape and motivate the behavior (e.g., Katherine Marshall, *Global Institutions of Religion: Ancient Movers, Modern Shakers* [New York: Routledge, 2013]). An exception to this approach is found in research that explores the manner in which Muslim social service organizations are shaped and influenced by Islamic values (Susumu Nejima, ed., *NGOs in the Muslim World: Faith and Social Services* [London: Routledge, 2015]). Furthermore, research has focused on the manner in which extremist and fundamentalist organizations use theological rationale to justify discrimination, violence, and misogyny (e.g., Juergensmeyer, *Terror in the Mind of God*; Appleby, *Ambivalence of the Sacred*; and Michael Jerryson, Mark Juergensmeyer, and Margo Kitts, eds., *The Oxford Handbook of Religion and Violence* [Oxford, UK: Oxford University Press, 2013]).

2   Séverine Deneulin and Masooda Bano, *Religion in Development: Rewriting the Secular Script* (London: Zed Books, 2009), 63.

3   Bahá'í World Centre, *One Common Faith*.

4   *Oxford English Dictionary*, "Substrate."

5   Ibid.

6   Ibid.

7   Lehmann, *Religious NGOs*, 42. The existence and flourishing of RNGOs have brought into sharp relief the dynamic aspects of religion: religious communities are continually evolving—in both form and substance—to give expression to their teachings in continually changing sociocultural contexts. For example, religious organizations that have existed for hundreds of years are refashioning themselves as "NGOs."

8   Thomas S. Kuhn, *The Structure of Scientific Revolutions*, 3rd ed. (Chicago, IL: University of Chicago Press, 1996).

9   Ibid.

10 Thomas S. Kuhn, "Scientific Revolutions as Changes of World View," in *Can Theories Be Refuted?: Essays on the Duhem-Quine Thesis*, ed. Sandra G. Harding (Boston, MA: Reidel Pub. Co., 1976), 133.

11 See Michel Foucault, *The Archaeology of Knowledge* (New York: Pantheon, 1972).

12 Foucault, *Order of Things*.

13 Michel Foucault, *Madness and Civilization: A History of Insanity in the Age of Reason* (New York: Pantheon, 1965).

14 David Ford, *Theology: A Very Short Introduction* (Oxford, UK: Oxford University Press, 2013), 9.

15 Bahá'u'lláh, *Kitáb-i-Aqdas (Most Holy Book): "Multilinear" Translation Project and Glossary*, ed. Jonah Winters (1999), n. 110, *Bahá'í Library Online*, accessed June 10, 2020, http://bahai-library.com/provisionals/aqdas/aqdas186.notes.html.

16 Ibid.

17 'Abdu'l-Bahá, *Promulgation*, 140.

18 Bahá'u'lláh, *Gleanings*, 198.

19 While individuals may be conscious of the foundational moral commitments of their respective organization, that doesn't imply that this understanding is fixed. As experience accumulates, understanding of the elements of the substrate may evolve and be refined.

20 Pierre Bourdieu, *Algeria 1960* (Cambridge, UK: Cambridge University Press, 1979), vii.

21 Ibid.

22 Pierre Bourdieu, *Distinction: A Social Critique of the Judgement of Taste* (London: Routledge, 1984), 170.

23 Shoghi Effendi, "A Statement by Shoghi Rabbani to Mr. Justice Emil Sandstrom, Chairman, United Nations Special Committee on Palestine," United Nations, April

6, 1948, http://unispal.un.org/UNISPAL.NSF/0/0074E155E7831EE385257061006 8A609.

24 I am grateful to Dr. Caity Bolton for this comment.

25 Universal House of Justice to the Bahá'ís of Iran, 2.

26 Ibid.

27 The Bahá'í perspective of history has much in common with the concept of "axiality" (Jaspers, *Origin and Goal of History*) and echoes thinkers who focused on the changeable, fluid, evolutionary dimensions of history and religion, such as G. W. F. Hegel, Charles Darwin, and Alfred North Whitehead. For an incisive analysis of prevalent narratives of religious history, see Schewel, Benjamin, *Seven Ways of Looking at Religion: The Major Narratives* (New Haven, CT: Yale University Press, 2017).

28 Universal House of Justice to the Bahá'ís of Iran, 2.

29 Shoghi Effendi, *World Order*, 155.

30 Universal House of Justice to the Bahá'ís of Iran, 3.

31 Ibid.

32 Shoghi Effendi, *Promised Day*, 5.

33 According to the Bahá'í Faith, there have always been Prophets (or Manifestations of God); while we have the historical record of those mentioned here, the names of others, according to Shoghi Effendi, have been "lost in the mists of ancient history" (Helen Hornby, ed., *Lights of Guidance: A Bahá'í Reference File* [New Delhi: Bahá'í Publishing Trust, 1988], 503).

34 Bahá'u'lláh, *Hidden Words*, Arabic no. 67.

35 Bahá'u'lláh, *Gleanings*, 213.

36 'Abdu'l-Bahá, *Promulgation*, 140.

37 Shoghi Effendi, *World Order*, 36.

38 Universal House of Justice to the Bahá'ís of the World, October 23, 1983, *Bahai.org*, accessed September 23, 2019, http://www.bahai.org/library/authoritative-texts/the-universal-house-of-justice/messages/19831020_001/1#346303577.

39 Shoghi Effendi, *World Order*, 43.

40 'Abdu'l-Bahá, *Selections*, 31.

41 Bahá'u'lláh, *Gleanings*, 286.

42 Universal House of Justice to the Bahá'ís of Egypt, December 21, 2006, *Bahai.org*, accessed September 23, 2019, http://www.bahai.org/library/authoritative-texts/the-universal-house-of-justice/messages/#d=20061221_001&f=f1, 2.

43 Bahá'u'lláh, *Gleanings*, 215.

44 Shoghi Effendi, *World Order*, 43.

45 'Abdu'l-Bahá, *Paris Talks*, 130.

46 Shoghi Effendi, *World Order*, 145. The Administrative Order was established by the founder of the Bahá'í Faith and elaborated by successive leaders of the Bahá'í community between 1897 and 1957.

47   Shoghi Effendi, *World Order*, 43.

48   Elections take place each year by secret ballot. There is no campaigning or electioneering; people vote according to the promptings of their conscience for those whom they deem possess the appropriate characteristics for service. Elections take place in all communities in which there are nine or more Baháʾís.

49   Shoghi Effendi, *World Order*, 154.

50   Ibid., 23.

51   The Constitution of the Universal House of Justice, adopted in 1972, provides its Terms of Reference: "The provenance, the authority, the duties, the sphere of action of the Universal House of Justice all derive from the revealed Word of Baháʾuʾlláh which, together with the interpretations and expositions of the Centre of the Covenant and of the Guardian of the Cause—who, after ʿAbduʾl-Bahá, is the sole authority in the interpretation of Baháʾí Scripture—constitute the binding terms of reference of the Universal House of Justice and are its bedrock foundation" (Universal House of Justice, "Constitution of the Universal House of Justice," 1966, *Bahai.org*, accessed September 23, 2019, http://universalhouseofjustice.bahai.org/constitution/constitution-universal-house-justice).

52   Shoghi Effendi, *World Order*, 23.

53   Ibid., 41.

54   Ibid.

55   Ibid., 42.

56   Acharya, *Rethinking Power*.

Chapter 4

1   "Here is the machinery," wrote Trygve Lie, the United Nations' first secretary-general. "It is for the peoples of the United Nations and their governments to see that its full potentialities are realized" (United Nations Office of Public Information, "Preface," in *United Nations Yearbook 1946–1947* [New York: United Nations, 1947], iii).

2   Wendy Brown, *Edgework: Critical Essays on Knowledge and Politics* (Princeton, NJ: Princeton University Press, 2005), 14.

3   Amitav Acharya and Barry Buzan, *The Making of Global International Relations: Origins and Evolution of IR at Its Centenary* (Cambridge, UK: Cambridge University Press, 2019), 2.

4   Acharya, *Rethinking Power*, 55. Consider for example the seminal document the Catholic Church issued during the Second Vatican Council, *Gaudium et Spes*, which notes that "the Church has always had the duty of scrutinizing the signs of the times and of interpreting them in the light of the Gospel." The document

provides a reading of contemporary reality in this light, asserting that "the human race is involved in a new stage of history" and that it has "passed from a rather static concept of reality to a more dynamic, evolutionary one." It goes on to examine the social order and the role of the church within it (Pope Paul VI, *Gaudium et Spes*, December 7, 1965, *Papal Archive*, The Holy See, accessed February 2, 2020, http://www.vatican.va/archive/hist_councils/ii_vatican_council/ documents/vat-ii_cons_19651207_gaudium-et-spes_en.html).

5   In the weeks and days before the conference, San Francisco would witness an influx of people from fifty countries, including some 1,700 delegates and assistants and over 2,600 newspaper and radio reporters (Stanley Meisler, *United Nations: A History*, rev. ed. [New York: Grove/Atlantic, 2011], 16).

6   The Charter was considered so valuable that it had its own parachute, but the person accompanying it didn't (Jean E. Krasno, *The Founding of the United Nations: International Cooperation as Evolutionary Process* [Academic Council on the United Nations System, 2001], 8–9.)!

7   *The Bahá'í World, 1944–1946*, 18.

8   Ibid. When the General Assembly held its first meeting in London in January 1946, the British Bahá'í community sent a welcome letter to delegates from all fifty-one nations (Ibid., 16).

9   In order to carry out the research, I drew on archival documents from the National Bahá'í Archives in Wilmette, Illinois. In particular, I studied the correspondence between the central actors of this period: (1) the first representative of the Bahá'í community to the United Nations, Mrs. Mildred Mottahedeh; (2) the secretary of the National Spiritual Assembly of the United States, the Bahá'í institution that provided administrative oversight of the BIC office; (3) the second representative, Mr. Victor Araujo, who succeeded Mrs. Mottahedeh, Mr. Victor Araujo; and (4) relevant UN agencies. In addition, of central importance, are the letters written by Shoghi Effendi, which provided the overall vision for the nature and purpose of the engagement as well as the broader historical perspective.

10 Heather M. Dubois and Janna Hunter-Bowman, "The Intersection of Christian Theology and Peacebuilding," in *Religion, Conflict, and Peacebuilding*, ed. Atalia Omer, R. Scott Abbleby, and David Little (New York: Oxford University Press, 2015), 582.

11 Shoghi Effendi, *World Order*, 42.

12 "That ... all-pervasive ... change, which we associate with the stage of maturity inevitable in the life of the individual and the development of the fruit must ... have its counterpart in the evolution of the organization of human society" (Shoghi Effendi, *World Order*, 163–4).

13 Victor de Araujo, Victor de Araujo to National Spiritual Assemblies, July 1, 1970, Bahá'í International Community United Nations Office Archives, New York.

14 This is well captured by the US representative to the United Nations in his remarks in the General Assembly welcoming Dag Hammarskjöld as the new secretary-general: "As Mr. Hammarskjöld takes up his duties, he becomes part of a living organization which has gone further towards organizing peace and organizing security than any other body in modern history ... Today an international organization must represent different cultures and different races, unlike the Council of Europe, which, more than a century ago, was conceived as a group of sovereigns, products of the same civilization and background, to maintain the stability of Europe" (United Nations General Assembly, General Assembly Seventh Session [New York: United Nations, April 10, 1953], 700, *UN.org*, https://www.un.org/ga/search/view_doc.asp?symbol=A/PV.426).

15 Acharya and Buzan, *Making of Global*, 302.

16 Bahá'í World Centre, *One Common Faith*.

17 Universal House of Justice to the Bahá'ís of Iran.

18 Ibid.

19 The International Covenant on Civil and Political Rights entered into force in 1976.

20 The International Covenant on Economic, Social and Cultural Rights entered into force in 1976.

21 Universal House of Justice to the Bahá'ís of Iran.

22 National Spiritual Assembly of the Bahá'ís of the United States and Canada, "National Spiritual Assembly of the United States and Canada to Trygve Lie (August 28, 1948)," Bahá'í International Community United Nations Office Archives, New York.

23 Chadwick Alger, "The Emerging Roles of NGOs in the UN System: From Article 71 to a People's Millennium Assembly," *Global Governance* 8, no. 1 (2002): 93.

24 United Nations, Charter of the United Nations, 1 UNTS XVI, June 26, 1945, art. 71, http://www.un.org/en/charter-united-nations/.

25 Peter Willetts, *The "Conscience of the World": The Influence of Non-Governmental Organisations in the U.N. System* (Washington, DC: The Brookings Institution, 1996), 27.

26 Chadwick, "Emerging Roles," 93.

27 The roots could be traced as far back as the Geneva Conventions of 1864 and the International Slavery Convention of 1926; with a basis for such formalized relationships captured in the Charter—in Article 71, specifically—a new world of possibilities opened up. The 1972 UN Conference on the Human Environment (Stockholm, Sweden) and the 1975 UN First World Conference on Women (Mexico City, Mexico) are considered among the milestones in the emergence and influence of NGOs in the international arena. We will return to the question of Article 71 and its central importance a little later on in the chapter.

28 In their early days, the role of NGOs was to support the public education work of the United Nations, publicize the rights and freedoms in the UDHR, and awaken new interest and understanding.

29 Bahá'í International Community letter to Mr. Dag Hammarskjold, May 23, 1955, in *The Baha'i World, 1954–1963*, vol. 13 (Haifa: Israel: Baha'i World Center, 1970), 796–7.

30 National Spiritual Assembly of the Bahá'ís of the United States and Canada, "A Baha'i Declaration of Human Obligations and Rights," presented to the first session of the United Nations Commission on Human Rights, Lake Success, NY, February 1, 1947, *BIC.org*, accessed September 22, 2019, http://www.bic.org/statements/bahai-declaration-human-obligations-and-rights.

31 Shoghi Effendi, *World Order*, 202.

32 Manfred B. Steger and Paul James, "Levels of Subjective Globalization: Ideologies, Imaginaries, Ontologies," *Perspectives on Development and Technology* 12, no. 1–2 (2013): 35.

33 See Michael Karlberg, "Western Liberal Democracy as New World Order?" in *The Bahá'í World, 2005–2006* (Haifa, Israel: Bahá'í World Centre, 2007), 133–56, *Bahai. org*, http://www.bahai.org/documents/essays/karlberg-dr-michael/western-liberal-democracy-new-world-order.

34 Acharya and Buzan, *Making of Global*, 3.

35 National Spiritual Assembly of the Bahá'ís of the United States and Canada, letter to Mr. Trygve Lie.

36 National Spiritual Assembly of the Bahá'ís of the United States and Canada, "Bahá'í Declaration."

37 Ibid.

38 Shoghi Effendi, *World Order*, 202.

39 Bahá'í International Community, "Proposals for Charter Revision Submitted to the United Nations by the Bahá'í International Community," May 23, 1955, *BIC. org*, http://www.bic.org/statements/proposals-charter-revision-submitted-united-nations-bah%C3%A1%C3%AD-international-community.

40 Ibid.

41 Ibid.

42 John Paul Lederach, *The Little Book of Conflict Transformation* (Intercourse, PA: Good Books, 2003), 37.

43 "The Bahá'í Faith and the United Nations: The Beginnings of the Bahá'í Relationship with the United Nations," in *The Bahá'í World, 1954–1963*, vol. 13 (Haifa, Israel: Bahá'í World Centre, 1970), 785.

44 Shoghi Effendi, *Citadel of Faith* (Wilmette, IL: US Bahá'í Publishing Trust, 1980), 33.

45 The National Spiritual Assembly of Canada was formed shortly thereafter.

46 "The Bahá'í Faith and the United Nations," 785.

47 *The Bahá'í World, 1946–1950*, vol. 11 (Wilmette, IL: Bahá'í Publishing Trust, 1981), 520–5.

48 In 1967, the Universal House of Justice assumed the oversight of the BIC.

49 "The Genocide Convention," *United Nations Office on Genocide Prevention and the Responsibility to Protect*, United Nations, accessed May 12, 2020, http://www. un.org/en/genocideprevention/genocide-convention.shtml.

50 "The Bahá'í Faith and the United Nations," 791.

51 Ibid.

52 Ibid.

53 Ibid., 791–2.

54 The twelve Assemblies that gave input were as follows: Iran, Iraq, India-Pakistan-Burma, Australia-New Zealand, Egypt-Sudan, Germany-Austria, Italy-Switzerland, British Isles, Canada, Central America, South America, and the United States. The Charter Revision Conference was preceded by a "Festival of Faith" held in the San Francisco Cow Palace and attended by 15,000 people. Bahá'ís were counted among the various faith representatives.

55 Bahá'í International Community, letter to Mr. Dag Hammarskjöld, 796–7.

56 Bahá'í International Community, The Work of Bahá'ís in Promotion of Human Rights, statement prepared for the United Nations Conference on Human Rights, Geneva, Switzerland, May 19–20, 1948, Office of the Secretary, US United Nations Representative and Bahá'í International Community Files, National Bahá'í Archives, the United States.

57 Mildred Mottahedeh, letter to Horace Holley, February 1, 1949, Office of the Secretary, US United Nations Representative and Bahá'í International Community Files, National Bahá'í Archives, the United States.

58 Bahá'í International Community, Report of the Bahá'í Activities in Relation to the United Nations (1947–52), Bahá'í International Community United Nations Office Archives, New York.

59 Mottahedeh, letter to Horace Holley.

60 For example, BIC representative Mildred Mottahedeh was nominated to chair a UN committee to oversee national meetings of NGOs in all UN member states (1949 UN Conference on International NGOs), while BIC representative Ugo Giachery was nominated by the UN Department of Public Information to chair the committee on "special problems of UN information in Europe" and was unanimously accepted by the delegates. As committee chair, Giachery became part of the steering committee for the 1951 Regional Conference on NGOs. At the 1950 UN Conference on International NGOs in Geneva, only 3 out of the 103 NGOs represented sent a full five-member delegation; the BIC was among the three (Bahá'í International Community, Report of the Bahá'í Activities).

61 Shoghi Effendi, *World Order*, 64.

62 Bahá'í International Community, Suggestions for Bahá'í Delegates to UN NGO Conferences, 1950, Bahá'í International Community United Nations Office Archives, New York.

63 Mildred Mottahedeh, Report of the Delegates of the BIC to the Fourth Conference of the International NGOs, June 26–28, 1950, Bahá'í International Community United Nations Office Archives, New York.

64 Ibid.

Chapter 5

1   Allen K. Jones cited in Ghanea, *Human Rights*, 7–8.

2   For more about the Báb's life and teachings, see Hasan Balyuzi, *The Báb: The Herald of the Day of Days* (Oxford, UK: George Ronald, 1973) and Saiedi, *Gate of the Heart.*

3   Geoffrey Cameron, "The Bahá'í Community and Public Policy: The Bahá'í Refugee Resettlement Program (1981–1989)," in *Religion and Public Discourse in an Age of Transition: Reflections on Bahá'í Practice and Thought*, ed. Geoffrey Cameron and Benjamin Schewel (Waterloo, Ontario, CA: Wilfrid Laurier University Press, 2018), 257.

4   Firuz Kazemzadeh, "The Bahá'ís in Iran: Twenty Years of Repression," *Social Research* 67, no. 2 (2000): 538.

5   Ghanea describes their predicament as being effectively rendered "juridical non-persons" (Ghanea, *Human Rights*, 102).

6   Karlberg, "Constructive Resilience," 227. All charges have been found to be baseless and have been completely rejected by United Nations human rights bodies as well as by recognized scholars.

7   Richard Falk quoted in Ghanea, *Human Rights*, 102.

8   In 1980, all nine members of the National Spiritual Assembly of Iran were arrested and never heard from again. After a re-election, eight of the nine elected members were arrested and executed. Bahá'ís elected a third assembly: all were arrested, some were tortured, and four were executed. See Kazemzadeh, "Bahá'ís in Iran," 536–58.

9   *The Bahá'í World, 1950–1954*, vol. 12 (Wilmette, IL: Bahá'í Publishing Trust, 1956), 419.

10 Margaret E. Keck and Kathryn Sikkink, *Activists beyond Borders: Advocacy Networks in International Politics* (Ithaca, NY: Cornell University Press, 1998); Willetts, *"Conscience of the World."*

11 Consultative status is rooted in Article 71 of the UN Charter, which stipulates that "[t]he Economic and Social Council may make suitable arrangements for

consultation with non-governmental organizations which are concerned with matters within its competence." Accredited organizations must meet the criteria for "special competence in areas of activity of concern to the Council" and be recognized internationally for such expertise (United Nations, Charter of the United Nations).

12 United Nations Office of Public Information, "Non-Governmental Organizations in Consultative Status (as of December 31, 1970)," in *Yearbook of the United Nations 1970*, vol. 24 (New York: United Nations, 1972), 626–9.

13 Religiously affiliated NGOs in consultative status with the United Nations in 1970: Bahá'í International Community, International Council on Jewish Social and Welfare Services, Catholic International Union for Social Service, International Young Christian Workers, Commission of the Churches on International Affairs, Pax Romana, Consultative Council of Jewish Organizations, Salvation Army, Co-ordinating Board of Jewish Organizations, World Alliance of Young Men's Christian Associations, Friends World Committee for Consultation (Quaker), World Federation of Catholic Youth, International Catholic Child Bureau, World Jewish Congress, International Catholic Migration Commission, World Muslim Congress, International Catholic Union of the Press, World Student Christian Federation, International Christian Union of Business Executives, World Union of Catholic Women's Organizations, International Conference of Catholic Charities, World Young Women's Christian Association, International Council of Jewish Women, and World's Woman's Christian Temperance Union.

14 "Activities of the Bahá'í International Community Relating to Persecution," in *The Bahá'í World, 1979–1983*, vol. 18 (Haifa, Israel: Bahá'í World Centre, 1986), 414.

15 The building was the House of the Báb, the forerunner of Bahá'u'lláh, founder of the Bahá'í Faith.

16 "Activities of the Bahá'í International Community Relating to Persecution," 414.

17 Ibid., 415. The human rights bodies addressed by the BIC included: UN Center for Human Rights, UN Sub-Commission on Prevention of Discrimination and Protection of Minorities, UN Commission on Human Rights, UN Working Group on Enforced or Involuntary Disappearances, UN Committee on the Elimination of Racial Discrimination, International Labor Organization, and UN Committee against Torture.

18 This was the first UN agency to put the Bahá'í case on the UN agenda.

19 The Third Committee of the United Nations General Assembly deals with social, humanitarian affairs, and human rights issues. There are five other committees of the United Nations General Assembly, each addressing a different set of issues: First Committee—Disarmament & International Security; Second Committee—Economic & Financial; Fourth Committee—Special Political & Decolonization; Fifth Committee—Administrative & Budgetary; Sixth Committee—Legal.

20 Ghanea, *Human Rights,* 105.

21 Ibid.

22 Ibid., 108.

23 Sub-Commission on Prevention of Discrimination and Protection of Minorities, Question of the Violation of Human Rights and Fundamental Freedoms Including Policies of Racial Discrimination and Segregation and of Apartheid, in All Countries: Report of the Sub-Commission under Commission on Human Rights, Resolution 8 (XXXIII), September 9, 1981, operative para. 1.

24 *Bahá'í World, 1979–1983,* 422.

25 Universal House of Justice to the Bahá'ís of the World, January 26, 1982, *Bahai.org,* accessed September 23, 2019, https://www.bahai.org/library/authoritative-texts/sea rch?q=26+January+1982#s=messages-universal-house-justice.

26 United Nations General Assembly, Situation of the Human Rights in the Islamic Republic of Iran, A/RES/40/141, December 13, 1985, operative para. 8.

27 In the 1970s, the Commission on Human Rights began to look more systematically at specific countries violating human rights. As Ghanea notes, even as late as the 1970s, "UN human rights bodies were reluctant to mention particular States by name … this was, in fact, deemed as exceeding the limits of 'domestic jurisdiction'" (Ghanea, *Human Rights* 106). It took the Commission on Human Rights nearly thirty years to begin to look at specific countries as violators of human rights.

28 Universal House of Justice to the Bahá'ís of Iran, June 23, 2009, *Bahá'í World News Service,* accessed September 23, 2019, http://news.bahai.org/story/720/.

29 Universal House of Justice, "The Prosperity of Humankind," 1992, *Bahai.org,* accessed September 23, 2019, http://www.bahai.org/library/other-literature/ official-statements-commentaries/prosperity-humankind/prosperity-humankind. pdf?0dfc93cd.

30 Arash Abizadeh, "Politics beyond War: Ulrich Gollmer's Contribution to Bahá'í Political Thought," *World Order* 35, no. 3 (2004): 19.

31 Ibid.

32 Ibid., 21.

33 A principled adherence to modes of communicative action doesn't preclude engagement with or respect for partners who use more traditional political, or "strategic" approaches to achieve noble ends.

34 Ghanea, *Human Rights*, 8.

35 Cameron, "Bahá'í Community," 271.

36 Derek H. Davis, "The Evolution of Religious Freedom as a Universal Human Right: Examining the Role of the 1981 United Nations Declaration on the Elimination of All Forms of Intolerance and of Discrimination Based on Religion or Belief," *BYU Law Review* 217 (2002): 217–36, *BYU Law,* accessed March 6, 2020, http:// digitalcommons.law.byu.edu/lawreview/vol2002/iss2/2.

37   United Nations General Assembly, "Declaration on the Elimination of All Forms of Intolerance and of Discrimination Based on Religion or Belief," A/RES/36/55, November 25, 1981, http://www.refworld.org/docid/3b00f02e40.html.

38   United Nations General Assembly, "Convention against Torture and Other Cruel, Inhuman or Degrading Treatment or Punishment," *Treaty Series* 1465 (December 10, 1984): 85, http://www.refworld.org/docid/3ae6b3a94.html. As of 2020, Iran is not a party to this convention.

39   Cameron, "Baháʼí Community," 272.

40   Universal House of Justice to the Baháʼís of the World, January 26, 1982.

41   Universal House of Justice to All National Spiritual Assemblies, February 26, 1979, *Bahai.org*, ccessed September 23, 2019, http://www.bahai.org/library/authoritative-texts/search?q=26±February±1979#s=messages-universal-house-justice.

42   For further details, see Karlberg, "Constructive Resilience," 237. While the program was raided in 1998, with Iranian security officials breaking into some 500 homes, confiscating material, and arresting dozens of faculty, it was able to continue its operations. It provides higher education to Iranian students to this day. *The New York Times* referred to it as an "elaborate act of communal self-preservation" (Ethan Bronner, "Iran Closes University Run Covertly by the Bahais," *New York Times*, October 29, 1998, *Nytimes.com*, accessed September 23, 2019, http://www.nytimes.com/1998/10/29/world/iran-closes-university-run-covertly-by-the-bahais.html). See also Cameron and Ghanea, "Baháʼís in the Middle East," 176.

43   John Hutchinson, "Introduction: Global Perspectives on Religion, Nationalism and Politics," in *Religions in Movement: The Local and the Global in Contemporary Faith Traditions*, ed. Robert W. Hefner et al. (New York: Routledge, 2013), 9.

44   Susanne Hoeber Rudolph, "Introduction: Religion, States and Transnational Civil Society," in *Transnational Religion and Fading States*, ed. Susanne Hoeber Rudolph and James Piscatori (Boulder, CO: Westview Press, 1997), 2.

45   Carrette, "Paradox of Globalization," 46.

46   Shoghi Effendi, *World Order*, 19.

47   Daniel H. Nexon, "Religion and International Relations: No Leap of Faith Required," in *Religion and International Relations Theory*, ed. Jack Snyder (New York: Columbia University Press, 2011), 145–6.

48   This is prior to the period covered in this chapter but informs the subsequent elements in the table.

49   The Universal House of Justice, elected every five years, was designated by Shoghi Effendi as the supreme legislative body of the Administrative Order. Learn more at http://universalhouseofjustice.bahai.org/unique-institution.

50   For a description of the first election, see "The Universal House of Justice" in *The Baháʼí World,* 1963–8, 425–30.

51 Prior to 1967, the National Spiritual Assembly of the United States guided the work of the BIC.

52 Universal House of Justice, Department of the Secretariat to the National Spiritual Assembly of the Bahá'ís of the United States, December 7, 1983, *Bahai.org*, accessed September 23, 2019, http://www.bahai.org/library/authoritative-texts/the-universal-house-of-justice/messages/19831207_001/1#611484718. The sentence before the quoted excerpt reads: "Actions perceived to be appropriate within the framework of American society can be counterproductive when viewed in the broader framework of a world community."

53 Universal House of Justice, Constitution.

54 "The provenance, the authority, the duties, the sphere of action of the Universal House of Justice all derive from the revealed Word of Bahá'u'lláh which, together with the interpretations and expositions of the Centre of the Covenant and of the Guardian of the Cause—who, after 'Abdu'l-Bahá, is the sole authority in the interpretation of Bahá'í Scripture—constitute the binding terms of reference of the Universal House of Justice and are its bedrock foundation" (Ibid.).

55 Ibid.

56 The full translation into English of Bahá'u'lláh's laws (Kitáb-i-Aqdas, "Most Holy Book") would be published in 1993. For further treatment of the subject of Bahá'í Law, see Danesh, *Dimensions of Bahá'í Law*.

57 Sipilä would send messages of support to the 1977 Asian Bahá'í Women's conference in New Delhi; the 1978 West African Bahá'í Women's Conference in Monrovia, Liberia; and special greetings to the West African Bahá'í Women's Conference. She writes, "I know that the Bahá'í community supports fully the goals of the UN Decade for Women" (*The Bahá'í World, 1976–1979*, vol. 17 [Haifa, Israel: Bahá'í World Centre, 1981], 234).

58 The conference in Mexico was attended by 133 governments (113 member state delegations were headed by women), 114 NGOs, and 4,000 NGO delegates (Louis Emmerij, Richard Jolly, and Thomas G. Weiss, *Ahead of the Curve?: UN Ideas and Global Challenges* [Bloomington, IN: Indiana University Press, 2001], 82). For the first time, the United Nations evaluated the extent of problems and conditions of women in varying nations, specifically separating data by sex to bring to light the level of inequality and discrimination toward women (Devaki Jain, *Women, Development, and the UN: A Sixty-Year Quest for Equality and Justice* [Bloomington, IN: Indiana University Press, 2005], 64).

59 Jain, *Women*, 74.

60 These were the United Nations Research and Training Institute for the Advancement of Women (INSTRAW, 1980) and the United Nations Development Fund for Women (UNIFEM, 1976). They were the first global institutions at the United Nations assigned to women since the creation of the Commission on the Status of Women in 1946.

61 Emmerij, Jolly, and Weiss, *Ahead of the Curve*, 82. According to Jain, "Defining discrimination and setting up normative standards and mechanisms to identify and remedy" were among the greatest accomplishments of UN system related to women (*Women*, 89).

62 Judith P. Zinsser, "From Mexico to Copenhagen to Nairobi: The United Nations Decade for Women, 1975–1985," *Journal of World History* 13, no. 1 (2002): 142–3, www.jstor.org/stable/20078945.

63 United Nations General Assembly, "World Conference of the International Women's Year," A/RES/3520, December 15, 1975, http://www.refworld.org/docid/3b00f1a814.html.

64 Note that authoritative Baháʼí writings include those written by Baháʼu'lláh, ʻAbdu'l-Bahá, and Shoghi Effendi.

65 United Nations Research Institute for Social Development, "UNRISD Research and Policy Brief 11: Religion, Politics, and Gender Equality," May 2011, *United Nations Research Institute for Social Development*, http://www.unrisd.org/publications/rpb11e.

66 Emma Tomalin, ed., *Gender, Faith and Development*, Working in Gender & Development (Oxford, UK: Oxfam, 2011), 4, http://oxfamilibrary.openrepository.com/bitstream/handle/10546/144042/bk-gender-faith-development-290911-en.pdf?sequence=3&isAllowed=y.

67 ʻAbdu'l-Baha, *Selections*.

68 Baháʼí International Community, International Instruments and National Standards Relating to the Status of Women: Implementation of the Declaration on the Elimination of Discrimination against Women and Related Instruments, Commission on the Status of Women, E/CN.6/NGO/252, January 11, 1974, 3.

69 Universal House of Justice to all National Spiritual Assemblies, May 25, 1975, *Bahai.org*, accessed September 23, 2019, http://www.bahai.org/library/authoritative-texts/the-universal-house-of-justice/messages/19750525_001/19750525_001.xhtml?c2a175ae.

70 For a more complete list, see Baháʼí International Community, *Activities in the Baháʼí World Community to Improve the Status of Women during the United Nations Decade for Women*, Report presented to the World Conference to Review and Appraise the Achievements of the United Nations Decade for Women: Equality, Development and Peace (Nairobi, Kenya: Baháʼí International Community, July 15, 1985), *BIC.org*, http://www.bic.org/statements/activities-bahai-world-community-improve-status-women-during-united-nations-decade-women.

71 For a more complete list of BIC engagement in NGO committees during this period, see *The Baháʼí World, 1983–1986*, vol. 19 (Haifa, Israel: Baháʼí World Centre, 1994), 381.

72 Ibid., 381.

73 Ibid., 385.

74 The Convention on the Elimination of All Forms of Discrimination against Women was ratified in September 1981, faster than any previous human rights convention.

75 Moojan Momen quoted in Cameron and Ghanea, "Bahá'ís in the Middle East," 174. According to some estimates, by 1918–19, Bahá'í schools in Iran "accounted for about 10 percent of primary and secondary education in the country" (Cameron and Ghanea, "Bahá'ís in the Middle East," 174).

76 Ann Boyles, "Towards the Goal of Full Partnership: One Hundred and Fifty Years of the Advancement of Women," in *The Bahá'í World, 1993–1994*, vol. 22 (Haifa, Israel: Bahá'í World Centre, 1994), 237–76, *Bahai.org*, accessed September 23, 2019, http://www.bahai.org/documents/essays/boyles-ann/towards-goal-full-partnership.

77 Bahá'í International Community, International Instruments, 3.

78 Otto Diane, "'Gender Comment': Why Does the UN Committee on Economic, Social, and Cultural Rights Need a General Comment on Women?" *Canadian Journal of Women and the Law*, 14, no. 1 (2002): 18–19.

79 Ibid.

80 Jain, *Women*, 93.

81 The recipients included Argentina, Brazil, Costa Rica, Dahomey (present-day Benin), Dominican Republic, Ecuador, Fiji, Finland, Ghana, Gilbert and Ellice Islands, Guatemala, Hawaii, Honduras, Jamaica, Kenya, Laos, Mauritius, the Netherlands, Niger, Reunion, Spain, Swaziland, Thailand, Togo, United Republic of Tanzania, and the Winward Islands.

82 Bahá'í International Community, "The Spiritual Basis for Equality," Statement distributed at the NGO Forum '85 (Nairobi, Kenya: Bahá'í International Community, July 10, 1985), 2.

83 For further details about the BIC's engagement in gender equality issues at the United Nations, see Julia Berger, "A New Politics of Engagement: The Bahá'í International Community, the United Nations, and Gender Equality," in *Religion in Public Discourse in an Age of Transition: Reflections on Bahá'í Practice and Thought*, ed. Geoffrey Cameron and Benjamin Schewel (Waterloo, Ontario, CA: Wilfrid Laurier University Press, 2018), 221–54.

84 *Bahá'í World, 1983–1986*, 398.

85 In Bahá'í elections, individuals do not run or nominate candidates for elected office. Each elector votes for those individuals "who can best combine the necessary qualities of unquestioned loyalty, of selfless devotion, of a well-trained mind, of recognized ability and mature experience" (Shoghi Effendi, *Bahá'í Administration* [Wilmette, IL: US Bahá'í Publishing Trust, 1974], 88).

86 Universal House of Justice to the Bahá'ís of the World," March 25, 2007, *Bahai.org*, accessed September 23, 2019, http://www.bahai.org/library/authoritative-texts/the-universal-house-of-justice/messages/20070325_001/1#126035670.

87 Members of the community over the age of twenty-one are eligible to vote.

88 *Bahá'í World, 1983–1986*, 401.

89 Ibid., 402.

90 Bahá'í International Community, International Instruments.

91 Ibid.

92 Ibid.

93 Universal House of Justice, Ridván Message 1985, April 21, 1985, *Bahai.org*, accessed September 23, 2019, http://www.bahai.org/library/authoritative-texts/search?q=ridvan+1985#s=messages-universal-house-justice.

Chapter 6

1 United Nations Office of Public Information, "International Year of Peace," in *Yearbook of the United Nations 1970*, vol. 24 (New York: United Nations, 1972), 122.

2 As Jeffrey Haynes reminds us, the significant rise in the number of RNGOs was also associated with this period (*EUI Working Papers: Faith-Based Organisations at the United Nations* [San Domenico di Fiesole, Italy: European University Institute Press, 2013], 57).

3 Universal House of Justice, *Ridván Message 1985*, 1.

4 In response to the severity of the persecution, the Universal House of Justice mobilized national Bahá'í communities to mount diplomatic and public information campaigns worldwide in order to acquaint government officials with the situation in Iran, to familiarize them with the nature and aims of the Bahá'í community (as these had been grossly distorted through Iranian media), and to make use of all available international mechanisms and processes to stem the persecution. By 1986, UN diplomats and missions from most countries had learned of the situation of the Bahá'ís, as well as the aims and activities of the global Bahá'í community.

5 Germany's constitutional High Court ruled that the Bahá'í Administrative Order was inseparable from Bahá'í belief and community life—a judgment with far-reaching implications in a country in which the Bahá'í Faith had long been misrepresented as a "cult." The nature of Bahá'í elected bodies in Germany had been challenged by local authorities as being technically incompatible with the requirements of German civil law (Universal House of Justice, "The German Court's Legal Recognition of Assembly Status," in *The Bahá'í World, 1983–1986*, vol. 19 [Haifa, Israel: Bahá'í World Centre, 1998], 571–608).

6 The Brazilian Chamber of Deputies held a special session to pay tribute to Bahá'u'lláh on the one hundredth anniversary of his ascension. On April 22, 1987, Mr. Donald Barrett, secretary-general of the Bahá'í International Community, and Mr. Shimon Perez, vice-premier and foreign minister of Israel, signed an agreement stating that "Israel recognizes the members of the Bahá'í Faith as a recognized

religious community in Israel ... and confirms that the Bahá'í World Centre is the world spiritual and administrative centre of the Bahá'í world community and that the Universal House of Justice in Haifa is the Head of the Bahá'í Faith" (*The Bahá'í World, 1986–1992*, vol. 20 [Haifa, Israel: Bahá'í World Centre, 1998], 192).

7   In 1986, there were 148 registered National Spiritual Assemblies and 4,627,800 Bahá'ís (David B. Barrett, "Religion: World Religious Statistics," in *1988 Encyclopedia Britannica Book of the Year*, ed. Daphne Daune and Louise Watson [Chicago, IL: Encyclopedia Britannica, 1988], 303).

8   Ibid.

9   Universal House of Justice to the Meeting of the Senior Officers of the United Nations Office and the Office of Public Information, October 29, 1986, *Bahai.org*, accessed September 23, 2019, http://www.bahai.org/library/authoritative-texts/the-universal-house-of-justice/messages/#d=19861029_001&f=f1.

10   Universal House of Justice, *Ridván 1985 Message*.

11   Universal House of Justice, "The Six Year International Teaching Plan," in *The Bahá'í World, 1986–1992*, vol. 20 (Haifa, Israel: Bahá'í World Centre, 1998), 131.

12   Universal House of Justice to the Meeting of the Senior Officers. It is important to note that this chapter doesn't attempt to summarize the totality of the BIC's work between 1986 and 2008.

13   Universal House of Justice, "The Promise of World Peace," 1985, *Bahai.org*, accessed September 23, 2019, http://www.bahai.org/library/authoritative-texts/the-universal-house-of-justice/messages/#d=19851001_001&f=f1.

14   This designation was given to 315 organizations and 58 cities around the world.

15   Oliver P. Richmond, "Reclaiming Peace in International Relations," *Millennium: Journal of International Studies* 36, no. 3 (May 2008): 439.

16   John Paul Lederach, "Spirituality and Religious Peacebuilding," in *Religion, Conflict, and Peacebuilding*, ed. Atalia Omer, R. Scott Appleby, and David Little (New York: Oxford University Press, 2015), 550.

17   Nader Saiedi, "Replacing the Sword with the Word: Bahá'u'lláh's Concept of Peace," *The Bahá'í World*, accessed September 15, 2019, http://bahaiworld.bahai.org/articles/replacing-sword-word/.

18   United Nations, Charter, 1.

19   Boutros Boutros-Ghali, *An Agenda for Peace: Preventive Diplomacy, Peacemaking and Peace-Keeping*. Report of the Secretary General Pursuant to the Statement Adopted by the Summit Meeting of the Security Council on January 31, 1992, S/24111 (New York: United Nations, 1992).

20   Both Boutros-Ghali's *Agenda for Peace* and the United Nations' Report of the Panel on United Nations Peace Operations ("Brahimi Report") identify three dimensions of UN peace operations: (a) conflict-prevention and peacemaking; (b) peacekeeping; and (c) peacebuilding. In 2004, expanding the concept further still,

the UN Secretary-General's High-Level Panel on Threats, Challenges and Change concluded that contemporary threats to peace now include "a whole range of issues that have not traditionally been considered as part of the peace and security nexus at all—poverty, environmental degradation, pandemic diseases and the spread of organized crime" (Richmond, "Reclaiming Peace," 439–40).

21 Richmond defines "liberal peace" as "an institutional peace to provide international governance and guarantees, a constitutional peace to ensure democracy and free trade, and a civil peace to ensure freedom and rights within society" ("Reclaiming Peace," 439–40). See also Oliver P. Richmond, *The Transformation of Peace* (New York: Palgrave, 2005), 2.

22 Richmond, "Reclaiming Peace," 441.

23 Scholar of religion and conflict Atalia Omer notes that the "theological genre resonates with works on forgiveness, nonviolence and reconciliation that ... seek to identify an ethics and practice of reconciliation and peace from within the resources of a given tradition" (Atalia Omer, "Religious Peacebuilding: The Exotic, the Good, and the Theatrical," in *The Oxford Handbook of Religion, Conflict, and Peacebuilding*, ed. Atalia Omer, R. Scott Appleby, and David Little [New York: Oxford University Press, 2015], 8). A growing body of scholars is beginning to address the religious and spiritual resources for peacebuilding, among them: James Heft, ed., *Beyond Violence: Religious Sources of Social Transformation in Judaism, Christianity, and Islam* (New York: Fordham University Press, 2004); Tanya B. Schwartz, *Faith-Based Organizations in Transnational Peacebuilding* (New York: Rowman & Littlefield International, 2018); and Joyce S. Dubensky, ed., *Peacemakers in Action: Profiles in Religious Peacebuilding*, vol. 2 (New York: Cambridge University Press, 2016).

24 Dubois and Hunter-Bowman, "Intersection," 569.

25 A detailed examination of this multi-faceted concept is beyond the scope of this chapter. For more on this subject, see Saiedi, "Replacing the Sword with the Word."

26 Bahá'u'lláh, *Gleanings*, 286.

27 Shoghi Effendi, *World Order*, 41.

28 Note that Shoghi Effendi refers to various types of diversity, including ethnic origins, climate, history, language, tradition, thought, and habit.

29 Vivienne Jabri, *War and the Transformation of Global Politics* (London: Palgrave, 2007), 268.

30 Shoghi Effendi, *World Order*, 42.

31 United Nations Economic and Social Council, "Constitution of the United Nations Educational, Scientific and Cultural Organization," November 16, 1945, in *Basic Texts: 2018 Edition* (Paris: UNESCO, 2018), 6.

32 Universal House of Justice, "Promise of World Peace."

33 Bahá'u'lláh, *Tablets*, 67.

34 Bahá'í International Community, "Prosperity of Humankind."

35 Universal House of Justice, "Promise of World Peace," 1.

36 Bahá'í International Community, "A Turning Point for All Nations," October 1, 1995, *Bahai.org*, accessed September 22, 2019, http://www.bahai.org/library/other-literature/official-statements-commentaries/turning-point-all-nations/#r=tpan_en-title.

37 Bahá'í International Community, "Peace among the Nations," 1, Bahá'í International Community United Nations Office Archives, New York.

38 Bahá'í World Centre, "External Affairs Strategy," Internal Memo to National Spiritual Assemblies and to the Bahá'í International Community Office at the United Nations (October 10, 1994) (Haifa, Israel: Bahá'í World Centre, 1994), 1.

39 Ibid.

40 Shoghi Effendi, *World Order*, 162.

41 For a further discussion about this distinction, see Universal House of Justice, "Promise of World Peace," section 2.

42 United Nations Economic and Social Council, Constitution, 1.

43 Dubois and Hunter-Bowman, "Intersection," 576.

44 Talal Asad, *Formations of the Secular: Christianity, Islam, Modernity* (Stanford, CA: Stanford University Press, 2003), 179. Similarly, theologian Charles Taylor contrasts "ordinary time" and "higher time" (Charles Taylor, *A Secular Age* [Cambridge, MA: Harvard University Press, 2007], 547).

45 Dubois and Hunter-Bowman, "Intersection," 572.

46 Bahá'í World Centre, "External Affairs Strategy," 1.

47 Ibid.

48 Ibid.

49 Richard Jolly, Louis Emmerij, and Thomas G. Weiss, *UN Ideas That Changed the World* (Bloomington, IN: Indiana University Press, 2009), 1.

50 It is the difference, for example, between advocating for more funding for the education of girls and the consideration of the broader role of girls and boys in the flourishing of society, as well as the conditions required for them to carry out this role.

51 During the period in question, the BIC participated actively in the following major UN summits (not an exhaustive list): World Summit for Children (1990); World Conference on Education for All (1990); UN Conference on Environment and Development (1992); World Conference on Human Rights (1993); UN Global Conference on Sustainable Development of Small Island Developing States (1994); International Conference on Population and Development (1994); Fourth World Conference on Women (1995); World Summit on Social Development (1995); Second UN Conference on Human Settlements (1996); World Food Summit (1996); World Youth Forum (1996, 1998, 2001); Millennium Summit (2000); World Conference against Racism, Racial Discrimination, Xenophobia, and Related Intolerance (2001);

Special Session of the General Assembly on Children (2002); World Assembly on Ageing (2002); World Summit on Sustainable Development (2002); World Summit on the Information Society (2003); and the 2005 World Summit (High-Level Plenary Meeting of the sixtieth session of the UN General Assembly).

52 Nora McKeon, *The United Nations and Civil Society: Legitimizing Global Governance—Whose Voice?* (London: Zed Books, 2009), 10.

53 Note that in 1989 the BIC established an Office for the Environment.

54 *Agenda 21: Programme of Action for Sustainable Development; Rio Declaration on Environment and Development* is the final text of agreements negotiated by governments at the "Earth Summit."

55 The BIC was one of thirteen NGOs selected by UNCED secretariat, from over 1,400 accredited NGOs, to make an oral statement to the plenary session of the summit (Bahá'í International Community, "Participation of the Bahá'í International Community Office of the Environment in the Process Leading up to and Including the United Nations World Summit for Social Development," 3–4).

56 The Earth Charter was spearheaded by Maurice Strong and Mikhail Gorbachev in 1987 in response to the World Commission on Environment and Development's call for a new charter to guide the transition to sustainable development. The initiative gave rise to unprecedented worldwide consultations concerning the ethical and moral foundations of sustainable development. The BIC participated extensively throughout the entire process, both in terms of submitting suggested text and playing a leadership role among civil society. Although the BIC was not able to endorse the final version of the charter, it continued to support the initiative that sought to establish widespread agreement on such principles.

57 The Peace Monument was built by the BIC and the Bahá'í community of Brazil for the conference. The top of the monument bears the words of Bahá'u'lláh: "The earth is but one country, and mankind its citizens," and inside is deposited soil from nearly 150 countries. The monument "also served as a very high profile example of a project which fostered collaboration between … NGOs, the business sector, local, state and national government bodies, and the governments of many nations" (Bahá'í International Community, "Participation of the Bahá'í International Community Office of the Environment in the Process Surrounding the United Nations Conference on Environment and Development" [UNCED/Earth Summit: December 1989–June 1992], 88, Bahá'í International Community United Nations Office Archives, New York).

58 In 1992, the BIC established an Office for the Advancement of Women (OAW), which guided the formation and efforts of over fifty national OAW offices throughout the world.

59 United Nations Entity for Gender Equality and the Empowerment of Women, "The Beijing Platform for Action: Inspiration Then and Now," *UN Women*, accessed September 23, 2019, https://beijing20.unwomen.org/en/about.

60 Of the 2,000 NGOs accredited to the conference, 50 were given the opportunity to present an oral statement. The BIC gave its spot to representatives of the Moscow Center for Gender Studies as a way of enabling the voices of women from Russia to be heard in this venue.

61 United Nations General Assembly, *Copenhagen Declaration on Social Development.*

62 Of the over 2,400 registered organizations, only 40 NGOs and NGO coalitions were able to make statements during the ten plenary sessions. (Bahá'í International Community, "Report on Bahá'í Participation in the World Summit for Social Development and the Parallel NGO Forum '95," 5. Bahá'í International Community United Nations Archives, New York)

63 Bahá'í International Community, Participation of the Bahá'í International Community Office of the Environment in the Process Leading up to and Including the United Nations World Summit for Social Development (March 6–12, 1995) and the Parallel NGO Forum '95 (March 2–12, 1995), 5, Bahá'í International Community United Nations Office Archives, New York.

64 Bahá'í International Community, "Bahá'í United Nations Representative Addresses World Leaders at Millennium Summit," March 6, 2000, *Bahai.org*, accessed September 25, 2019, http://www.bic.org/news/bahai-united-nations-representative-addresses-world-leaders-millennium-summit-0.

65 As nearly all statements refer to more than one theme, the total number of statements in the chart far exceeds the number of statements issued. A full 45 percent of the statements concerned human rights; of these, about 25 percent addressed the persecution of the Bahá'í community in Iran and were delivered at successive sessions of the (then) Commission on Human Rights and its various mechanisms. It must be noted that many of the human rights statements belong to a special category, that is, they were not seeking to influence ideas more broadly per se but were often trying to appeal to the international community to address and stem the acute, persistent, and debilitating persecution of the Bahá'í community in Iran.

66 A number of internal and external factors shaped the BIC decision to issue a statement to the United Nations. External factors included, for example, incidents of persecution of the Bahá'í community requiring urgent diplomatic attention. (The BIC issued forty statements during this period addressing the issue of the persecution of the Bahá'í community in Iran.) They also included UN-driven factors such as the number of opportunities to issue statements on particular issues (including the number of UN bodies/agencies addressing particular issues, UN conferences, international years, anniversaries, regional meetings), opportunities to provide input on draft UN documents and reports, and opportunities to co-draft or co-sign NGO statements. BIC-driven factors are intimately associated with the impetus to give expression to the substrate. In addition to substrate-driven ones,

there were also human resource factors (for instance, existing expertise on a given issue, availability of BIC staff and resources), as well as any specific instructions or requests from the Universal House of Justice.

67 These statements included: "The Promise of World Peace" (1985, International Year of Peace); "World Citizenship: A Global Ethic for Sustainable Development" (1993, UN Commission for Sustainable Development); "A Turning Point for All Nations" (1995, fiftieth Anniversary of the United Nations); "The Greatness Which Might Be Theirs" (1995, UN Fourth World Conference on Women); "The Prosperity of Humankind" (1995, World Summit for Social Development); "Valuing Spirituality in Development" (1998, World Faiths Development Dialogue); "Who Is Writing the Future? Reflections on the Twentieth Century" (1999, general); "Freedom to Believe: Upholding the Universal Standard of Human Rights" (2005, Response to UNDP Human Development Report); "The Search for Values in an Age of Transition" (2005, sixtieth Anniversary of the United Nations); and "Beyond Legal Reform: Culture and Capacity in the Eradication of Violence against Women and Girls" (2006, general). National Spiritual Assemblies were encouraged to translate the statements into their respective languages.

68 Bahá'í International Community, "Prosperity."

69 Bahá'í International Community, "Overcoming Corruption and Safeguarding Integrity in Public Institutions," May 28, 2001, *BIC.org*, accessed September 23, 2019, https://www.bic.org/statements/overcoming-corruption-and-safeguarding-integrity-public-institutions-bahai-perspective.

70 Universal House of Justice, "Promise," 1.

71 Bahá'í International Community, "Beyond Legal Reforms: Culture and Capacity in the Eradication of Violence against Women and Girls," July 2, 2006, *BIC.org*, accessed September 23, 2019, http://www.bic.org/statements/beyond-legal-reforms-culture-and-capacity-eradication-violence-against-women-and-girls.

72 Bahá'í International Community, "Religious Values and the Measurement of Poverty and Prosperity," Bahá'í International Community United Nations Archives, New York.

73 Bahá'í International Community, "Prosperity of Humankind."

74 Ibid.

75 Ibid. References to this concept are found in other BIC statements: "Often the target populations of poverty eradication projects are perceived as masses of undernourished people, overwhelmed by their circumstances and needs rather than capable agents of change in their communities. The challenge for development efforts is to find methods that allow individuals and communities to solve their own problems; the ability of a community to take on more complex social issues is a key indicator of progress" (Bahá'í International Community, "A New Framework for Global Prosperity," Submission to the 2006 Commission on Social Development

on the Review of the First United Nations Decade for the Eradication of Poverty, January 1, 2006, *BIC.org*, accessed September 23, 2019, http://www.bic.org/statements/new-framework-global-prosperity).

76 Bahá'í International Community, "The Role of Religion in Promoting the Advancement of Women," Statement to the United Nations Fourth World Conference on Women, September 13, 1995, *BIC.org*, accessed September 23, 2019, http://www.bic.org/statements/role-religion-promoting-advancement-women.

77 The Bahá'í community saw the conferences as milestones in the long march toward the Lesser Peace: the global community was developing and demonstrating its capacity to come together, conference after conference, to consult on issues of global import on an unprecedented scale. In the report of its participation at the Earth Summit, the BIC noted that among its aims at the conference was "unify[ing] efforts of NGOs," both among themselves and between NGOs and governments; among it aims at the World Summit for Social Development was "influenc[ing] processes of the Lesser Peace"; among its aims at the Fourth Women's Conference in Beijing was "be[ing] of service to conference organizers" (Bahá'í International Community, "Report of Bahá'í Participation in the Fourth World Conference on Women (September 4–15, 1995)," Bahá'í International Community United Nations Office Archives, New York).

78 Bahá'í International Community, "Turning Point," 7.

79 Universal House of Justice, "Promise of World Peace."

80 Bahá'í International Community, "Who Is Writing the Future?: Reflections on the Twentieth Century," February 1999, *Bahai.org*, accessed September 22, 2019, http://www.bahai.org/documents/bic-opi/who-writing-future.

81 While the question of methods used by religious NGOs at the United Nations has received some attention in the literature, it nevertheless belies a narrow understanding of the operation of normative foundations of such processes. As one scholar notes, "Whenever a process is used by an RNGO that displays a religious, spiritual, or faith-inspired nature, identity or language, this process can be seen as a 'religious process'" (Verena Beittinger-Lee, "Blessing or Bother?: Religion and Religious NGOs at the UN in New York," in *Religion, NGOs and the United Nations: Visible and Invisible Actors in Power*, ed. Jeremy Carrette and Hugh Miall [London: Bloomsbury, 2017], 149). The challenge of such an approach is that without an awareness of the substrate, the researcher does not fully appreciate the manner in which the organization is acting on its understanding of particular normative foundations. How does a researcher recognize that an orientation toward particular forms of deliberation is inspired by a religious tradition?

82 In the months and years leading up to the conferences, the BIC was invited and/or elected to leadership roles in many committees (e.g., a BIC representative was elected to the Global Facilitating Committee of the Fourth World Conference on Women and invited as convener of the NGO Forum Working Group for this conference).

83 Religion Counts, *Religion and Public Policy*, 37.

84 Ibid.

85 The Bahá'í International Community's Office of Public Information elaborates that the Lesser Peace "implies the achievement of a relationship among [the nations] that will enable them to resolve questions of international import through consultation rather than war" (Bahá'í International Community, "Peace among the Nations").

86 This is significant because BIC representatives do not put their names forward for election; rather, they are nominated by their peers, and a committee vote determines the selection of the candidate.

87 The International Steering Committee consisted of the NGO Forum coordinator, the chairs of the three planning groups, the president of the Conference of NGOs (CONGO), and the past coordinator of Forum 1985. The committee was responsible for setting the tone and agenda for the then-largest-to-date gathering of NGOs. The BIC representative served on this committee from 1992 to 1995. During the Beijing conference, the BIC representative was also the chair of the NGO Planning Group in New York ("NGO Focal Point"), and another Bahá'í representative was elected to chair the Indigenous Women's Caucus. The BIC representative in Geneva was elected to the position of convener of the Geneva Working Group on the Beijing NGO Forum ("Forum '95'").

88 This is the largest NGO committee at the United Nations. The BIC has been elected to the position of chair or to other executive office positions on this committee almost every year from 1992 until the end of this period.

89 The CONGO's vision is to be the primary support and platform for a civil society represented by a global community of informed, empowered, and committed NGOs that fully participate with the United Nations in decision-making and programs leading to a better world, a world of economic and social justice. For details, see Conference of NGOs in Consultative Relationship with the United Nations, "Vision, Mission and Objectives," *NGOCongo.org*, accessed September 2019, http://www.ngocongo.org/who-we-are/vision-mission-and-objectives.

90 Others include chair of NGO committees on human rights, freedom of religion or belief, social development, UNIFEM, UNICEF, Task Forces on UN Reform, Task Force on Access to the UN; as well as executive positions on NGO committees on human settlements, development, youth, family, and the UN Department of Public Information.

91 Jeffrey Haynes, *Faith-Based Organizations at the United Nations* (New York: Palgrave, 2014), 169.

92 Bahá'í International Community, "Report of Bahá'í Participation in the Fourth World Conference on Women," 6.

93 Universal House of Justice to the Bahá'ís of Iran.

94 Lawrence Arturo, personal e-mail to the author, February 10, 2017. Another example of this is the BIC's role on the Facilitation Committee of the Gender Equality Architecture Reform Campaign (2006–10), which mobilized over 300 NGOs—both secular and religious—to join together to advocate for the creation of UN Women—a new UN entity that consolidated the work of four disparate UN bodies working on gender equality.

95 Bahá'í World Centre, "External Affairs Strategy," 1.

96 Bahá'í International Community, "Role of Religion."

97 Bahá'í World Centre, "External Affairs Strategy," 6.

98 The BIC was involved at national, regional, and international levels in preparatory meetings. BIC representatives attended regional and preparatory committee meetings ("PrepComs"), were involved in caucuses, and interacted extensively with government and UN officials on drafting documents. Some National Spiritual Assemblies also participated in national consultations leading up to these conferences.

99 They were also the largest delegation of NGOs at the official Habitat Conference and possibly the largest contingent of representatives of an NGO at the NGO Forum (Bahá'í International Community, "Participation of the Bahá'í International Community Office of the Environment in the Process Leading Up to and Including the Second UN Conference on Human Settlements—Habitat II (June 3–14, 1996) and the Parallel NGO Forum (May 30–June 14, 1996)," 2, Bahá'í International Community United Nations Office Archives, New York).

100 For further details, see Bahá'í International Community, *Human Rights Education Training Manual*, Bahá'í International Community United Nations Office Archives, New York.

Chapter 7

1 Universal House of Justice to the Bahá'ís of Iran.

2 Razavi, "Bahá'í Participation," 179.

3 Bahá'í World Centre, "External Affairs Strategy," 4–5. During this time, the Universal House of Justice described the Bahá'í community's engagement in society in terms of three interrelated areas: efforts to expand and develop the Bahá'í community, social action (encompassing social and economic development), and participation in the discourses of society. See Universal House of Justice, Ridván Message 2010, April 2, 2010, *Bahai.org*, accessed June 10, 2020 http://www.bahai.org/library/authoritative-texts/the-universal-house-of-justice/messages/20100421_001/1#178319844.

4 Bahá'u'lláh, *The Tabernacle of Divine Unity: Bahá'u'lláh's Responses to Manikchi Sahib and Other Writings* (Haifa, Israel: Bahá'í World Centre, 2006), 5.

5 Foucault, *Archaeology of Knowledge*, 49.

6 Michael Karlberg, "The Power of Discourse and the Discourse of Power: Pursuing Peace through Discourse Intervention," *International Journal of Peace Studies* 10, no. 1 (2005): 1, http://www.jstor.org/stable/41852070. Foucault argues that it is a combination of power, knowledge, and truth that generates the effects of a discourse (Sara Mills, *Discourse* [New York: Routledge, 1997], 15).

7 For more details, see Foucault, *Madness and Civilization*. He carried out a similar analysis with respect to the development of the history of medicine in *The Birth of the Clinic: An Archeology of Medical Perception* (London: Tavistock, 1973).

8 Bahá'í International Community, "Bahá'í International Community's Quadrennial Report (2010–2013)," 6–7.

9 Universal House of Justice to the Bahá'ís of Iran.

10 Bahá'í World Centre, "External Affairs Strategy."

11 Universal House of Justice to the Bahá'ís of Iran.

12 Turan Kayaoğlu, "Giving an Inch Only to Lose a Mile: Muslim States, Liberalism, and Human Rights in the United Nations," *Human Rights Quarterly* 36, no. 1 (2014): 74, doi.org/10.1353/hrq.2014.0004.

13 Ibid., 64.

14 Ibid., 70.

15 Kerstin Martens, *NGOs and the United Nations: Institutionalization, Professionalization and Adaptation* (New York: Palgrave, 2005).

16 These reports are required of all NGOs in consultative status.

17 The Millennium Development Goals (MDGs) were eight international development goals, set by UN Member States in the year 2000, to be achieved by 2015. The goals were: eradicate extreme poverty and hunger; to achieve universal primary education; promote gender equality and empower women; reduce child mortality; improve maternal health; combat HIV/AIDS, malaria, and other diseases; ensure environmental sustainability; and develop a global partnership for development. The Sustainable Development Goals (SDGs) succeeded the MDGs in 2016.

18 Bahá'í International Community, "Bahá'í International Community's Quadrennial Report (2010–2013)," 6–7.

19 The agencies included the UN Population Fund (UNFPA), the Joint United Nations Programme on HIV/AIDS (UNAIDS), the United Nations Children's Fund (UNICEF), the UN Development Programme (UNDP), and the UN High Commissioner for Refugees (UNHCR). In formulating its guidelines, the UNDP invited the BIC Offices to comment on an early draft of the guidelines. In response, the BIC offered to convene a consultation so as to enable wider input on the draft.

20 United Nations Children's Fund, *Partnering with Religious Communities for Children* (New York: UNICEF, 2000), 51.

21 Ibid., 54–5.

22 United Nations Population Fund, "Guidelines for Engaging Faith-Based Organizations (FBOs) as Agents of Change" (New York: UNFPA, 2009), 3, *UNFPA. org*, accessed September 23, 2019, https://www.unfpa.org/sites/default/files/resource-pdf/fbo_engagement.pdf.

23 Azza Karam, "Concluding Thoughts on Religion and the United Nations: Redesigning the Culture of Development," *CrossCurrents* 60, no. 3 (2010): 472, doi:10.1111/j.1939-3881.2010.00143.x.

24 Haynes, *Faith-Based Organizations*, 170.

25 Kayaoğlu, "Giving an Inch," 72–3.

26 Haynes, *Faith-Based Organizations*, 482.

27 The BIC's annual reports during this (and the previous) period document extensive engagement in civil society processes aimed at strengthening human rights mechanisms, such as the Human Rights Council, its special procedures, and the Universal Periodic Review. BIC representatives during this period served as presidents of both the New York- and Geneva-based NGO Committees on Freedom of Religion or Belief, as a member of the European Platform on Religious Intolerance and Discrimination, and were invited to speak on panels addressing human rights and religions, the defamation of religions, and discrimination against religious minorities.

28 Berger, "New Politics," 223.

29 Clarke and Jennings, "Introduction."

30 "Exploring the Role of Religion in Europe, BIC Hosts Event at European Parliament," May 13, 2019, *BIC.org*, accessed May 31, 2019, http://www.bic.org/news/exploring-role-religion-europe-bic-hosts-event-european-parliament.

31 Ibid.

32 United Nations General Assembly, "Report of the Secretary-General on the Work of the Organization (2011)," A/66/1, 4, Dag Hammarskjöld Library, New York. It was the call from civil society, for example, that urged the United Nations to institute dramatic changes to its gender equality institutions. After a widespread four-year campaign (2006–10) involving NGOs across a wide spectrum of expertise—including religious and faith-based organizations—UN Women, a new UN entity, was created.

33 United Nations General Assembly, "Report of the Secretary-General on the Work of the Organization (2015)," UN.org, accessed September 23, 2019, http://www.un.org/en/ga/search/view_doc.asp?symbol=A/70/1. The United Nations launched a worldwide social media campaign to solicit civil society input on the articulation of the Sustainable Development Goals, exerting unprecedented effort to bring all peoples to bear on the creation of an international development agenda that would reflect the aspirations of countries large and small; urban and rural populations; the voices of men, women, girls, and boys; and a variety of socioeconomic realities.

34 United Nations General Assembly, "Report of the Secretary-General on the Work of the Organization (2016)," A/71/1, 4, Dag Hammarskjöld Library, New York.

35 United Nations General Assembly, "Report of the Secretary-General on the Work of the Organization (2011)," 1.

36 Brown, *Edgework*, 73–4; emphasis added.

37 Ibid.

38 Ibid.

39 United Nations General Assembly, "UN75 People's Declaration & Plan for Global Action: Humanity at a Crossroads: Global Solutions for Global Challenges," May 14–15, 2020, *UN.org*, accessed May 31, 2020, http://www.un.org/pga/74/wp-content/uploads/sites/99/2020/05/Updated-Final-Peoples-Declaration-and-Plan-of-Global-Action-2-JJ-edit-1.pdf.

40 Bani Dugal, "Women, Faith, and Human Rights," October 2, 2017, *BIC.org*, accessed May 31, 2020, http://www.bic.org/perspectives/women-faith-and-human-rights.

41 Universal House of Justice to the Bahá'ís of Iran.

42 Universal House of Justice to the Conference of the Continental Boards of Counsellors, December 28, 2010, *Bahai.org*, accessed September 23, 2019, https://www.bahai.org/library/authoritative-texts/search?q=28+December+2010#s=messages-universal-house-justice.

43 Bahá'í International Community, Influencing Culture, Draft concept note, 1, Bahá'í International Community United Nations Office Archives, New York.

44 Ibid., 2.

45 United Nations General Assembly, "Report of the Secretary-General on the Work of the Organization," 9.

46 Bahá'í International Community, "Bahá'í International Community's United Nations Office and Representation to the European Union: Year in Review 2012," 5, Bahá'í International Community United Nations Office Archives, New York.

47 "When a meeting, or part thereof, is held under the Chatham House Rule, participants are free to use the information received, but neither the identity nor the affiliation of the speaker(s), nor that of any other participant, may be revealed" (Chatham House, "Chatham House Rule," *ChathamHouse.org*, accessed September 23, 2019, https://www.chathamhouse.org/chatham-house-rule#). The aim is to encourage openness of discussion and facilitate the sharing of information.

48 See Serik Tokbolat, "Ensuring Substantive Collaboration with Civil Society in Implementing Agenda 2030," September 28, 2016, *BIC.org*, accessed September 23, 2019, http://www.bic.org/perspectives/perspective-ensuring-substantive-collaboration-civil-society-implementing-agenda-2030.

49 Atwood, *From the Inside Out*, 17.

50 Religion Counts, *Religion and Public Policy*, 37.

51 For further details, see Berger, "New Politics."

52 United Nations Entity for Gender Equality and the Empowerment of Women, "Beijing Platform." The "Platform for Action" outlines "12 Critical Areas of Concern."

53 The Facilitation Committee included representatives of the Center for Global Leadership, the International Planned Parenthood Federation, the International Women's Health Coalition, the Women's Environment and Development Organization, and the World Federalist Movement.

54 These included the Office of the Special Advisor on Gender Issues and Advancement of Women, the United Nations Development Fund for Women (UNIFEM), the Division for the Advancement of Women, and the United Nations International Research and Training Institute for the Advancement of Women.

55 For more details, see Faith and Feminism Working Group, "Objectives," *FaothFem. com*, accessed September 24, 2019, http://sites.google.com/bic.org/faithfem-com/objectives?authuser=0.

56 Faith and Feminism Working Group, "Oral Statement to the 60th Session of the Commission on the Status of Women," March 14–24, 2016, http://static1. squarespace.com/static/55120ecae4b01593abadc441/t/56f9745a906340974484b be2/1459188826781/FaithFemOralStatementCSW.docx.pdf. The statement was delivered by BIC representative Saphira Rameshfar, a member of the working group's Steering Committee, who had been invited to do so by the committee.

57 Bahá'í International Community, "Bahá'í International Community's Quadrennial Report UN (2010–2013)," 7.

58 Bahá'í International Community, "Empowerment as a Mechanism for Social Transformation: Bahá'í International Community's Contribution to the 51st Session of the Commission for Social Development," November 15, 2012, Bahá'í International Community United Nations Office Archive, New York; emphasis added.

59 Bahá'í International Community, "Beyond Mere Economics: A Moral Inquiry into the Roots of Empowerment," *BIC.org*, accessed September 23, 2019, http://www.bic. org/sites/default/files/pdf/status_of_women_final.pdf.

60 Bahá'í International Community, "Rising Together: Building the Capacity to Recover from Within," May 17, 2016, *BIC.org*, accessed September 23, 2019, http:// www.bic.org/statements/rising-together-building-capacity-recover-within.

61 Bahá'í International Community, "Beyond Balancing the Scales: The Roots of Equity, Justice and Prosperity for All," October 12, 2012, *BIC.org*, accessed September 23, 2019, http://www.bic.org/statements/beyond-balancing-scales-roots-equity-justice-and-prosperity-all; emphasis added.

62 Bahá'í International Community, "Summoning Our Common Will: A Bahá'í Contribution to the United Nations Global Development Agenda," October 13,

2015, *BIC.org*, accessed September 23, 2019, http://www.bic.org/statements/
summoning-our-common-will-bahai-contribution-united-nations-global-
development-agenda.

63 Ibid.

64 Ibid.

65 Bahá'í International Community, "Rising Together."

66 Bahá'í International Community, "Beyond Balancing"; emphasis added.

67 Although, of course, this is not the only consideration, these decisions also are
shaped by the BIC's own priority areas and the availability of human resources.

68 Bahá'í World Centre, "National and International External Affairs Endeavors of the
Worldwide Bahá'í Community," October 20, 2014, http://xn–80aab4a4d.xn–p1acf/
images/9/97/National_and_International_External_Affairs_Endeavours_of_the_
Worldwide.pdf.

69 Ibid.

70 Bahá'í International Community, "Bahá'í International Community's United
Nations Office," 3.

71 Bahá'í International Community, "BIC Offers Fresh Perspective at UN's Largest
Gathering on Gender Equality," March 25, 2019, *BIC.org*, accessed May 31, 2020,
http://www.bic.org/news/bic-offers-fresh-perspective-uns-largest-gathering-
gender-equality.

72 United Nations, *Beijing Declaration and Platform of Action, Adopted at the Fourth
World Conference on Women*, October 27, 1995, *Refworld.org*, accessed June 12,
2020, http://www.refworld.org/docid/3dde04324.html.

73 Bahá'í International Community, "Glimpses into the Spirit of Gender Equality:
Mwinilunga, Zambia," March 4, 2020, *BIC.org*, accessed May 31, 2020, http://
www.bic.org/news/glimpses-spirit-gender-equality-mwinilunga-zambia;
Bahá'í International Community, "Glimpses into the Spirit of Gender Equality:
Hasankheda, India," February 20, 2020, *BIC.org*, accessed May 31, 2020, http://
www.bic.org/news/glimpses-spirit-gender-equality-hasankheda-india; Bahá'í
International Community, "Glimpses into the Spirit of Gender Equality: Kejau,
Malaysia," February 27, 2020, *BIC.org*, accessed May 31, 2020, http://www.bic.
org/news/glimpses-spirit-gender-equality-kejau-malaysia; Bahá'í International
Community, "Glimpses into the Spirit of Gender Equality: Riohacha, Colombia,"
February 12, 2020, *BIC.org*, accessed May 31, 2020, http://www.bic.org/news/
glimpses-spirit-gender-equality-riohacha-colombia.

74 Bahá'í International Community, "Rising Generations: Weaving a New Tapestry of
Community Life," January 25, 2018, *BIC.org*, accessed May 31, 2020, http://www.
bic.org/statements/rising-generations-weaving-new-tapestry-community-life.

75 See, for example, Bahá'í International Community, "Summoning Our Common
Will"; Bahá'í International Community, "Builders of Civilization: Youth and the

Advancement of Humankind," May 2, 2014, *BIC.org*, accessed May 31, 2020, https://www.bic.org/statements/Builders-Civilization-Youth-and-Advancement-Humankind; Bahá'í International Community, "Rethinking Prosperity: Forging Alternatives to a Culture of Consumerism," May 3, 2020, *BIC.org*, accessed May 31, 2020, http://www.bic.org/statements/rethinking-prosperity-forging-alternatives-culture-consumerism.

76 Bahá'í International Community, "Bahá'í International Community's United Nations Office: Year in Review. (January 2013–August 2013)," 4, Bahá'í International Community United Nations Office Archives, New York.

77 Bahá'í International Community, "Rethinking Prosperity," 4.

78 See, for example, Serik Tokbolat, "Climate Education in and beyond the Classroom," July 23, 2015, *BIC.org*, accessed May 31, 2020, http://www.bic.org/perspectives/climate-education-and-beyond-classroom; Daniel Perell, "Why Participation Will Be So Important in Advancing the Post-2015 Agenda. Or: Zeroing in on the Zero Draft," June 17, 2015, *BIC.org*, accessed May 31, 2020, http://www.bic.org/perspectives/why-participation-will-be-so-important-advancing-post-2015-agenda-or-zeroing-zero-draft. Perspective pieces also generally did not require the approval of the Universal House of Justice and, as such, could be made public more quickly.

79 For example: Bahá'í International Community, "Interview with GEAR Campaign Representatives Part 1," July 30, 2010, *BIC.org*, accessed September 23, 2019, https://www.bic.org/videos/interview-gear-campaign-representatives-part-1. The BIC interviewed members of the leadership team of the Gender Equality Architecture Reform Campaign (BIC representative among them) to discuss the role of the campaign in the passage of the UN resolution to establish UN Women.

80 Bahá'í International Community, "Bahá'í International Community's United Nations Office Year in Review. (January 2013–August 2013)," 5.

81 Ibid.

82 Bahá'í World Centre, "National and International External Affairs," 8.

83 This list includes only the roles held by representatives at the BIC Office in New York.

84 The Faith and Feminism Working Group is a civil society-led coalition, targeting the gender equality discourse at the United Nations. It is comprised of faith-based organizations, scholars, secular organizations, and social justice groups working toward gender equality through the lens of faith and feminism. See https://sites.google.com/bic.org/faithfem-com/home?authuser=0, accessed June 14, 2020.

85 UNIFEM (the United Nations Development Fund for Women) was established in 1976 to provide financial and technical assistance to programs and initiatives that promoted women's human rights, political participation, and economic security. In 2011, UNIFEM was merged into UN Women, a composite entity of the UN, with

International Research and Training Institute for the Advancement of Women, Office of the Special Adviser on Gender Issues, and Division for the Advancement of Women.

86 The NGO Forum plans all civil society-related events for the annual meetings of the UN Commission on the Status of Women, which is attended by thousands of civil society representatives from around the world.

87 The NGO Major Group facilitates the participation of NGOs in processes related to the "High Level Political Forum," which is the main United Nations platform that reviews progress toward the Sustainable Development Goals (SDGs) at the global level.

88 The Working Group on Girls is a coalition of over eighty national and international NGOs dedicated to promoting the human rights of the girl child in all areas and stages of her life, advancing the inclusion and status of girls and assisting them to develop their full potential as women. See https://girlsrights.org, accessed June 14, 2020.

Chapter 8

1 Foucault, *Order of Things*, 168.
2 Consider the differences between concepts such as *ummah* (Islam), *sangha* (Buddhism), *kehillah* (Judaism)—they generally signify "community" but are also distinct in the way they understand the construction, role, and nature of that entity.
3 David Palmer, "Religion, Spiritual Principles, and Civil Society," in *Religion and Public Discourse in an Age of Transition: Reflections on Bahá'í Practice and Thought*, ed. Benjamin Schewel and Geoffrey Cameron (Waterloo, Ontario, CA: Wilfrid Laurier University Press, 2018), 44.
4 Ibid., 45.
5 Acharya and Buzan, *Making of Global*, 286.
6 Ibid., 3.
7 Peter M. Haas, "Introduction: Epistemic Communities and International Policy Coordination," *International Organization* 46, no. 1 (1992): 3, http://www.jstor.org/stable/2706951.
8 Paul Cloke, "Theo-Ethics and Radical Faith-Based Praxis in the Postsecular City," in *Exploring the Postsecular: The Religious, the Political, and the Urban*, ed. Arie L. Molendijk, Justin Beaumont, and Christoph Jedan (Leiden, the Netherlands: Brill, 2010), 210.
9 Universal House of Justice to the Bahá'ís of Iran.
10 See, for example, Asad, *Formations of the Secular*, and Taylor, *Secular Age*.

11 See Dubois and Bowman, "Intersection of Christian Theology," and Jarem
    Sawatsky, "Extending the Peacebuilding Timeframe: Revising Lederach's Integrative
    Framework," *Peace Research* 37, no. 1 (2005): 123–30, http://www.jstor.org/
    stable/24469691.

12 Brown, *Edgework*, 14.

13 Universal House of Justice, "Promise of World Peace," 2.

14 Victor de Araujo, Letter to National Spiritual Assemblies, July 1, 1970, Baháʼí
    International Community United Nations Office Archives, New York.

15 Acharya and Buzan, *Making of Global*, 303.

16 The Baháʼí community sees the UN conferences as milestones in the long march
    toward the Lesser Peace. The global community has been developing and
    demonstrating its capacity to come together, conference after conference, to consult
    on issues of global import on an unprecedented scale.

17 Shoghi Effendi, *World Order*, 43.

18 Ibid.

19 Karlberg, "Western Liberal Democracy," 134.

20 Ibid., 146.

21 Ibid., 136.

22 For example, Alexis de Tocqueville, *Democracy in America* (Chicago, IL: University
    of Chicago Press, 2002); Robert D. Putnam, "Bowling Alone: America's Declining
    Social Capital," *Journal of Democracy* 6, no. 1 (1995): 65–78. Of course, it is
    important to acknowledge that people come together not only around progressive
    causes but also to support racist, fanatical, and violent aims. The aims and values of
    the organization are just as, if not more, important as the collaboration itself.

23 Shoghi Effendi, *Promised Day*, 118.

24 Byrd, *Quaker Ways*, xv.

25 Baháʼí World Centre, "The Baháʼí Administrative Order," *Bahai.org*, accessed
    September 22, 2019, http://www.bahai.org/beliefs/essential-relationships/
    administrative-order/.

26 Shoghi Effendi, *World Order*, 154.

27 Universal House of Justice, Constitution, 4.

28 For more about the BIC Office in Geneva, see Baháʼí International Community,
    "United Nations Offices," *BIC.org*, accessed September 23, 2019, https://www.bic.
    org/offices/united-nations.

29 For more on this subject, see Ghanea, *Human Rights*; Baháʼí International
    Community, *The Baha'i Question Revisited: Persecution and Resilience in Iran* (New
    York: BIC, 2016), *BIC.org*, accessed May 31, 2020, http://www.bic.org/sites/default/
    files/pdf/iran/thebahaiquestionrevisited_final_160839e.pdf. For detailed, up-to-
    date coverage of the BIC's work in this area, see Baháʼí International Community,

"Situation of Baha'is in Iran," *BIC.org*, accessed September 23, 2019, http://www.bic.
org/focus-areas/situation-iranian-bahais.

30 For an exploration of the Bahá'í perspective on human rights see, for example,
John Barnabas Leith, "A More Constructive Encounter: A Bahá'í View of Religion
and Human Rights," in *Does God Believe in Human Rights?: Essays on Religion and
Human Rights*, ed. Nazila Ghanea, Alan Stephens, and Raphael Walden (Leiden,
the Netherlands: Brill, 2007), 121–44; Brian D. Lepard, *A Bahá'í Perspective on
International Human Rights Law* (Hong Kong: Juxta, 2012).

Bibliography

'Abdu'l-Bahá. *The Secret of Divine Civilization*. Wilmette, IL: US Bahá'í Publishing Trust, 1957.

'Abdu'l-Bahá. *Paris Talks*. 11th ed. London: UK Bahá'í Publishing Trust, 1972.

'Abdu'l-Bahá. *Selections from the Writings of 'Abdu'l-Bahá*. Haifa, Israel: Bahá'í World Centre, 1982a.

'Abdu'l-Bahá. *The Promulgation of Universal Peace*. 2nd ed. Wilmette, IL: US Bahá'í Publishing Trust, 1982b.

'Abdu'l-Bahá. *The Will and Testament of 'Abdu'l-Bahá*. Wilmette, IL: US Bahá'í Publishing Trust, 1990.

Abizadeh, Arash. "Politics beyond War: Ulrich Gollmer's Contribution to Bahá'í Political Thought." *World Order* 35, no. 3 (2004): 19–23.

Acharya, Amitav. *Rethinking Power, Institutions and Ideas in World Politics: Whose IR?* Abingdon, Oxon, UK: Routledge, 2014.

Acharya, Amitav, and Barry Buzan. *The Making of Global International Relations: Origin and Evolution of IR at Its Centenary*. Cambridge, UK: Cambridge University Press, 2019.

"Activities of the Bahá'í International Community Relating to Persecution." In *The Bahá'í World, 1979–1983*. Vol. 18, 414–15. Haifa, Israel: Bahá'í World Centre, 1986.

Alger, Chadwick. "The Emerging Roles of NGOs in the UN System: From Article 71 to a People's Millennium Assembly." *Global Governance* 8, no. 1 (2002): 93–117.

Amanat, Abbas. *Resurrection and Renewal: The Making of the Babi Movement in Iran, 1844–1850*. Ithaca, NY: Cornell University Press, 1989.

Andrews, Fannie Fern. "The Central Organization for a Durable Peace." *The Annals of the American Academy of Political and Social Science* 66, no. 1 (1916): 16–21. doi. org/10.1177/000271621606600104

Appleby, R. Scott. *The Ambivalence of the Sacred: Religion, Violence, and Reconciliation*. Oxford, UK: Rowman & Littlefield, 2000.

Araujo, Victor de. Letter from Victor de Araujo to National Spiritual Assemblies, July 1, 1970. Bahá'í International Community United Nations Office Archives, New York.

Arturo, Lawrence. Personal e-mail to the author, February 10, 2017.

Asad, Talal. *Formations of the Secular: Christianity, Islam, Modernity*. Stanford, CA: Stanford University Press, 2003.

Atwood, David. *From the Inside Out: Observations on Quaker Work at the United Nations*. Australia: The Religious Society of Friends, 2012.

Bahador, Babak, and Nazila Ghanea, eds. *Processes of Lesser Peace*. Oxford, UK: George Ronald, 2003.

Bahá'í International Community. "The Work of Bahá'ís in Promotion of Human Rights." Statement prepared for the United Nations Conference on Human Rights. Geneva, Switzerland. May 19–20, 1948. Office of the Secretary, United Nations Representative and Bahá'í International Community Files, National Bahá'í Archives, United States.

Bahá'í International Community. "Suggestions for Bahá'í Delegates to UN NGO Conferences." 1950 Bahá'í International Community United Nations Office Archives, New York.

Bahá'í International Community. "Letter to Mr. Dag Hammarskjöold, May 23, 1955." In *The Bahá'í World, 1954–1963*. Vol. 13, 796–7. Haifa, Israel: Bahá'í World Centre, 1970.

Bahá'í International Community. International Instruments and National Standards Relating to the Status of Women: Implementation of the Declaration on the Elimination of Discrimination against Women and Related Instruments. Commission on the Status of Women. E/CN.6/NGO/252. January 11, 1974.

Bahá'í International Community. *Activities in the Bahá'í World Community to Improve the Status of Women during the United Nations Decade for Women*. Report presented to the World Conference to Review and Appraise the Achievements of the United Nations Decade for Women: Equality, Development and Peace. Nairobi, Kenya: Bahá'í International Community, July 15, 1985. *BIC.org*. http://www.bic.org/ statements/activities-bahai-world-community-improve-status-women-during-united-nations-decade-women

Bahá'í International Community. "The Spiritual Basis for Equality." Statement distributed at the NGO Forum '85. Nairobi, Kenya: Bahá'í International Community, July 10, 1985.

Bahá'í International Community. "The Role of Religion in Promoting the Advancement of Women." Statement to the United Nations Fourth World Conference on Women. September 13, 1995. *BIC.org*. Accessed September 23, 2019. http://www.bic.org/ statements/role-religion-promoting-advancement-women

Bahá'í International Community. "A Turning Point for All Nations." October 1, 1995. *Bahai. org*. Accessed September 22, 2019. http://www.bahai.org/library/other-literature/official-statements-commentaries/turning-point-all-nations/#r=tpan_en-title

Bahá'í International Community. "Who Is Writing the Future?: Reflections on the Twentieth Century." February 1999. *Bahai.org*. Accessed September 22, 2019. http:// www.bahai.org/documents/bic-opi/who-writing-future

Bahá'í International Community. "Bahá'í United Nations Representative Addresses World Leaders at Millennium Summit." March 6, 2000. *Bahai.org*. Accessed September 23, 2019. http://www.bic.org/news/bahai-united-nations-representative-addresses-world-leaders-millennium-summit-0

Bahá'í International Community. "Overcoming Corruption and Safeguarding Integrity in Public Institutions." May 28, 2001. *BIC.org*. Accessed September 23, 2019. http:// www.bic.org/statements/overcoming-corruption-and-safeguarding-integrity-public-institutions-bahai-perspective

Bahá'í International Community. "A New Framework for Global Prosperity." Submission to the 2006 Commission on Social Development on the Review of the First United Nations Decade for the Eradication of Poverty. January 1, 2006a. *BIC.org.* Accessed September 23, 2019. http://www.bic.org/statements/new-framework-global-prosperity

Bahá'í International Community. "Beyond Legal Reforms: Culture and Capacity in the Eradication of Violence against Women and Girls." July 2, 2006b. *BIC.org.* Accessed September 23, 2019, https://www.bic.org/statements/beyond-legal-reforms-culture-and-capacity-eradication-violence-against-women-and-girls

Bahá'í International Community. *The Bahá'í Question: Cultural Cleansing in Iran.* New York: Bahá'í International Community, 2008.

Bahá'í International Community. "Interview with GEAR Campaign Representatives." July 30, 2010. *BIC.org.* Accessed September 23, 2019. http://www.bic.org/videos/interview-gear-campaign-representatives-part-1

Bahá'í International Community. "Beyond Balancing the Scales: The Roots of Equity, Justice and Prosperity for All." October 12, 2012a. *Bahai.org.* Accessed September 23, 2019. www.bic.org/statements/beyond-balancing-scales-roots-equity-justice-and-prosperity-all#SRiVP8TRjZbdVpR5.99

Bahá'í International Community. "Empowerment as a Mechanism for Social Transformation: Bahá'í International Community's Contribution to the 51st Session of the Commission for Social Development." November 15, 2012b. Bahá'í International Community United Nations Office Archive, New York.

Bahá'í International Community. *Bahá'í International Community's Quadrennial Report (2010–2013).* New York: Bahá'í International Community, 2014a. Bahá'í International Community United Nations Office Archives, New York.

Bahá'í International Community. "Builders of Civilization: Youth and the Advancement of Humankind." May 2, 2014b. *BIC.org.* Accessed May 31, 2020. https://www.bic.org/statements/builders-civilization-youth-and-advancement-humankind

Bahá'í International Community. "Summoning Our Common Will: A Bahá'í Contribution to the United Nations Global Development Agenda." October 13, 2015. *BIC.org.* Accessed September 23, 2019. http://www.bic.org/statements/summoning-our-common-will-Bahai-contribution-united-nations-global-development-agenda

Bahá'í International Community. *The Bahá'í Question Revisited: Persecution and Resilience in Iran.* New York: Bahá'í International Community, 2016. *BIC. org.* Accessed May 31, 2020. http://www.bic.org/sites/default/files/pdf/iran/thebahaiquestionrevisited_final_160839e.pdf

Bahá'í International Community. "Rising Generations: Weaving a New Tapestry of Community Life." January 25, 2018. *BIC.org.* Accessed May 31, 2020. http://www.bic.org/statements/rising-generations-weaving-new-tapestry-community-life

Bahá'í International Community. "BIC Offers Fresh Perspective at UN's Largest Gathering on Gender Equality." March 25, 2019. *BIC.org.* Accessed May 31, 2020. https://www.bic.org/news/bic-offers-fresh-perspective-uns-largest-gathering-gender-equality

Bahá'í International Community. "Beyond Mere Economics: A Moral Inquiry into the Roots of Empowerment." *BIC.org.* Accessed September 23, 2019. http://www.bic.org/sites/default/files/pdf/status_of_women_final.pdf

Bahá'í International Community. "Situation of Baha'is in Iran." *BIC.org.* Accessed September 23, 2019. http://www.bic.org/focus-areas/situation-iranian-bahais

Bahá'í International Community. "The Prosperity of Humankind." *BIC.org.* Accessed September 23, 2019. http://www.bic.org/statements/prosperity-humankind

Bahá'í International Community. "Glimpses into the Spirit of Gender Equality: Hasankheda, India." February 20, 2020a. *BIC.org.* Accessed May 31, 2020. http://www.bic.org/news/glimpses-spirit-gender-equality-hasankheda-india

Bahá'í International Community. "Glimpses into the Spirit of Gender Equality: Kejau, Malaysia." February 27, 2020b. *BIC.org.* Accessed May 31, 2020. http://www.bic.org/news/glimpses-spirit-gender-equality-kejau-malaysia

Bahá'í International Community. "Glimpses into the Spirit of Gender Equality: Mwinilunga, Zambia." March 4, 2020c. *BIC.org.* Accessed May 31, 2020. http://www.bic.org/news/glimpses-spirit-gender-equality-mwinilunga-zambia

Bahá'í International Community. "Glimpses into the Spirit of Gender Equality: Riohacha, Colombia." February 12, 2020d. *BIC.org.* Accessed May 31, 2020. http://www.bic.org/news/glimpses-spirit-gender-equality-riohacha-colombia

Bahá'í International Community. "Rethinking Prosperity: Forging Alternatives to a Culture of Consumerism." May 3, 2020e. *BIC.org.* Accessed May 31, 2020. http://www.bic.org/statements/rethinking-prosperity-forging-alternatives-culture-consumerism

Bahá'í International Community. "Bahá'í International Community's United Nations Office and Representation to the European Union: Year in Review (2012)." Bahá'í International Community United Nations Office Archives, New York.

Bahá'í International Community. "Bahá'í International Community's United Nations Office: Year in Review (January 2013–August 2013)." Bahá'í International Community United Nations Office Archives, New York.

Bahá'í International Community. *Human Rights Education Training Manual.* Bahá'í International Community United Nations Office Archives, New York.

Bahá'í International Community. "Influencing Culture, Draft Concept Note." Bahá'í International Community United Nations Office Archives, New York.

Bahá'í International Community. "Participation of the Bahá'í International Community Office of the Environment in the Process Leading up to and Including the United Nations World Summit for Social Development (March 6–12, 1995) and the Parallel NGO Forum '95 (March 2–12, 1995)." Bahá'í International Community United Nations Office Archives, New York.

Bahá'í International Community. "Participation of the Bahá'í International Community Office of the Environment in the Process Leading up to and Including the Second UN Conference on Human Settlements—Habitat II (June 3–14, 1996) and the Parallel NGO Forum (May 30–June 14, 1996)." Bahá'í International Community United Nations Office Archives, New York.

Bahá'í International Community. "Participation of the Bahá'í International Community Office of the Environment in the Process Surrounding the United Nations Conference on Environment and Development (UNCED/Earth Summit). December 1989–June 1992." Bahá'í International Community United Nations Office Archives, New York.

Bahá'í International Community. "Peace among the Nations." Bahá'í International Community United Nations Office Archives, New York.

Bahá'í International Community. "Religious Values and the Measurement of Poverty and Prosperity." Bahá'í International Community United Nations Office Archives, New York.

Bahá'í International Community. "Report of the Bahá'í Activities in Relation to the United Nations (1947–1952)." Bahá'í International Community United Nations Office Archives, New York.

Bahá'í International Community. "Report of Bahá'í Participation in the Fourth World Conference on Women (September 4–15, 1995)." Bahá'í International Community United Nations Office Archives, New York.

Bahá'í International Community. "Report on Bahá'í Participation in the World Summit for Social Development and the Parallel NGO Forum '95." Bahá'í International Community United Nations Office Archives, New York.

Bahá'í World Centre. "External Affairs Strategy." Internal Memo to National Spiritual Assemblies and to the Bahá'í International Community Office at the United Nations (October 10, 1994). Haifa, Israel: Bahá'í World Centre, 1994.

Bahá'í World Centre. *One Common Faith*. Haifa, Israel: Bahá'í World Centre, 2005.

Bahá'í World Centre. "National and International External Affairs Endeavors of the Worldwide Bahá'í Community (October 20, 2014)." Haifa, Israel: Bahá'í World Centre, 2014.

Bahá'í World Centre. "The Bahá'í Administrative Order." *Bahai.org*. Accessed September 22, 2019. http://www.bahai.org/beliefs/essential-relationships/administrative-order/

Bahá'í World Centre. "The Life and Work of Shoghi Effendi." *Bahai.org*. Accessed September 23, 2019.

Bahá'u'lláh. *Proclamation of Bahá'u'lláh*. Wilmette, IL: US Bahá'í Publishing Trust, 1978.

Bahá'u'lláh. *Tablets of Bahá'u'lláh Revealed after the Kitáb-i-Aqdas*. Haifa, Israel: Bahá'í World Centre, 1978.

Bahá'u'lláh. *The Hidden Words of Bahá'u'lláh*. Translated by Shoghi Effendi. Wilmette, IL: US Bahá'í Publishing Trust, 1985.

Bahá'u'lláh. *Gleanings from the Writings of Bahá'u'lláh*. Wilmette, IL: US Bahá'í Publishing Trust, 1990.

Bahá'u'lláh. *The Summons of the Lord of Hosts*. Haifa: Bahá'í World Centre, 2002. http://bahai-library.com/bahaullah_summons_lord_hosts

Bahá'u'lláh. *Kitáb-i-Aqdas (Most Holy Book): "Multilinear" Translation Project and Glossary*. Edited by Jonah Winters. *Bahá'í Library Online*. Accessed June 10, 2020. http://bahai-library.com/provisionals/aqdas/aqdas186.notes.html

Balyuzi, Hasan M. *The Báb: The Herald of the Day of Days*. Oxford, UK: George Ronald, 1973.

Balyuzi, Hasan M. *Bahá'u'lláh: The King of Glory*. Oxford, UK: George Ronald, 1991.

Barrett, David. B. "Religion: World Religious Statistics." In *1988 Encyclopedia Britannica Book of the Year*, edited by Daphne Daune and Louise Watson, 303. Chicago, IL: Encyclopedia Britannica, 1988.

Beittinger-Lee, Verena. "Blessing or Bother? Religion and Religious NGOs at the UN in New York." In *Religion, NGOs and the United Nations: Visible and Invisible Actors in Power*, edited by Jeremy Carrette and Hugh Miall, 119–54. London: Bloomsbury, 2017a.

Beittinger-Lee, Verena. "Catholicism at the United Nations in New York." In *Religion, NGOs and the United Nations: Visible and Invisible Actors in Power*, edited by Jeremy Carrette and Hugh Miall, 177–94. London: Bloomsbury, 2017b.

Beittinger-Lee, Verena, and Hugh Miall. "Islam, the OIC, and the Defamation of Religions Controversy." In *Religion, NGOs and the United Nations: Visible and Invisible Actors in Power*, edited by Jeremy Carrette and Hugh Miall, 155–75. London: Bloomsbury, 2017.

Bellah, Robert N. *Beyond Belief: Essays on Religion in a Post-Traditionalist World*. Berkeley, CA: University of California Press, 1991.

Berger, Julia. "Religious Nongovernmental Organizations: An Exploratory Analysis." *Voluntas: International Journal of Voluntary and Nonprofit Organizations* 14, no. 1 (2003): 15–39. doi:10.1023/A:1022988804887

Berger, Julia. "A New Politics of Engagement: The Bahá'í International Community, the United Nations, and Gender Equality." In *Religion and Public Discourse in an Age of Transition: Reflections on Bahá'í Practice and Thought*, edited by Benjamin Schewel and Geoffrey Cameron, 221–54. Waterloo, Ontario, CA: Wilfrid Laurier University Press, 2018.

Berger, Peter L. *Sacred Canopy: Elements of a Sociological Theory of Religion*. New York: Random House, 1990.

Berger, Peter L. "Secularism in Retreat." *The National Interest* 46 (1996/97): 3.

Boehle, Josef. "Religious NGOs at the UN and the Millennium Development Goals: An Introduction." *Global Change, Peace & Security* 22, no. 3 (2010a): 275–96. doi:10.1080/14781158.2010.510241

Boehle, Josef. "The UN System and Religious Actors in the Context of Global Change." *CrossCurrents* 60, no. 3 (September 2010b): 383–401. doi:1111/j.1939-3881.2010.00138.x

Bourdieu, Pierre. *Algeria 1960*. Cambridge, UK: Cambridge University Press, 1979.

Bourdieu, Pierre. *Distinction: A Social Critique of the Judgment of Taste*. London: Routledge, 1984.

Boutros-Ghali, Boutros. *An Agenda for Peace: Preventive Diplomacy, Peacemaking and Peace-Keeping*. Report of the Secretary General Pursuant to the Statement Adopted by the Summit Meeting of the Security Council on January 31, 1992. S/24111. New York: United Nations, 1992.

Boy, John D., and John Torpey. "Inventing the Axial Age: The Origins and Uses of a Historical Concept." *Theory and Society* 42, no. 3 (May 2013): 241–59. doi:10.1007/ s11186-013-9193-0

Boyles, Ann. "Towards the Goal of Full Partnership: One Hundred and Fifty Years of the Advancement of Women." In *The Bahá'í World, 1993–1994.* Vol. 22, 237–76. Haifa, Israel: Bahá'í World Centre, 1994.

Braunstein, Ruth, Todd N. Fuist, and Rhys H. Williams, eds. *Religion and Progressive Activism: New Stories about Faith and Politics.* Religion and Social Transformation. New York: New York University Press, 2017.

Bronner, Ethan. "Iran Closes University Run Covertly by the Bahais." *New York Times.* October 29, 1998. *Nytimes.com.* Accessed September 23, 2019. http://www.nytimes. com/1998/10/29/world/iran-closes-university-run-covertly-by-the-bahais.html

Brown, Wendy. *Edgework: Critical Essays on Knowledge and Politics.* Princeton, NJ: Princeton University Press, 2005.

Byrd, Robert O. *Quaker Ways in Foreign Policy.* Toronto: University of Toronto Press, 1960.

Cameron, Geoffrey. "The Bahá'í Community and Public Policy: The Bahá'í Refugee Resettlement Program (1981–1989)." In *Religion and Public Discourse in an Age of Transition: Reflections on Bahá'í Practice and Thought,* edited by Geoffrey Cameron and Benjamin Schewel, 255–80. Waterloo, Ontario, CA: Wilfrid Laurier University Press, 2018.

Cameron, Geoffrey, and Benjamin Schewel, eds. *Religion and Public Discourse in an Age of Transition: Reflections on Bahá'í Practice and Thought.* Waterloo, Ontario, CA: Wilfrid Laurier University Press, 2018.

Camilleri, Joseph A. "Postsecularist Discourse in an 'Age of Transition.'" *Review of International Studies* 38, no. 5 (2012): 1019–39. doi:10.1017/S0260210512000459

Carrette, Jeremy. "The Paradox of Globalization: Quakers, Religious NGOs, and the United Nations." In *Religions in Movement: The Local and the Global in Contemporary Faith Traditions,* edited by Robert W. Hefner, John Hutchinson, Sara Mels and Christiane Timmerman, 37–56. London: Routledge, 2013.

Carrette, Jeremy, and Hugh Miall, eds. *Religion, NGOs and the United Nations: Visible and Invisible Actors in Power.* London: Bloomsbury, 2017.

Chatham House. "Chatham House Rule." *ChathamHouse.org.* Accessed September 23, 2019. http://www.chathamhouse.org/chatham-house-rule#

Clarke, Gerard, and Michael Jennings. "Introduction." In *Development, Civil Society and Faith-Based Organizations: Bridging the Sacred and the Secular,* edited by Gerard Clarke and Michael Jennings. New York: Palgrave, 2008.

Cloke, Paul. "Theo-Ethics and Radical Faith-Based Praxis in the Postsecular City." In *Exploring the Postsecular: The Religious, the Political and the Urban,* edited by Arie L. Molendijk, Justin Beaumont, and Christoph Jedan, 223–42. Leiden, Netherlands: Brill, 2010.

Conference of NGOs in Consultative Relationship with the United Nations. "Vision,
    Mission and Objectives." *NGOCongo.org*. Accessed September 22, 2019. http://www.
    ngocongo.org/who-we-are/vision-mission-and-objectives

Connolly, William E. "Biology, Politics, Creativity." *Perspectives on Politics* 11, no. 2
    (June 2013): 508–11. doi:10.1017/S1537592713000935

Danesh, Roshan. *Dimensions of Baháʼí Law*. Wilmette, IL: Baháʼí Publishing, 2019.

Davis, Derek H. "The Evolution of Religious Freedom as a Universal Human Right:
    Examining the Role of the 1981 United Nations Declaration on the Elimination
    of All Forms of Intolerance and of Discrimination Based on Religion or Belief."
    BYU Law Review 217, no. 2002: 217–36. *BYU Law*. Accessed March 6, 2020. http://
    digitalcommons.law.byu.edu/lawreview/vol2002/iss2/2

Deneulin, Séverine, and Carole Rakodi. 2011. "Revisiting Religion: Development
    Studies Thirty Years On." *World Development* 39, no. 1 (January 2011): 45–54.
    doi:10.1016/j.worlddev.2010.05.007

Deneulin, Séverine, and Masooda Bano, *Religion in Development: Rewriting the Secular
    Script*. London: Zed Books, 2009.

Diane, Otto. "'Gender Comment': Why Does the UN Committee on Economic, Social,
    and Cultural Rights Need a General Comment on Women?" *Canadian Journal of
    Women and the Law* 14, no. 1 (2002): 1–48.

Dubensky, Joyce S., ed. *Peacemakers in Action*. Vol. 2. New York: Cambridge University
    Press, 2016.

Dubois, Heather M., and Janna Hunter-Bowman. "The Intersection of Christian
    Theology and Peacebuilding." In *Religion, Conflict, and Peacebuilding*, edited
    by Atalia Omer, R. Scott Appleby, and David Little, 569–89. New York: Oxford
    University Press, 2015.

Dugal, Bani. "Women, Faith, and Human Rights." October 2, 2017. *BIC.org*. Accessed
    May 31, 2020. http://www.bic.org/perspectives/women-faith-and-human-rights

Effendi, Shoghi. "A Statement by Shoghi Rabbani to Mr. Justice Emil Sandstrom,
    Chairman, United Nations Special Committee on Palestine." United Nations. April
    6, 1948. http://unispal.un.org/UNISPAL.NSF/0/0074E155E7831EE385257061006
    8A609

Effendi, Shoghi. *The Baháʼí Faith: 1844–1952: Information Statistical and Comparative*.
    Wilmette, IL: Baháʼí Publishing Committee, 1953.

Effendi, Shoghi. *Baháʼí Administration*. Wilmette, IL: US Bahaʼi Publishing Trust, 1974.

Effendi, Shoghi. *God Passes By*. Wilmette, IL: US Baháʼí Publishing Trust, 1979.

Effendi, Shoghi. *Citadel of Faith: Messages to America 1947–1957*. Wilmette, IL: Baháʼí
    Publishing Trust, 1980a.

Effendi, Shoghi. *The Promised Day Is Come*. Rev. ed. Wilmette, IL: Baháʼí Publishing
    Trust, 1980b.

Effendi, Shoghi. *The World Order of Baháʼuʼlláh*. Wilmette, IL: Baháʼí Publishing Trust,
    1991.

Eisenstadt, Samuel N. "Multiple Modernities in an Age of Globalization." *Canadian
    Journal of Sociology* 24, no. 2 (1999): 283–95.

Emmerij, Louis, Richard Jolly, and Tomas G. Weiss. *Ahead of the Curve?: UN Ideas and Global Challenges*. Bloomington, IN: Indiana University Press, 2001.

Ewing, Sovaida Ma'ani. *Collective Security within Reach*. Oxford, UK: George Ronald, 2007.

"Exploring the Role of Religion in Europe, the BIC Hosts Event at European Parliament." May 13, 2019. *BIC.org*. Accessed May 31, 2019. http://www.bic.org/news/exploring-role-religion-europe-bic-hosts-event-european-parliament

Faith and Feminism Working Group. "Oral Statement to the 60th Session of the Commission on the Status of Women." March 14–24, 2016. Accessed September 22, 2019. http://static1.squarespace.com/static/55120ecae4b01593abadc441/t/56f9745a906340974484bbe2/1459188826781/FaithFemOralStatementCSW.docx.pdf

Faith and Feminism Working Group. "Objectives." *FaothFem.com*. Accessed September 24, 2019. https://sites.google.com/bic.org/faithfem-com/objectives?authuser=0

Farid-Arbab, Sona. *Moral Empowerment: In Quest of a Pedagogy*. Wilmette, IL: Bahá'í Publishing, 2017.

Ford, David. *Theology: A Very Short Introduction*. Oxford, UK: Oxford University Press, 2013.

Foucault, Michel. *Madness and Civilization: A History of Insanity in the Age of Reason*. New York: Pantheon, 1965.

Foucault, Michel. *The Order of Things: An Archeology of the Human Sciences*. London: Tavistock, 1970.

Foucault, Michel. *The Archaelogy of Knowledge*. New York: Pantheon, 1972.

Foucault, Michel. *The Birth of the Clinic: An Archeology of Medical Perception*. London: Tavistock, 1973.

Fulkerson, Mary McClintock, and Sheila Briggs, eds. *The Oxford Handbook of Feminist Theology*. Oxford, UK: Oxford University Press, 2012.

Ghanea, Nazila. *Human Rights, the U.N. and the Bahá'ís in Iran*. Oxford, UK: George Ronald Publisher, 2003.

Gilbert, Martin. *A History of the Twentieth Century: The Concise Edition of the Acclaimed World History*. New York: HarperCollins, 2001.

Gollmer, Ulrich. "Bahá'í Political Thought." In *Making the Crooked Straight: A Contribution to Bahá'í Apologetics*, edited by Udo Schaefer, Nicola Towfigh, and Ulrich Gollmer, translated by Geraldine Schuckelt, 418–47. Oxford, UK: George Ronald, 2000.

Haas, Peter M. "Introduction: Epistemic Communities and International Policy Coordination." *International Organization* 46, no. 1 (Winter 1992): 1–35. http://www.jstor.org/stable/2706951

Habermas, Jürgen. "Notes on a Post-Secular Society." *New Perspectives Quarterly* 25, no. 4 (October 2008). https://doi.org/10.1111/j.1540-5842.2008.01017.x

Hands of the Cause of God Residing in the Holy Land, ed. *The Bahá'í Faith, 1844–1963: Information and Statistical Comparison*. Vol. 128. Ramat Gan, Peli: PEC Printing Works, 1963.

Haynes, Jeffrey. *EUI Working Papers: Faith-Based Organisations at the United Nations.* San Domenico di Fiesole, Italy: European University Institute Press, 2013.

Haynes, Jeffrey. *Faith-Based Organizations at the United Nations.* New York: Palgrave, 2014.

Hedges, Chris. "What Every Person Should Know about War (Excerpt)." *New York Times.* July 6, 2003. http://www.nytimes.com/2003/07/06/books/chapters/what-every-person-should-know-about-war.html

Heft, James, ed. *Beyond Violence: Religious Sources of Social Transformation in Judaism, Christianity, and Islam.* New York: Fordham University Press, 2004.

Hoffmann, Bruce. "'Holy Terror': The Implications of Terrorism Motivated by a Religious Imperative." *Studies in Conflict and Terrorism* 18, no. 4 (1995): 271–84. doi:10.1080/10576109508435985

Holley, Marion. "The Bahá'í Faith and the San Francisco Conference." In *The Bahá'í World: A Biennial International Record (1944–1946).* Vol. X, 741–51. Wilmette, IL: Bahá'í Publishing Trust, 1946.

Hornby, Helen, ed. *Lights of Guidance: A Bahá'í Reference File.* New Delhi: Bahá'í Publishing Trust, 1988.

Hugo, Victor. "The History of a Crime: The Testimony of an Eye-Witness." 1877. Translated by T. H. Joyce and Arthur Locker. Retrieved from http://www.gutenberg.org/files/10381/10381-h/10381-h.htm

Hutchinson, John. "Introduction: Global Perspectives on Religion, Nationalism and Politics." In *Religions in Movement: The Local and the Global in Contemporary Faith Traditions*, edited by Robert W. Hefner, John Hutchinson, Sara Mels and Christiane Timmerman, 9–18. New York: Routledge, 2013.

Iran Human Rights Documentation Center. *A Faith Denied: The Persecution of the Bahá'ís of Iran.* New Haven, CT: IHRDC, 2006.

Jabri, Vivienne. *War and the Transformation of Global Politics.* London: Palgrave, 2007.

Jain, Devaki. *Women, Development, and the UN: A Sixty-Year Quest for Equality and Justice*, edited by United Nations Intellectual History Project. Bloomington, IN: Indiana University Press, 2005.

Jaspers, Karl. *The Origin and Goal of History.* New York: Routledge, 2010.

Jerryson, Michael, Mark Juergensmeyer, and Margo Kitts, eds. *The Oxford Handbook of Religion and Violence.* Oxford, UK: Oxford University Press, 2013.

Jolly, Richard, Louis Emmerij, and Tomas G. Weiss. *UN Ideas That Changed the World.* Bloomington, IN: Indiana University Press, 2009.

Juergensmeyer, Mark. *Terror in the Mind of God: The Global Rise of Religious Violence.* 3rd ed. Berkeley, CA: University of California Press, 2003.

Juergensmeyer, Mark, Margo Kitts, and Michael Jerryson, eds. *The Oxford Handbook of Religion and Violence.* Oxford, UK: Oxford University Press, 2015.

Karam, Azza. "Concluding Thoughts on Religion and the United Nations: Redesigning the Culture of Development." *CrossCurrents* 60, no. 3 (September 2010): 462–74. doi:10.1111/j.1939-3881.2010.00143.x

Karlberg, Michael. *Beyond the Culture of Contest: From Adversarialism to Mutualism in an Age of Interdependence*. Oxford, UK: George Ronald Publisher, 2004.

Karlberg, Michael. "The Power of Discourse and the Discourse of Power: Pursuing Peace through Discourse Intervention." *International Journal of Peace Studies* 10, no. 1 (Spring/Summer 2005): 1–25. http://www.jstor.org/stable/41852070.

Karlberg, Michael. "Western Liberal Democracy as New World Order?" In *The Bahá'í World 2005–2006*, 133–56. Haifa, Israel: Bahá'í World Centre, 2007. *Bahai.org*. Accessed September 22, 2019. http://www.bahai.org/documents/essays/karlberg-dr-michael/western-liberal-democracy-new-world-order.

Karlberg, Michael. "Constructive Resilience: The Bahá'í Response to Oppression." *Peace & Change* 35, no. 2 (March 2010): 222–57. doi:org/10.1111/j.1468-0130.2009.00627.x

Kayaoğlu, Turan. "Islam in the United Nations: The Liberal Limits of Postsecularism." Paper presented at "The Postsecular in International Politics," University of Sussex, October 27–28, 2011.

Kayaoğlu, Turan. "Giving an Inch Only to Lose a Mile: Muslim States, Liberalism, and Human Rights in the United Nations." *Human Rights Quarterly* 36, no. 1 (February 2014): 61–89. doi.org/10.1353/hrq.2014.0004

Kazemzadeh, Firuz. "The Bahá'ís in Iran: Twenty Years of Oppression," *Social Research* 67, no. 2 (Summer 2000): 537–58. http://www.jstor.org/stable/40971483.

Keck, Margaret E., and Kathryn Sikkink. *Activists beyond Borders: Advocacy Networks in International Politics*. Ithaca, NY: Cornell University Press, 1998.

Kessler, Michael Jon. *Political Theology for a Plural Age*. Oxford, UK: Oxford University Press, 2013.

Khan, Janet, and Peter Khan. *Advancement of Women: A Bahá'í Perspective*. Wilmette, IL: Bahá'í Publishing Trust, 2003.

King, Richard. *Orientalism and Religion: Postcolonial Theory, India and "The Mystic East."* London: Routledge, 1999.

Krasno, Jean E. *The Founding of the United Nations: International Cooperation as Evolutionary Process*. Academic Council on the United Nations System, 2001.

Kuhn, Thomas S. "Scientific Revolutions as Changes of World View." In *Can Theories Be Refuted?: Essays on the Duhem-Quine Thesis*, edited by Sandra G. Harding, 133–54. Boston, MA: Reidel Pub. Co., 1976.

Kuhn, Thomas S. *The Structure of Scientific Revolutions*. 3rd ed. Chicago, IL: University of Chicago Press, 1996.

Lederach, John Paul. *The Little Book of Conflict Transformation*. Intercourse, PA: Good Books, 2003.

Lederach, John Paul. "Spirituality and Religious Peacebuilding." In *Religion, Conflict, and Peacebuilding*, edited by Atalia Omer, R. Scott Appleby, and David Little, 542–66. New York: Oxford University Press, 2015.

Lehmann, Karsten. *Religious NGOs in International Relations: The Construction of "the Religious" and "the Secular."* Routledge Studies in Religion and Politics. New York: Routledge, 2016.

Leith, John Barnabas. "A More Constructive Encounter: A Bahá'í View of Religion and Human Rights." In *Does God Believe in Human Rights? Essays on Religion and Human Rights*, edited by Nazila Ghanea, Alan Stephens, and Raphael Walden, 121–44. Leiden, Netherlands: Brill, 2007.

Lepard, Brian D. *Rethinking Humanitarian Intervention: A Fresh Legal Approach Based on Fundamental Ethical Principles in International Law and World Religions*. University Park, PA: Pennsylvania State University Press, 2003.

Lepard, Brian D. *A Bahá'í Perspective on International Human Rights Law*. Hong Kong: Juxta, 2012.

Lerche, Charles. *Healing the Body Politic*. Oxford, UK: George Ronald Publisher, 2004.

Marshall, Katherine. *Global Institutions of Religion: Ancient Movers, Modern Shakers*. New York: Routledge, 2013.

Martens, Kerstin. *NGOs and the United Nations: Institutionalization, Professionalization and Adaptation*. New York: Palgrave Macmillan, 2005.

Mavelli, Luca, and Fabio Petito. "The Postsecular in International Relations: An Overview." *Review of International Studies* 38, no. 2 (December 2012): 931–42. doi. org/10.1017/S026021051200040X

Mazower, Mark. *Governing the World: The History of an Idea, 1815 to the Present*. New York: Penguin, 2013.

McKeon, Nora. *The United Nations and Civil Society: Legitimating Global Governance—Whose Voice?* London: Zed Books, 2009.

McMullen, Michael. *The Bahá'í: The Religious Construction of a Global Identity*. New Brunswick, NJ: Rutgers University Press, 2000.

Meisler, Stanley. *United Nations: A History*. Rev. ed. New York: Grove/Atlantic, 2011.

Mills, Sara. *Discourse*. London and New York: Routledge, 1997.

Molejdijk Arie, L., Justin Beaumont, and Christoph Jedan, eds. *Exploring the Post-Secular: The Religious, the Political, and the Urban*. Leiden, Netherlands: Brill, 2010.

Mottahedeh, Mildred. Letter to Horace Holley, February 1, 1949. Office of the Secretary, United Nations Representative and Bahá'í International Community Files. National Bahá'í Archives, United States.

Mottahedeh, Mildred. "Report of the Delegates of the BIC to the Fourth Conference of the International NGOs (June 26–28, 1950)." Bahá'í International Community United Nations Office Archives, New York.

Murphy-Graham, Erin. *Opening Minds, Improving Lives: Education and Women's Empowerment in Honduras*. Nashville, TN: Vanderbilt University Press, 2012.

National Spiritual Assembly of the Bahá'ís of the United States and Canada. "A Bahá'í Declaration of Human Obligations and Rights." Presented to the first session of the United Nations Commission on Human Rights. Lake Success, NY, February 1, 1947. *BIC.org*. Accessed September 22, 2019. https://www.bic.org/statements/bahai-declaration-human-obligationsand-rights

National Spiritual Assembly of the Bahá'ís of the United States and Canada. "National Spiritual Assembly of the United States and Canada to Trygve Lie (August 28, 1948)." Bahá'í International Community United Nations Office Archives, New York.

National Spiritual Assembly of the Bahá'ís of the United States and Canada. *The Bahá'í World, 1930–1932*. Vol. 4. New York: Bahá'í Publishing Committee, 1933.

National Spiritual Assembly of the Bahá'ís of the United States. *The Bahá'í World, 1944–1946*. Vol. 10. Wilmette, IL: Bahá'í Publishing Trust, 1948.

National Spiritual Assembly of the Bahá'ís of the United States and Canada. *The Bahá'í World, 1946–1950*. Vol. 11. Wilmette, IL: Bahá'í Publishing Trust, 1981.

National Spiritual Assembly of the Bahá'ís of the United States. *The Bahá'í World, 1950–1954*. Vol. 12. Wilmette, IL: Bahá'í Publishing Trust, 1956.

Negele, Gundula. "Engagement for Religious Freedom at the United Nations: The Contribution of the Bahá'ís." In *Human Rights and Religion in Educational Contexts*, edited by Manfred L. Pirner, Johannes Lähnemann, and Heiner Bielefeldt, 91–103. Switzerland: Springer International Publishing, 2016.

Nejima, Susumu, ed. *NGOs in the Muslim World: Faith and Social Services*. New York: Routledge, 2015.

Nexon, Daniel H. "Religion and International Relations: No Leap of Faith Required," In *Religion and International Relations Theory*, edited by Jack Snyder, 141–67. New York: Columbia University Press, 2011.

Nietzsche, Friedrich. *The Gay Science: With a Prelude in Rhymes and an Appendix of Songs*. Translated by Walter Kaufmann. New York: Vintage, 1974.

Omer, Atalia. "Religious Peacebuilding: The Exotic, the Good, and the Theatrical." In *The Oxford Handbook of Religion, Conflict, and Peacebuilding*, edited by Atalia Omer, R. Scott Appleby, and David Little, 3–32. New York: Oxford University Press, 2015.

Osterhammel, Jürgen. *The Transformation of the World: A Global History of the Nineteenth Century*. America in the World. Princeton, NJ: Princeton University Press, 2014.

Oxford English Dictionary. s.v. "Substrate." n.p.

Palmer, David. "Religion, Spiritual Principles, and Civil Society." In *Religion and Public Discourse in an Age of Transition: Reflections on Bahá'í Practice and Thought*, edited by Benjamin Schewel and Geoffrey Cameron, 37–69. Waterloo, Ontario, CA: Wilfrid Laurier University Press, 2018.

Perowell, Daniel. "Why Participation Will Be So Important in Advancing the Post-2015 Agenda. Or: Zeroing in on the Zero Draft." June 17, 2015. *BIC.org*. Accessed May 31, 2020. http://www.bic.org/perspectives/why-participation-will-be-so-important-advancing-post-2015-agenda-or-zeroing-zero-draft

Petersen, Marie Juul. "International Religious NGOs at the United Nations: A Study of a Group of Religious Organizations." November 17, 2010. *The Journal of Humanitarian Assistance*. http://sites.tufts.edu/jha/archives/847

Pope Paul VI. "Address of the Holy Father Paul VI to the United Nations Organization." New York: The Permanent of Observer Mission of the Holy See to the United Nations. October 4, 1965a. http://holyseemission.org/contents/statements/address-of-the-holy-father-paul-vi-to-the-united-nations-organization.php

Pope Paul VI. *Gaudium et Spes*. December 7, 1965b. *Papal Archive*. Accessed February 2, 2020, http://www.vatican.va/archive/hist_councils/ii_vatican_council/documents/vat-ii_cons_19651207_gaudium-et-spes_en.html

Putnam, Robert D. "Bowling Alone: America's Declining Social Capital," *Journal of Democracy* 6, no. 1 (1995): 65–78.

Razavi, Shahriar. "Bahá'í Participation in Public Discourse: Some Considerations Related to History, Concepts, and Approaches." In *Religion and Public Discourse in an Age of Transition: Reflections on Bahá'í Practice and Thought*, edited by Benjamin Schewel and Geoffrey Cameron, 163–90. Waterloo, Ontario, CA: Wilfrid Laurier University Press, 2018.

Religion Counts. *Religion and Public Policy at the UN*. Observatory on the Universality of Rights. April 2002. https://www.oursplatform.org/wp-content/uploads/Catholics-for-Choice-Religion-Counts-Religion-and-Public-Policy-at-the-UN-1.pdf

Richards, Michael, and Paul R. Waibel. *Twentieth-Century Europe: A Brief History, 1900 to the Present*. 3rd ed. Malden, MA: Wiley, 2014.

Richmond, Oliver P. *The Transformation of Peace*. New York: Palgrave, 2005.

Richmond, Oliver P. "Reclaiming Peace in International Relations." *Millennium: Journal of International Studies* 36, no. 3 (May 2008): 439–70. doi.org/10.1177/03058298080 360030401

Rossi, Joseph S. *Uncharted Territory: The American Catholic Church at the United Nations, 1946–1972*. Washington, DC: Catholic University of America Press, 2006.

Rudolph, Susanne Hoeber. "Introduction: Religion, States and Transnational Civil Society." In *Transnational Religion and Fading States*, edited by Susanne Hoeber Rudolph and James Piscatori, 1–26. Boulder, CO: Westview Press, 1997.

Saiedi, Nader. *Logos and Civilization: Spirit, History, and Order in the Writings of Bahá'u'lláh*. Bethesda, MD: University Press of Maryland, 2000.

Saiedi, Nader. *Gate of the Heart: Understanding the Writings of the Báb*. Waterloo, Ontario, CA: Wilfrid Laurier University Press, 2008.

Saiedi, Nader. "Replacing the Sword with the Word: Bahá'u'lláh's Concept of Peace." *The Bahá'í World*. Accessed September 15, 2019. http://bahaiworld.bahai.org/articles/replacing-sword-word

Sawatsky, Jarem. "Extending the Peacebuilding Timeframe: Revising Lederach's Integrative Framework," *Peace Research* 37, no. 1 (2005): 123–30, http://www.jstor.org/stable/24469691.

Schaefer, Udo. *Bahá'í Ethics in Light of Scripture*. Vol. 1. Oxford, UK: George Ronald Publishing, 2007.

Schaefer, Udo. *Bahá'í Ethics in Light of Scripture*. Vol. 2. Oxford, UK: George Ronald Publishing, 2009.

Schewel, Benjamin. *Seven Ways of Looking at Religion: The Major Narratives*. New Haven, CT: Yale University Press, 2017.

Schewel, Benjamin. "Religion in an Age of Transition." In *Religion and Discourse in an Age of Transition: Reflections on Bahá'í Practice and Thought*, edited by Geoffrey

Cameron and Benjamin Schewel, 13–36. Waterloo, Ontario, CA: Wilfrid Laurier University Press, 2018.

Schwartz, Tanya B. *Faith-Based Organizations in Transnational Peacebuilding*. New York: Rowman & Littlefield International, 2018.

Shah, Timothy Samuel, Alfred Stepan, and Monica Duffy Toft, eds. *Rethinking Religion and World Affairs*. Oxford, UK: Oxford University Press, 2012.

Shahvar, Soli. *The Forgotten Schools: The Bahá'ís and Modern Education in Iran, 1899–1934*. London: I. B. Studies, 2009.

Sharon, Moshe, ed. *Studies in Modern Religions, Religions, Religious Movements and the Babi-Bahá'í Faiths*. Netherlands: Brill, 2004.

Siemann, Wolfram. *Metternich: Strategist and Visionary*. Cambridge, MA: Harvard University Press, 2019.

Slessarev-Jamir, Helene. *Prophetic Activism: Progressive Religious Justice Movements in Contemporary America*. New York: New York University Press, 2011.

Smart, Ninian. *Worldviews: Crosscultural Explorations of Human Beliefs*. 3rd ed. Upper Saddle River, NJ: Pearson, 1999.

Smith, Peter. *The Babi and Bahá'í Religions: From Messianic Shi'ism to a World Religion*. Cambridge, UK: Cambridge University Press, 1987.

Sohrabi, Nader. "Historicizing Revolutions: Constitutional Revolutions in the Ottoman Empire, Iran, and Russia, 1905–1908." *American Journal of Sociology* 100, no. 6 (May 1995): 1383–447. http://www.jstor.org/stable/2782676.

Steger, Manfred B, and Paul James. "Levels of Subjective Globalization: Ideologies, Imaginaries, Ontologies." *Perspectives on Development and Technology* 12, no. 1–2 (2013): 17–40. doi.org/10.1163/15691497-12341240

Stockman, Robert H. *The Bahá'í Faith in America: Origins, 1892–1900*. Wilmette, IL: Bahá'í Publishing Trust, 1985.

Stockman, Robert H. *'Abdu'l-Bahá in America*. Wilmette, IL: Bahá'í Publishing Trust, 2012.

Sub-Commission on Prevention of Discrimination and Protection of Minorities, Question of the Violation of Human Rights and Fundamental Freedoms Including Policies of Racial Discrimination and Segregation and of Apartheid, in All Countries: Report of the Sub-Commission under Commission on Human Rights, Resolution 8 (XXXIII), adopted at 929th meeting, September 9, 1981.

Taherzadeh, Adib. *The Revelation of Bahá'u'lláh*. 4 vols. Oxford, UK: George Ronald, 1974–87.

Taylor, Charles. *A Secular Age*. Cambridge, MA: Harvard University Press, 2007.

Tocqueville, Alexis de. *Democracy in America*. Chicago, IL: University of Chicago Press, 2002.

Toft, Monica Duffy, Daniel Philpott, and Timothy Samuel Shah. *God's Century: Resurgent Religion and Global Politics*. New York: W. W. Norton, 2011.

Tokbolat, Serik. "Climate Education in and beyond the Classroom." July 23, 2015. *BIC. org*. Accessed May 31, 2020. http://www.bic.org/perspectives/climate-education-and-beyond-classroom

Tokbolat, Serik. "Ensuring Substantive Collaboration with Civil Society in Implementing Agenda 2030." September 28, 2016. *BIC.org.* Accessed September 23, 2019. http://www.bic.org/perspectives/perspective-ensuring-substantive-collaboration-civil-society-implementing-agenda-2030

Tomalin, Emma, ed. *Gender, Faith and Development.* Working in Gender & Development. Oxford, UK: Oxfam, 2011. Retrieved from http://oxfamilibrary.openrepository.com/bitstream/handle/10546/144042/bk-gender-faith-development-290911-en.pdf?sequence=3&isAllowed=y

United Nations. Charter of the United Nations. 1 UNTS XVI. June 26, 1945. Article 71. http://www.un.org/en/charter-united-nations/

United Nations. *Beijing Declaration and Platform of Action, Adopted at the Fourth World Conference on Women.* October 27, 1995. *Refworld.org.* Accessed June 12, 2020. http://www.refworld.org/docid/3dde04324.html

United Nations Children's Fund. "Partnering with Religious Communities for Children." New York: UNICEF, 2000. https://www.unicef.org/about/partnerships/files/Partnering_with_Religious_Communities_for_Children_%28UNICEF%29.pdf

United Nations Economic and Social Council. Constitution of the United Nations Educational, Scientific and Cultural Organization. November 16, 1945. In *Basic Texts: 2018 Edition*, 6–18. Paris: UNESCO, 2018. Accessed September 23, 2019. http://unesdoc.unesco.org/ark:/48223/pf0000261751.page=6

United Nations Economic and Social Council. *List of Non-Governmental Organizations in Consultative Status with the Economic and Social Council as of 1 September 2016.* December 29, 2016. http://digitallibrary.un.org/record/1286140?ln=en

United Nations Entity for Gender Equality and the Empowerment of Women. "In Brief: Politics and Practice: A Guide for Gender-Responsive Implementation of the Global Compact for Migration." N.p.: UN Women, 2019. http://www.unwomen.org/-/media/headquarters/attachments/sections/library/publications/2018/guide-for-gender-responsive-implementation-of-the-global-compact-for-migration-en.pdf?la=en&vs=5533

United Nations Entity for Gender Equality and the Empowerment of Women. "The Beijing Platform for Action: Inspiration Then and Now." *UN Women.* Accessed September 23, 2019. http://beijing20.unwomen.org/en/about

United Nations General Assembly. "General Assembly Seventh Session: Official Records." New York: United Nations, April 10, 1953. Accessed November 24, 2017. http://www.un.org/ga/search/view_doc.asp?symbol=A/PV.426

United Nations General Assembly. World Conference of the International Women's Year. A/RES/3520. December 15, 1975. http://www.refworld.org/docid/3b00f1a814.html

United Nations General Assembly. "Declaration on the Elimination of All Forms of Intolerance and of Discrimination Based on Religion or Belief." A/RES/36/55. November 25, 1981. *Refworld.org.* Accessed April 25, 2020. http://www.refworld.org/docid/3b00f02e40.html

United Nations General Assembly. "Convention against Torture and Other Cruel, Inhuman or Degrading Treatment or Punishment." December 10, 1984. United Nations, *Treaty Series*, Vol. 1465 (December 10, 1984), 85. *Refworld.org.* Accessed April 25, 2020. http://www.refworld.org/docid/3ae6b3a94.html

United Nations General Assembly. "Situation of the Human Rights in the Islamic Republic of Iran." A/RES/40/141. 116th plenary meeting, December 13, 1985.

United Nations General Assembly. "Report of the Secretary-General on the Work of the Organization (2015)." *UN.org.* Accessed September 23, 2019. http://www.un.org/en/ga/search/view_doc.asp?symbol=A/70/1

United Nations General Assembly. "UN75 People's Declaration & Plan for Global Action: PEOPLE'S DECLARATION & PLAN FOR GLOBAL ACTION: Humanity at a Crossroads: Global Solutions for Global Challenges." May 14–15, 2020. *UN. org.* Accessed May 31, 2020. http://www.un.org/pga/74/wp-content/uploads/sites/99/2020/05/Updated-Final-Peoples-Declaration-and-Plan-of-Global-Action-2-JJ-edit-1.pdf

United Nations General Assembly. "Report of the Secretary-General on the Work of the Organization (2011)." A/66/1/. Dag Hammarskjöld Library, New York, 2011.

United Nations General Assembly. "Report of the Secretary-General on the Work of the Organization (2016)." A/71/1. Dag Hammarskjöld Library, New York, 2016.

United Nations Office on Genocide Prevention and the Responsibility to Protect. "The Genocide Convention." *United Nations Office on Genocide Prevention and the Responsibility to Protect.* Accessed May 12, 2020. http://www.un.org/en/genocideprevention/genocide-convention.shtml

United Nations Office of Public Information. "Preface." In *United Nations Yearbook 1945–1956*, iii. New York: United Nations, 1947.

United Nations Office of Public Information. "Non-Governmental Organizations in Consultative Status (as of 31 December 1970)." In *Yearbook of the United Nations 1970*. Vol. 24, 626–9. New York: United Nations, 1972.

United Nations Population Fund. "Guidelines for Engaging Faith-Based Organizations (FBOs) as Agents of Change." New York: UNFPA, 2009. *UNFPA.org.* Accessed September 23, 2019. http://www.unfpa.org/culture/docs/fbo_engagement.pdf

United Nations Research Institute for Social Development. "UNRISD Research and Policy Brief 11: Religion, Politics, and Gender Equality." May 2011. *United Nations Research Institute for Social Development.* http://www.unrisd.org/publications/rpb11e

Universal House of Justice. Constitution of the Universal House of Justice. 1966. *Bahai.org.* Accessed September 23, 2019. http://universalhouseofjustice.bahai.org/constitution/constitution-universal-house-justice

Universal House of Justice. To All National Spiritual Assemblies. February 26, 1979. *Bahai.org.* Accessed September 23, 2019. http://www.bahai.org/library/authoritative-texts/search?q=26+February+1979#s=messages-universal-house-justice

Universal House of Justice. To the Bahá'ís of the World. January 26, 1982. *Bahai.org.* Accessed September 23, 2019. https://www.bahai.org/library/authoritative-texts/sear ch?q=26+January+1982#s=messages-universal-house-justice.

Universal House of Justice. Department of the Secretariat to the National Spiritual Assembly of the Bahá'ís of the United States. December 7, 1983a. *Bahai.org.* Accessed September 23, 2019. http://www.bahai.org/library/authoritative-texts/the-universal-house-of-justice/messages/19831207_001/1#611484718

Universal House of Justice. To the Bahá'ís of the World. October 23, 1983b. *Bahai.org.* Accessed September 23, 2019. http://www.bahai.org/library/authoritative-texts/the-universal-house-of-justice/messages/19831020_001/1#346303577

Universal House of Justice. Ridván Message 1985. April 21, 1985. *Bahai.org.* Accessed September 23, 2019. http://www.bahai.org/library/authoritative-texts/the-universal-house-of-justice/messages/#d=19850421_001&f=f1-2

Universal House of Justice. "The Promise of World Peace." 1985. *Bahai.org.* Accessed September 23, 2019. http://www.bahai.org/library/authoritative-texts/the-universal-house-of-justice/messages/#d=19851001_001&f=f1

Universal House of Justice. To the Meeting of the Senior Officers of the United Nations Office and the Office of Public Information. October 29, 1986. *Bahai.org.* Accessed September 23, 2019. http://www.bahai.org/library/authoritative-texts/the-universal-house-of-justice/messages/#d=19861029_001&f=f1

Universal House of Justice. "The Bahá'í Faith and the United Nations: The Beginnings of the Bahá'í Relationship with the United Nations." In *The Bahá'í World, 1954–1963.* Vol. 13, 785. Haifa, Israel: Universal House of Justice, 1970.

Universal House of Justice. *The Bahá'í World, 1963–1968.* Vol. 14. Haifa, Israel: Universal House of Justice, 1974.

Universal House of Justice. *The Bahá'í World, 1976–1979.* Vol. 17. Haifa, Israel: Bahá'í World Centre, 1981.

Universal House of Justice. *The Bahá'í World, 1979–1983.* Vol. 18. Haifa, Israel: Bahá'í World Centre, 1986.

Universal House of Justice. *Ministry of the Custodians: An Account of the Stewardship of the Hands of the Cause 1957–1963.* Haifa, Israel: Bahá'í World Centre, 1992.

Universal House of Justice. *The Bahá'í World, 1983–1986.* Vol. 19. Haifa, Israel: Bahá'í World Centre, 1994.

Universal House of Justice. "The German Court's Legal Recognition of Assembly Status." In *The Bahá'í World 1983–1986.* Vol. 19, 571–608. Haifa: Bahá'í World Centre, 1998a.

Universal House of Justice. "The Six Year International Teaching Plan." In *The Bahá'í World, 1986–1992*, 115–91. Haifa, Israel: Bahá'í World Centre, 1998b.

Universal House of Justice. *The Bahá'í World, 1986–1992.* Vol. 20. Haifa, Israel: Bahá'í World Centre, 1998c.

Universal House of Justice. To the Bahá'ís of the World. March 25, 2007. *Bahai.org.* Accessed September 23, 2019. http://www.bahai.org/library/authoritative-texts/the-universal-house-of-justice/messages/20070325_001/1#126035670

Universal House of Justice. Ridván Message 2010. April 2, 2010a. *Bahai.org*. Accessed September 23, 2019. http://preview.bahai.org/library/authoritative-texts/the-universal-house-of-justice/messages/#d=20100421_001&f=f1

Universal House of Justice. To the Conference of the Continental Boards of Counsellors. December 28, 2010b. *Bahai.org*. Accessed September 23, 2019. https://www.bahai.org/library/authoritative-texts/search?q=28+December+2010#s=messages-universal-house-justice

Universal House of Justice. To the Baháʼís of Iran. March 2, 2013. *Bahai.org*. Accessed September 23, 2019. http://www.bahai.org/library/authoritative-texts/the-universal-house-of-justice/messages/#d=20130302_001&f=f1

Universal House of Justice. "Introduction." In *The Summons of the Lord of Hosts*, i–vii. Haifa, Israel: Baháʼí World Centre, 2017.

van den Hoonaard, Will C. *The Origins of the Baháʼí Community of Canada, 1898–1948*. Waterloo, Ontario, CA: Wilfrid Laurier University Press, 1996.

Venters, Louis. *No Jim Crow Church: The Origins of South Carolina's Baháʼí Community*. Gainesville, FL: University of Florida Press, 2015.

Weber, Max. *The Protestant Ethic and the Spirit of Capitalism*. New York: Scribner, 2001.

Weiner, Matthew. "Religion and the United Nations—Introduction." *CrossCurrents* 60, no. 3 (September 2010): 292–6. doi.org/10.1111/j.1939-3881.2010.00127.x

Willetts, Peter. *The "Conscience of the World": The Influence of Non-Governmental Organisations in the U.N. System*. Washington, DC: The Brookings Institution, 1996.

Wu, Zheng Xuan. "The Baháʼí International Community in Global Governance." PhD Diss., 2012. Fudan University, Shanghai, China.

Yazdani, Mina. "ʻAbdu'l-Bahá and the Iranian Constitutional Revolution: Embracing Principles while Disapproving Methodologies,." *Journal of Baháʼí Studies* 24, no. 1–2 (2014): 47–82.

Zinsser, Judith P. "From Mexico to Copenhagen to Nairobi: The United Nations Decade for Women, 1975–1985." *Journal of World History* 13, no. 1 (2002): 139–68. www.jstor.org/stable/20078945

Index